# The Vicar's Daug

George MacDonald

**Alpha Editions**

This edition published in 2024

ISBN : 9789362928863

Design and Setting By
**Alpha Editions**
www.alphaedis.com
Email - info@alphaedis.com

# Contents

# CHAPTER I.

## INTRODUCTORY.

I think that is the way my father would begin. My name is Ethelwyn Percivale, and used to be Ethelwyn Walton. I always put the Walton in between when I write to my father; for I think it is quite enough to have to leave father and mother behind for a husband, without leaving their name behind you also. I am fond of lumber-rooms, and in some houses consider them far the most interesting spots; but I don't choose that my old name should lie about in the one at home.

I am much afraid of writing nonsense; but my father tells me that to see things in print is a great help to recognizing whether they are nonsense or not. And he tells me, too, that his friend the publisher, who,—but I will speak of him presently,—his friend the publisher is not like any other publisher he ever met with before; for he never grumbles at any alterations writers choose to make,—at least he never says any thing, although it costs a great deal to shift the types again after they are once set up. The other part of my excuse for attempting to write lies simply in telling how it came about.

Ten days ago, my father came up from Marshmallows to pay us a visit. He is with us now, but we don't see much of him all day; for he is generally out with a friend of his in the east end, the parson of one of the poorest parishes in London,—who thanks God that he wasn't the nephew of any bishop to be put into a good living, for he learns more about the ways of God from having to do with plain, yes, vulgar human nature, than the thickness of the varnish would ever have permitted him to discover in what are called the higher orders of society. Yet I must say, that, amongst those I have recognized as nearest, the sacred communism of the early church—a phrase of my father's—are two or three people of rank and wealth, whose names are written in heaven, and need not be set down in my poor story.

A few days ago, then, my father, coming home to dinner, brought with him the publisher of the two books called, "The Annals of a Quiet Neighborhood," and "The Seaboard Parish." The first of these had lain by him for some years before my father could publish it; and then he remodelled it a little for the magazine in which it came out, a portion at a time. The second was written at the request of Mr. S., who wanted something more of the same sort; and now, after some years, he had begun again to represent to my father, at intervals, the necessity for another story to complete the *trilogy*, as he called it: insisting, when my father objected the difficulties of growing years and failing judgment, that indeed he owed it to him; for he had left him in the lurch, as it were, with an incomplete story, not to say an uncompleted series. My father still objected, and Mr. S. still urged, until, at length, my father said—this I learned afterwards, of course—"What would you say if I found you a substitute?" "That depends on who the substitute might be, Mr. Walton," said Mr. S. The result of their talk was that my father brought him home to dinner that day; and hence it comes, that, with some real fear and much metaphorical trembling, I am now writing this. I wonder if anybody will ever read it. This my first chapter shall be composed of a little of the talk that passed at our dinner-table that day. Mr. Blackstone was the only other stranger present; and he certainly was not much of a stranger.

"Do you keep a diary, Mrs. Percivale?" asked Mr. S., with a twinkle in his eye, as if he expected an indignant repudiation.

"I would rather keep a rag and bottle shop," I answered: at which Mr. Blackstone burst into one of his splendid roars of laughter; for if ever a man could laugh like a Christian who believed the world was in a fair way after all, that man was Mr. Blackstone; and even my husband, who seldom laughs at any thing I say with more than his eyes, was infected by it, and laughed heartily.

"That's rather a strong assertion, my love," said my father. "Pray, what do you mean by it?"

"I mean, papa," I answered, "that it would be a more profitable employment to keep the one than the other."

"I suppose you think," said Mr. Blackstone, "that the lady who keeps a diary is in the same danger as the old woman who prided herself in keeping a strict account of her personal expenses. And it always was correct; for when she could not get it to balance at the end of the week, she brought it right by putting down the deficit as *charity*."

"That's just what I mean," I said.

"But," resumed Mr. S., "I did not mean a diary of your feelings, but of the events of the day and hour."

"Which are never in themselves worth putting down," I said. "All that is worth remembering will find for itself some convenient cranny to go to sleep in till it is wanted, without being made a poor mummy of in a diary."

"If you have such a memory, I grant that is better, even for my purpose, much better," said Mr. S.

"For your purpose!" I repeated, in surprise. "I beg your pardon; but what designs can you have upon my memory?"

"Well, I suppose I had better be as straightforward as I know you would like me to be, Mrs. Percivale. I want you to make up the sum your father owes me. He owed me three books; he has paid me two. I want the third from you."

I laughed; for the very notion of writing a book seemed preposterous.

"I want you, under feigned names of course," he went on, "as are all the names in your father's two books, to give me the further history of the family, and in particular your own experiences in London. I am confident the history of your married life must contain a number of incidents which, without the least danger of indiscretion, might be communicated to the public to the great advantage of all who read them."

"You forget," I said, hardly believing him to be in earnest, "that I should be exposing my story to you and Mr. Blackstone at least. If I were to make the absurd attempt,—I mean absurd as regards my ability,—I should be always thinking of you two as my public, and whether it would be right for me to say this and say that; which you may see at once would render it impossible for me to write at all."

"I think I can suggest a way out of that difficulty, Wynnie," said my father. "You must write freely, all you feel inclined to write, and then let your husband see it. You may be content to let all pass that he passes."

"You don't say you really mean it, papa! The thing is perfectly impossible. I never wrote a book in my life, and"—

"No more did I, my dear, before I began my first."

"But you grew up to it by degrees, papa!"

"I have no doubt that will make it the easier for you, when you try. I am so far, at least, a Darwinian as to believe that."

"But, really, Mr. S. ought to have more sense—I beg your pardon, Mr. S.; but it is perfectly absurd to suppose me capable of finishing any thing my father has begun. I assure you I don't feel flattered by your proposal. I have got a man of more consequence for a father than that would imply."

All this time my tall husband sat silent at the foot of the table, as if he had nothing on earth to do with the affair, instead of coming to my assistance, when, as I thought, I really needed it, especially seeing my own father was of the combination against me; for what can be more miserable than to be taken for wiser or better or cleverer than you know perfectly well you are. I looked down the table, straight and sharp at him, thinking to rouse him by the most powerful of silent appeals; and when he opened his mouth very solemnly, staring at me in return down all the length of the table, I thought I had succeeded. But I was not a little surprised, when I heard him say,—

"I think, Wynnie, as your father and Mr. S. appear to wish it, you might at least try."

This almost overcame me, and I was very near,—never mind what. I bit my lips, and tried to smile, but felt as if all my friends had forsaken me, and were about to turn me out to beg my bread. How on earth could I write a book without making a fool of myself?

"You know, Mrs. Percivale," said Mr. S., "you needn't be afraid about the composition, and the spelling, and all that. We can easily set those to rights at the office."

He couldn't have done any thing better to send the lump out of my throat; for this made me angry.

"I am not in the least anxious about the spelling," I answered; "and for the rest, pray what is to become of me, if what you print should happen to be praised by somebody who likes my husband or my father, and therefore wants to say a good word for me? That's what a good deal of reviewing comes to, I understand. Am I to receive in silence what doesn't belong to me, or am I to send a letter to the papers to say that the whole thing was patched and polished at the printing-office, and that I have no right to more than perhaps a fourth part of the commendation? How would that do?"

"But you forget it is not to have your name to it," he said; "and so it won't matter a bit. There will be nothing dishonest about it."

"You forget, that, although nobody knows my real name, everybody will know that I am the daughter of that Mr. Walton who would have thrown his pen in the fire if you had meddled with any thing he wrote. They would be praising *me*, if they praised at all. The name is nothing. Of all things, to have praise you don't deserve, and not to be able to reject it, is the most miserable! It is as bad as painting one's face."

"Hardly a case in point," said Mr. Blackstone. "For the artificial complexion would be your own work, and the other would not."

"If you come to discuss that question," said my father, "we must all confess we have had in our day to pocket a good many more praises than we had a right to. I agree with you, however, my child, that we must not connive at any thing of the sort. So I will propose this clause in the bargain between you and Mr. S.; namely, that, if he finds any fault with your work, he shall send it back to yourself to be set right, and, if you cannot do so to his mind, you shall be off the bargain."

"But papa,—Percivale,—both of you know well enough that nothing ever happened to me worth telling."

"I am sorry your life has been so very uninteresting, wife," said my husband grimly; for his fun is always so like earnest!

"You know well enough what I mean, husband. It does *not* follow that what has been interesting enough to you and me will be interesting to people who know nothing at all about us to begin with."

"It depends on how it is told," said Mr. S.

"Then, I beg leave to say, that I never had an original thought in my life; and that, if I were to attempt to tell my history, the result would be as silly a narrative as ever one old woman told another by the workhouse fire."

"And I only wish I could hear the one old woman tell her story to the other," said my father.

"Ah! but that's because you see ever so much more in it than shows. You always see through the words and the things to something lying behind them," I said.

"Well, if you told the story rightly, other people would see such things behind it too."

"Not enough of people to make it worth while for Mr. S. to print it," I said.

"He's not going to print it except he thinks it worth his while; and you may safely leave that to him," said my husband.

"And so I'm to write a book as big as 'The Annals;' and, after I've been slaving at it for half a century or so, I'm to be told it won't do, and all my labor must go for nothing? I must say the proposal is rather a cool one to make,—to the mother of a family."

"Not at all; that's not it, I mean," said Mr. S.; "if you will write a dozen pages or so, I shall be able to judge by those well enough,—at least, I will take all the responsibility on myself after that."

"There's a fair offer!" said my husband. "It seems to me, Wynnie, that all that is wanted of you is to tell your tale so that other people can recognize the human heart in it,—the heart that is like their own, and be able to feel as if they were themselves going through the things you recount."

"You describe the work of a genius, and coolly ask me to do it. Besides, I don't want to be set thinking about my heart, and all that," I said peevishly.

"Now, don't be raising objections where none exist," he returned.

"If you mean I am pretending to object, I have only to say that I feel all one great objection to the whole affair, and that I won't touch it."

They were all silent; and I felt as if I had behaved ungraciously. Then first I felt as if I might *have* to do it, after all. But I couldn't see my way in the least.

"Now, what is there," I asked, "in all my life that is worth setting down,—I mean, as I should be able to set it down?"

"What do you ladies talk about now in your morning calls?" suggested Mr. Blackstone, with a humorous glance from his deep black eyes.

"Nothing worth writing about, as I am sure *you* will readily believe, Mr. Blackstone," I answered.

"How comes it to be interesting, then?"

"But it isn't. They—we—only talk about the weather and our children and servants, and that sort of thing."

"*Well!*" said Mr. S., "and I wish I could get any thing sensible about the weather and children and servants, and that sort of thing, for my magazine. I have a weakness in the direction of the sensible."

"But there never is any thing sensible said about any of them,—not that I know of."

"Now, Wynnie, I am sure you are wrong," said my father. "There is your friend, Mrs. Cromwell: I am certain she, sometimes at least, must say what is worth hearing about such matters."

"Well, but she's an exception. Besides, she hasn't any children."

"Then," said my husband, "there's Lady Bernard"—

"Ah! but she was like no one else. Besides, she is almost a public character, and any thing said about her would betray my original."

"It would be no matter. She is beyond caring for that now; and not one of her friends could object to any thing you who loved her so much would say about her."

The mention of this lady seemed to put some strength into me. I felt as if I did know something worth telling, and I was silent in my turn.

"Certainly," Mr. S. resumed, "whatever is worth talking about is worth writing about,—though not perhaps in the way it is talked about. Besides, Mrs. Percivale, my clients want to know more about your sisters, and little Theodora, or Dorothea, or—what was her name in the book?"

The end of it was, that I agreed to try to the extent of a dozen pages or so.

# CHAPTER II.

## I TRY.

I hope no one will think I try to write like my father; for that would be to go against what he always made a great point of,—that nobody whatever should imitate any other person whatever, but in modesty and humility allow the seed that God had sown in her to grow. He said all imitation tended to dwarf and distort the plant, if it even allowed the seed to germinate at all. So, if I do write like him, it will be because I cannot help it.

I will just look how "The Seaboard Parish" ends, and perhaps that will put into my head how I ought to begin. I see my father does mention that I had then been Mrs. Percivale for many years. Not so very many though,—five or six, if I remember rightly, and that is three or four years ago. Yes; I have been married nine years. I may as well say a word as to how it came about; and, if Percivale doesn't like it, the remedy lies in his pen. I shall be far more thankful to have any thing struck out on suspicion than remain on sufferance.

After our return home from Kilkhaven, my father and mother had a good many talks about me and Percivale, and sometimes they took different sides. I will give a shadow of one of these conversations. I think ladies can write fully as natural talk as gentlemen can, though the bits between mayn't be so good.

*Mother.*—I am afraid, my dear husband [This was my mother's most solemn mode of addressing my father], "they are too like each other to make a suitable match."

*Father.*—I am sorry to learn you consider me so very unlike yourself, Ethelwyn. I had hoped there was a very strong resemblance indeed, and that the match had not proved altogether unsuitable.

*Mother.*—Just think, though, what would have become of me by this time, if you had been half as unbelieving a creature as I was. Indeed, I fear sometimes I am not much better now.

*Father.*—I think I am, then; and I know you've done me nothing but good with your unbelief. It was just because I was of the same sort precisely that I was able to understand and help you. My circumstances and education and superior years—

*Mother.*—Now, don't plume yourself on that, Harry; for you know everybody says you look much the younger of the two.

*Father.*—I had no idea that everybody was so rude. I repeat, that my more years, as well as my severer education, had, no doubt, helped me a little further on before I came to know you; but it was only in virtue of the doubt in me that I was able to understand and appreciate the doubt in you.

*Mother.*—But then you had at least begun to leave it behind before I knew you, and so had grown able to help me. And Mr. Percivale does not seem, by all I can make out, a bit nearer believing in any thing than poor Wynnie herself.

*Father.*—At least, he doesn't fancy he believes when he does not, as so many do, and consider themselves superior persons in consequence. I don't know that it would have done you any great harm, Miss Ethelwyn, to have made my acquaintance when I was in the worst of my doubts concerning the truth of things. Allow me to tell you that I was nearer making shipwreck of my faith at a certain period than I ever was before or have been since.

*Mother.*—What period was that?

*Father.*—Just the little while when I had lost all hope of ever marrying you,—unbeliever as you counted yourself.

*Mother.*—You don't mean to say you would have ceased to believe in God, if he hadn't given you your own way?

*Father.*—No, my dear. I firmly believe, that, had I never married you, I should have come in the end to say, "*Thy will be done,*" and to believe that it must be all right, however hard to bear. But, oh, what a terrible thing it would have been, and what a frightful valley of the shadow of death I should have had to go through first!

[I know my mother *said* nothing more just then, but let my father have it all his own way for a while.]

*Father.*—You see, this Percivale is an honest man. I don't exactly know how he has been brought up; and it is quite possible he may have had such evil instruction in Christianity that he attributes to it doctrines which, if I supposed they actually belonged to it, would make me reject it at once as ungodlike and bad. I have found this the case sometimes. I remember once being astonished to hear a certain noble-minded lady utter some indignant words against what I considered a very weighty doctrine of Christianity; but, listening, I soon found that what she supposed the doctrine to contain was something considered vastly unchristian. This may be the case with Percivale, though I never heard him say a word of the kind. I think his difficulty comes mainly from seeing so much suffering in the world, that he cannot imagine the presence and rule of a good God, and therefore lies with religion rather than with Christianity as yet. I am all but certain, the only thing that will ever make him able to believe in a God at all is meditation on the Christian idea of God,—I mean the idea of God *in* Christ reconciling the world to himself,—not that pagan corruption of Christ in God reconciling him to the world. He will then see that suffering is not either wrath or neglect, but pure-hearted love and tenderness. But we must give him time, wife; as God has borne with us, we must believe that he bears with others, and so learn to wait in hopeful patience until they, too, see as we see.

And as to trusting our Wynnie with Percivale, he seems to be as good as she is. I should for my part have more apprehension in giving her to one who would be called a thoroughly religious man; for not only would the unfitness be greater, but such a man would be more likely to confirm her in doubt, if the phrase be permissible. She wants what some would call homoeopathic treatment. And how should they be able to love one another, if they are not fit to be married to each other? The fitness, seems inherent to the fact.

*Mother.*—But many a two love each other who would have loved each other a good deal more if they hadn't been married.

*Father.*—Then it was most desirable they should find out that what they thought a grand affection was not worthy of the name. But I don't think there is much fear of that between those two.

*Mother.*—I don't, however, see how that man is to do her any good, when *you* have tried to make her happy for so long, and all in vain.

*Father.*—I don't know that it has been all in vain. But it is quite possible she does not understand me. She fancies, I dare say, that I believe every thing without any trouble, and therefore cannot enter into her difficulties.

*Mother.*—But you have told her many and many a time that you do.

*Father.*—Yes: and I hope I was right; but the same things look so different to different people that the same words won't describe them to both; and it may seem to her that I am talking of something not at all like what she is feeling or thinking of. But when she sees the troubled face of Percivale, she knows that he is suffering; and sympathy being thus established between them, the least word of the one will do more to help the other than oceans of argument. Love is the one great instructor. And each will try to be good, and to find out for the sake of the other.

*Mother.*—I don't like her going from home for the help that lay at her very door.

*Father.*—You know, my dear, you like the Dean's preaching much better than mine.

*Mother.*—Now, that is unkind of you!

*Father.*—And why? [My father went on, taking no heed of my mother's expostulation.] Because, in the first place, it *is* better; because, in the second, it comes in a newer form to you, for you have got used to all my modes; in the third place, it has more force from the fact that it is not subject to the doubt of personal preference; and lastly, because he has a large, comprehensive way of asserting things, which pleases you better than my more dubitant mode of submitting them,—all very sound and good reasons: but still, why be so vexed with Wynnie?

[My mother was now, however, so vexed with my father for saying she preferred the Dean's preaching to his,—although I doubt very much whether it wasn't true,—that she actually walked out of the octagon room where they were, and left him to meditate on his unkindness. Vexed with herself the next moment, she returned as if nothing had happened. I am only telling what my mother told me; for to her grown daughters she is blessedly trusting.]

*Mother.*—Then if you will have them married, husband, will you say how on earth you expect them to live? He just makes both ends meet now: I suppose he doesn't make things out worse than they are; and that is his own account of the state of his affairs.

*Father.*—Ah, yes! that *is*—a secondary consideration, my dear. But I have hardly begun to think about it yet. There will be a difficulty there, I can easily imagine; for he is far too independent to let us do any thing for him.

*Mother.*—And you can't do much, if they would. Really, they oughtn't to marry yet.

*Father.*—Really, we must leave it to themselves. I don't think you and I need trouble our heads about it. When Percivale considers himself prepared to marry, and Wynnie thinks he is right, you may be sure they see their way to a livelihood without running in hopeless debt to their tradespeople.

*Mother.*—Oh, yes! I dare say: in some poky little lodging or other!

*Father.*—For my part, Ethelwyn, I think it better to build castles in the air than huts in the smoke. But seriously, a little poverty and a little struggling would be a most healthy and healing thing for Wynnie. It hasn't done Percivale much good yet, I confess; for he is far too indifferent to his own comforts to mind it: but it will be quite another thing when he has a young wife and perhaps children depending upon him. Then his poverty may begin to hurt him, and so do him some good.

* * * * *

It may seem odd that my father and mother should now be taking such opposite sides to those they took when the question of our engagement was first started, as represented by my father in "The Seaboard Parish." But it will seem inconsistent to none of the family; for it was no unusual thing for them to take opposite sides to those they had previously advocated,—each happening at the time, possibly enlightened by the foregone arguments of the other, to be impressed with the correlate truth, as my father calls the other side of a thing. Besides, engagement and marriage are two different things; and although my mother was the first to recognize the good of our being engaged, when it came to marriage she got frightened, I think. Any how, I have her authority for saying that something like this passed between her and my father on the subject.

Discussion between them differed in this from what I have generally heard between married people, that it was always founded on a tacit understanding of certain unmentioned principles; and no doubt sometimes, if a stranger had been present, he would have been bewildered as to the very meaning of what they were saying. But we girls generally understood: and I fancy we learned more from their differences than from their agreements; for of course it was the differences that brought out their minds most, and chiefly led us to think that we might understand. In our house there were very few of those mysteries which in some houses seem so to abound; and I think the openness with which every question, for whose concealment there was no special reason, was discussed, did more than even any direct instruction we received to develop what thinking faculty might be in us. Nor was there much reason to dread that my small brothers might repeat any thing. I remember hearing Harry say to Charley once, they being then eight and nine years old, "That is mamma's opinion, Charley, not yours; and you know we must not repeat what we hear."

They soon came to be of one mind about Mr. Percivale and me: for indeed the only *real* ground for doubt that had ever existed was, whether I was good enough for him; and for my part, I knew then and know now, that I was and am dreadfully inferior to him. And notwithstanding the tremendous work women are now making about their rights (and, in as far as they are their rights, I hope to goodness they may get them, if it were only that certain who make me feel ashamed of myself because I, too, am a woman, might perhaps then drop out of the public regard),—notwithstanding this, I venture the sweeping assertion, that every woman is not as good as every man, and that it is not necessary to the dignity of a wife that she should assert even equality with her husband. Let him assert her equality or superiority if he will; but, were it a fact, it would be a poor one for her to assert, seeing her glory is in her husband. To seek the chief place is especially unfitting the marriage-feast. Whether I be a Christian or not,—and I have good reason to doubt it every day of my life,—at least I see that in the New Jerusalem one essential of citizenship consists in knowing how to set the good in others over against the evil in ourselves.

There, now, my father might have said that! and no doubt has said so twenty times in my hearing. It is, however, only since I was married that I have come to see it for myself; and, now that I do see it, I have a right to say it.

So we were married at last. My mother believes it was my father's good advice to Percivale concerning the sort of pictures he painted, that brought it about. For certainly soon after we were engaged, he began to have what his artist friends called a run of luck: he sold one picture after another in a very extraordinary and hopeful manner. But Percivale says it was his love for me—indeed he does—which enabled him to see not only much deeper into things, but also to see much better the bloom that hangs about every thing, and so to paint much better pictures than before. He felt, he said, that he had a hold now where before he had only a sight. However this may be, he had got on so well for a while that he wrote at last, that, if I was willing to share his poverty, it would not, he thought, be absolute starvation; and I was, of course, perfectly content. I can't put in words—indeed I dare not, for fear of writing what would be, if not unladylike, at least uncharitable—my contempt for those women who, loving a man, hesitate to run every risk with him. Of course, if they cannot trust him, it is a different thing. I am not going to say any thing about that; for I should be out of my depth,—not in the least understanding how a woman can love a man to whom she cannot look up. I believe there are who can; I see some men married whom I don't believe any woman ever did or ever could respect; all I say is, I don't understand it.

My father and mother made no objection, and were evidently at last quite agreed that it would be the best thing for both of us; and so, I say, we were married.

I ought to just mention, that, before the day arrived, my mother went up to London at Percivale's request, to help him in getting together the few things absolutely needful for the barest commencement of housekeeping. For the rest, it had been arranged that we should furnish by degrees, buying as we saw what we liked, and could afford it. The greater part of modern fashions in furniture, having both been accustomed to the stateliness of a more artistic period, we detested for their ugliness, and chiefly, therefore, we desired to look about us at our leisure.

My mother came back more satisfied with the little house he had taken than I had expected. It was not so easy to get one to suit us; for of course he required a large room to paint in, with a good north light. He had however succeeded better than he had hoped.

"You will find things very different from what you have been used to, Wynnie," said my mother.

"Of course, mamma; I know that," I answered. "I hope I am prepared to meet it. If I don't like it, I shall have no one to blame but myself; and I don't see what right people have to expect what they have been used to."

"There is just this advantage," said my father, "in having been used to nice things, that it ought to be easier to keep from sinking into the sordid, however straitened the new circumstances may be, compared with the old."

On the evening before the wedding, my father took me into the octagon room, and there knelt down with me and my mother, and prayed for me in such a wonderful way that I was perfectly astonished and overcome. I had never known him to do any thing of the kind before. He was not favorable to extempore prayer in public, or even in the family, and indeed had often seemed willing to omit prayers for what I could not always count sufficient reason: he had a horror at their getting to be a matter of course, and a form; for then, he said, they ceased to be worship at all, and were a mere pagan rite, better far left alone. I remember also he said, that those, however good they might be, who urged attention to the forms of religion, such as going to church and saying prayers, were, however innocently, just the prophets of Pharisaism; that what men had to be stirred up to was to lay hold upon God, and then they would not fail to find out what religious forms they ought to cherish. "The spirit first, and then the flesh," he would say. To put the latter before the former was a falsehood, and therefore a frightful danger, being at the root of all declensions in the Church, and making ever-recurring earthquakes and persecutions and repentances and reformations needful. I find what my father used to say coming back so often now that I hear so little of it,—especially as he talks much less, accusing himself of having always talked too much,—and I understand it so much better now, that I shall be always in danger of interrupting my narrative to say something that he said. But when I commence the next chapter, I shall get on faster, I hope. My story is like a vessel I saw once being launched: it would stick on the stocks, instead of sliding away into the expectant waters.

# CHAPTER III.

## MY WEDDING.

I confess the first thing I did when I knew myself the next morning was to have a good cry. To leave the place where I had been born was like forsaking the laws and order of the Nature I knew, for some other Nature it might be, but not known to me as such. How, for instance, could one who has been used to our bright white sun, and our pale modest moon, with our soft twilights, and far, mysterious skies of night, be willing to fall in with the order of things in a planet, such as I have read of somewhere, with three or four suns, one red and another green and another yellow? Only perhaps I've taken it all up wrong, and I do like looking at a landscape for a minute or so through a colored glass; and if it be so, of course it all blends, and all we want is harmony. What I mean is, that I found it a great wrench to leave the dear old place, and of course loved it more than I had ever loved it. But I would get all my crying about that over beforehand. It would be bad enough afterwards to have to part with my father and mother and Connie, and the rest of them. Only it wasn't like leaving them. You can't leave hearts as you do rooms. You can't leave thoughts as you do books. Those you love only come nearer to you when you go away from them. The same rules don't hold with *thinks* and *things*, as my eldest boy distinguished them the other day.

But somehow I couldn't get up and dress. I seemed to have got very fond of my own bed, and the queer old crows, as I had called them from babyhood, on the chintz curtains, and the Chinese paper on the wall with the strangest birds and creeping things on it. It was a lovely spring morning, and the sun was shining gloriously. I knew that the rain of the last night must be glittering on the grass and the young leaves; and I heard the birds singing as if they knew far more than mere human beings, and believed a great deal more than they knew. Nobody will persuade me that the birds don't mean it; that they sing from any thing else than gladness of heart. And if they don't think about cats and guns, why should they? Even when they fall on the ground, it is not without our Father. How horridly dull and stupid it seems to say that "without your Father" means without *his knowing it.* The Father's mere *knowledge* of a thing—if that could be, which my father says can't—is not the Father. The Father's tenderness and care and love of it all the time, that is the not falling without him. When the cat kills the bird, as I have seen happen so often in our poor little London garden, God yet saves his bird from his cat. There is nothing so bad as it looks to our half-sight, our blinding perceptions. My father used to say we are all walking in a spiritual twilight, and are all more or less affected with twilight blindness, as some people are physically. Percivale, for one, who is as brave as any wife could wish, is far more timid than I am in crossing a London street in the twilight; he can't see what is coming, and fancies he sees what is not coming. But then he has faith in me, and never starts when I am leading him.

Well, the birds were singing, and Dora and the boys were making a great chatter, like a whole colony of sparrows, under my window. Still I felt as if I had twenty questions to settle before I could get up comfortably, and so lay on and on till the breakfast-bell rang: and I was not more than half dressed when my mother came to see why I was late; for I had not been late forever so long before.

She comforted me as nobody but a mother can comfort. Oh, I do hope I shall be to my children what my mother has been to me! It would be such a blessed thing to be a well of water whence they may be sure of drawing comfort. And all she said to me has come true.

Of course, my father gave me away, and Mr. Weir married us.

It had been before agreed that we should have no wedding journey. We all liked the old-fashioned plan of the bride going straight from her father's house to her husband's. The other way seemed a poor invention, just for the sake of something different. So after the wedding, we spent the time as we should have done any other day, wandering about in groups, or sitting and reading, only that we were all more smartly dressed; until it was time for an early dinner, after which we drove to the station, accompanied only by my father and mother. After they left us, or rather we left them, my husband did not speak to me for nearly an hour: I knew why, and was very grateful. He would not show his new face in the midst of my old loves and their sorrows, but would give me time to re-arrange the grouping so as myself to bring him in when all was ready for him. I know that was what he was thinking, or feeling rather; and I understood him perfectly. At last, when I had got things a little tidier inside me, and had got my eyes to stop, I held out my hand to him, and then—knew that I was his wife.

This is all I have got to tell, though I have plenty more to keep, till we get to London. There, instead of my father's nice carriage, we got into a jolting, lumbering, horrid cab, with my five boxes and Percivale's little portmanteau on the top of it, and drove away to Camden Town. It *was* to a part of it near the Regent's Park; and so our letters were always, according to the divisions of the post-office, addressed to Regent's Park, but for all practical intents we were in Camden Town. It was indeed a change from a fine old house in the country; but the street wasn't much uglier than Belgrave Square, or any other of those heaps of uglinesses, called squares, in the West End; and, after what I had been told to expect, I was surprised at the prettiness of the little house, when I stepped out of the cab and looked about me. It was stuck on like a swallow's nest to the end of a great row of commonplace houses, nearly a quarter of a mile in length, but itself was not the work of one of those wretched builders who care no more for beauty in what they build than a scavenger in the heap of mud he scrapes from the street. It had been built by a painter for himself, in the Tudor style; and though Percivale says the idea is not very well carried out, I like it much.

I found it a little dreary when I entered though,—from its emptiness. The only sitting-room at all prepared had just a table and two or three old-fashioned chairs in it; not even a carpet on the floor. The bedroom and dressing-room were also as scantily furnished as they well could be.

"Don't be dismayed, my darling," said my husband.

"Look here,"—showing me a bunch of notes,—"we shall go out to-morrow and buy all we want,—as far as this will go,—and then wait for the rest. It will be such a pleasure to buy the things with you, and see them come home, and have you appoint their places. You and Sarah will make the carpets; won't you? And I will put them down, and we shall be like birds building their nest."

"We have only to line it; the nest is built already."

"Well, neither do the birds build the tree. I wonder if they ever sit in their old summer nests in the winter nights."

"I am afraid not," I answered; "but I'm ashamed to say I can't tell."

"It is the only pretty house I know in all London," he went on, "with a studio at the back of it. I have had my eye on it for a long time, but there seemed no sign of a migratory disposition in the bird who had occupied it for three years past. All at once he spread his wings and flew. I count myself very fortunate."

"So do I. But now you must let me see your study," I said. "I hope I may sit in it when you've got nobody there."

"As much as ever you like, my love," he answered. "Only I don't want to make all my women like you, as I've been doing for the last two years. You must get me out of that somehow."

"Easily. I shall be so cross and disagreeable that you will get tired of me, and find no more difficulty in keeping me out of your pictures."

But he got me out of his pictures without that; for when he had me always before him he didn't want to be always producing me.

He led me into the little hall,—made lovely by a cast of an unfinished Madonna of Michael Angelo's let into the wall,—and then to the back of it, where he opened a small cloth-covered door, when there yawned before me, below me, and above me, a great wide lofty room. Down into it led an almost perpendicular stair.

"So you keep a little private precipice here," I said.

"No, my dear," he returned; "you mistake. It is a Jacob's ladder,—or will be in one moment more."

He gave me his hand, and led me down.

"This is quite a banqueting-hall, Percivale!" I cried, looking round me.

"It shall be, the first time I get a thousand pounds for a picture," he returned.

"How grand you talk!" I said, looking up at him with some wonder; for big words rarely came out of his mouth.

"Well," he answered merrily, "I had two hundred and seventy-five for the last."

"That's a long way off a thousand," I returned, with a silly sigh.

"Quite right; and, therefore, this study is a long way off a banqueting-hall."

There was literally nothing inside the seventeen feet cube except one chair, one easel, a horrible thing like a huge doll, with no end of joints, called a lay figure, but Percivale called it his bishop; a number of pictures leaning their faces against the walls in attitudes of grief that their beauty was despised and no man would buy them; a few casts of legs and arms and faces, half a dozen murderous-looking weapons, and a couple of yards square of the most exquisite tapestry I ever saw.

"Do you like being read to when you are at work?" I asked him.

"Sometimes,—at certain kinds of work, but not by any means always," he answered. "Will you shut your eyes for one minute," he went on, "and, whatever I do, not open them till I tell you?"

"You mustn't hurt me, then, or I may open them without being able to help it, you know," I said, closing my eyes tight.

"Hurt you!" he repeated, with a tone I would not put on paper if I could, and the same moment I found myself in his arms, carried like a baby, for Percivale is one of the strongest of men.

It was only for a few yards, however. He laid me down somewhere, and told me to open my eyes.

I could scarcely believe them when I did. I was lying on a couch in a room,—small, indeed, but beyond exception the loveliest I had ever seen. At first I was only aware of an exquisite harmony of color, and could not have told of what it was composed. The place was lighted by a soft lamp that hung in the middle; and when my eyes went up to see where it was fastened, I found the ceiling marvellous in deep blue, with a suspicion of green, just like some of the shades of a peacock's feathers, with a multitude of gold and red stars upon it. What the walls were I could not for some time tell, they were so covered with pictures and sketches; against one was a lovely little set of book-shelves filled with books, and on a little carved table stood a vase of white hot-house flowers, with one red camellia. One picture had a curtain of green silk before it, and by its side hung the wounded knight whom his friends were carrying home to die.

"O my Percivale!" I cried, and could say no more.

"Do you like it?" he asked quietly, but with shining eyes.

"Like it?" I repeated. "Shall I like Paradise when I get there? But what a lot of money it must have cost you!"

"Not much," he answered; "not more than thirty pounds or so. Every spot of paint there is from my own brush."

"O Percivale!"

I must make a conversation of it to tell it at all; but what I really did say I know no more than the man in the moon.

"The carpet was the only expensive thing. That must be as thick as I could get it; for the floor is of stone, and must not come near your pretty feet. Guess what the place was before."

"I should say, the flower of a prickly-pear cactus, full of sunlight from behind, which a fairy took the fancy to swell into a room."

"It was a shed, in which the sculptor who occupied the place before me used to keep his wet clay and blocks of marble."

"Seeing is hardly believing," I said. "Is it to be my room? I know you mean it for my room, where I can ask you to come when I please, and where I can hide when any one comes you don't want me to see."

"That is just what I meant it for, my Ethelwyn,—and to let you know what I *would* do for you if I could."

"I hate the place, Percivale," I said. "What right has it to come poking in between you and me, telling me what I know and have known—for, well, I won't say how long—far better than even you can tell me?"

He looked a little troubled.

"Ah, my dear!" I said, "let my foolish words breathe and die."

I wonder sometimes to think how seldom I am in that room now. But there it is; and somehow I seem to know it all the time I am busy elsewhere.

He made me shut my eyes again, and carried me into the study.

"Now," he said, "find your way to your own room."

I looked about me, but could see no sign of door. He took up a tall stretcher with a canvas on it, and revealed the door, at the same time showing a likeness of myself,—at the top of the Jacob's ladder, as he called it, with me foot on the first step, and the other half way to the second. The light came from the window on my left, which he had turned into a western window, in order to get certain effects from a supposed sunset. I was represented in a white dress, tinged with the rose of the west; and he had managed, attributing the phenomenon to the inequalities of the glass in the window, to suggest one rosy wing behind me, with just the shoulder-roof of another visible.

"There!" he said. "It is not finished yet, but that is how I saw you one evening as I was sitting here all alone in the twilight."

"But you didn't really see me like that!" I said.

"I hardly know," he answered. "I had been forgetting every thing else in dreaming about you, and—how it was I cannot tell, but either in the body or out of the body there I saw you, standing just so at the top of the stair, smiling to me as much as to say, 'Have patience. My foot is on the first step. I'm coming.' I turned at once to my easel, and before the twilight was gone had sketched the vision. To-morrow, you must sit to me for an hour or so; for I will do nothing else till I have finished it, and sent it off to your father and mother."

I may just add that I hear it is considered a very fine painting. It hangs in the great dining-room at home. I wish I were as good as he has made it look.

The next morning, after I had given him the sitting he wanted, we set out on our furniture hunt; when, having keen enough eyes, I caught sight of this and of that and of twenty different things in the brokers' shops. We did not agree about the merits of everything by which one or the other was attracted; but an objection by the one always turned the other, a little at least, and we bought nothing we were not agreed about. Yet that evening the hall was piled with things sent home to line our nest. Percivale, as I have said, had saved up some money for the purpose, and I had a hundred pounds my father had given me before we started, which, never having had more than ten of my own at a time, I was eager enough to spend. So we found plenty to do for the fortnight during which time my mother had promised to say nothing to her friends in London of our arrival. Percivale also keeping out of the way of his friends, everybody thought we were on the Continent, or somewhere else, and left us to ourselves. And as he had sent in his pictures to the Academy, he was able to take a rest, which rest consisted in working hard at all sorts of upholstery, not to mention painters' and carpenters' work; so that we soon got the little house made into a very warm and very pretty nest. I may mention that Percivale was particularly pleased with a cabinet I bought for him on the sly, to stand in his study, and hold his paints and brushes and sketches; for there were all sorts of drawers in it, and some that it took us a good deal of trouble to find out, though he was clever enough to suspect them from the first, when I hadn't a thought of such a thing; and I have often fancied since that that cabinet was just like himself, for I have been going on finding out things in him that I had no idea were there when I married him. I had no idea that he was a poet, for instance. I wonder to this day why he never showed me any of his verses before we were married. He writes better poetry than my father,—at least my father says so. Indeed, I soon came to feel very ignorant and stupid beside him; he could tell me so many things, and especially in art (for he had thought about all kinds of it), making me understand that there is no end to it, any more than to the Nature which sets it going, and that the more we see into Nature, and try to represent it, the more ignorant and helpless we find ourselves, until at length I began to wonder whether God might not have made the world so rich and full just to teach his children humility. For a while I felt quite stunned. He very much wanted me to draw; but I thought it was no use trying, and, indeed, had no heart for it. I spoke to my father about it. He said it was indeed of no use, if my object was to be able to think much of myself, for no one could ever succeed in that in the long run; but if my object was to reap the delight of the truth, it was worth while to spend hours and hours on trying to draw a single tree-leaf, or paint the wing of a moth.

# CHAPTER IV.

## JUDY'S VISIT.

The very first morning after the expiry of the fortnight, when I was in the kitchen with Sarah, giving her instructions about a certain dish as if I had made it twenty times, whereas I had only just learned how from a shilling cookery-book, there came a double knock at the door. I guessed who it must be.

"Run, Sarah," I said, "and show Mrs. Morley into the drawing-room."

When I entered, there she was,—Mrs. Morley, *alias* Cousin Judy.

"Well, little cozzie!" she cried, as she kissed me three or four times, "I'm glad to see you gone the way of womankind,—wooed and married and a'!
Fate, child! inscrutable fate!" and she kissed me again.

She always calls me little coz, though I am a head taller than herself. She is as good as ever, quite as brusque, and at the first word apparently more overbearing. But she is as ready to listen to reason as ever was woman of my acquaintance; and I think the form of her speech is but a somewhat distorted reflex of her perfect honesty. After a little trifling talk, which is sure to come first when people are more than ordinarily glad to meet, I asked after her children. I forget how many there were of them, but they were then pretty far into the plural number.

"Growing like ill weeds," she said; "as anxious as ever their grandfathers and mothers were to get their heads up and do mischief. For my part I wish I was Jove,—to start them full grown at once. Or why shouldn't they be made like Eve out of their father's ribs? It would be a great comfort to their mother."

My father had always been much pleased with the results of Judy's training, as contrasted with those of his sister's. The little ones of my aunt Martha's family were always wanting something, and always looking care-worn like their mother, while she was always reading them lectures on their duty, and never making them mind what she said. She would represent the self-same thing to them over and over, until not merely all force, but all sense as well, seemed to have forsaken it. Her notion of duty was to tell them yet again the duty which they had been told at least a thousand times already, without the slightest result. They were dull children, wearisome and uninteresting. On the other hand, the little Morleys were full of life and eagerness. The fault in them was that they wouldn't take petting; and what's the good of a child that won't be petted? They lacked that something which makes a woman feel motherly.

"When did you arrive, cozzie?" she asked.

"A fortnight ago yesterday."

"Ah, you sly thing! What have you been doing with yourself all the time?"

"Furnishing."

"What! you came into an empty house?"

"Not quite that, but nearly."

"It is very odd I should never have seen your husband. We have crossed each other twenty times."

"Not so *very* odd, seeing he has been my husband only a fortnight."

"What is he like?"

"Like nothing but himself."

"Is he tall?"

"Yes."

"Is he stout?"

"No."

"An Adonis?"

"No."

"A Hercules?"

"No."

"Very clever, I believe."

"Not at all."

For my father had taught me to look down on that word.

"Why did you marry him then?"

"I didn't. He married me."

"What did you marry him for then?"

"For love."

"What did you love him for?"

"Because he was a philosopher."

"That's the oddest reason I ever heard for marrying a man."

"I said for loving him, Judy."

Her bright eyes were twinkling with fun.

"Come, cozzie," she said, "give me a proper reason for falling in love with this husband of yours."

"Well, I'll tell you, then," I said; "only you mustn't tell any other body; he's got such a big shaggy head, just like a lion's."

"And such a huge big foot,—just like a bear's?"

"Yes, and such great huge hands! Why, the two of them go quite round my waist! And such big eyes, that they look right through me; and such a big heart, that if he saw me doing any thing wrong, he would kill me, and bury me in it."

"Well, I must say, it is the most extraordinary description of a husband I ever heard. It sounds to me very like an ogre."

"Yes; I admit the description is rather ogrish. But then he's poor, and that makes up for a good deal."

I was in the humor for talking nonsense, and of course expected of all people that Judy would understand my fun.

"How does that make up for any thing?"

"Because if he is a poor man, he isn't a rich man, and therefore not so likely to be a stupid."

"How do you make that out?"

"Because, first of all, the rich man doesn't know what to do with his money, whereas my ogre knows what to do without it. Then the rich man wonders in the morning which waistcoat he shall put on, while my ogre has but one, besides his Sunday one. Then supposing the rich man has slept well, and has done a fair stroke or two of business, he wants nothing but a well-dressed wife, a well-dressed dinner, a few glasses of his favorite wine, and the evening paper, well-diluted with a sleep in his easy chair, to be perfectly satisfied that this world is the best of all possible worlds. Now my ogre, on the other hand"—

I was going on to point out how frightfully different from all this my ogre was,—how he would devour a half-cooked chop, and drink a pint of ale from the public-house, &c., &c., when she interrupted me, saying with an odd expression of voice,—

"You are satirical, cozzie. He's not the worst sort of man you've just described. A woman might be very happy with him. If it weren't such early days, I should doubt if you were as comfortable as you would have people think; for how else should you be so ill-natured?"

It flashed upon me, that, without the least intention, I had been giving a very fair portrait of Mr. Morley. I felt my face grow as red as fire.

"I had no intention of being satirical, Judy," I replied.

"I was only describing a man the very opposite of my husband."

"You don't know mine yet," she said. "You may think"—

She actually broke down and cried. I had never in my life seen her cry, and I was miserable at what I had done. Here was a nice beginning of social relations in my married life!

I knelt down, put my arms round her, and looked up in her face.

"Dear Judy," I said, "you mistake me quite. I never thought of Mr. Morley when I said that. How should I have dared to say such things if I had? He is a most kind, good man, and papa and every one is glad when he comes to see us. I dare say he does like to sleep well,—I know Percivale does; and I don't doubt he likes to get on with what he's at: Percivale does, for he's ever so much better company when he has got on with his picture; and I know he likes to see me well dressed,—at least I haven't tried him with any thing else yet, for I have plenty of clothes for a while; and then for the dinner, which I believe was one of the points in the description I gave, I wish Percivale cared a little more for his, for then it would be easier to do something for him. As to the newspaper, there I fear I must give him up, for I have never yet seen him with one in his hand. He's *so* stupid about some things!"

"Oh, you've found that out! have you? Men *are* stupid; there's no doubt of that. But you don't know my Walter yet."

I looked up, and, behold, Percivale was in the room! His face wore such a curious expression that I could hardly help laughing. And no wonder: for here was I on my knees, clasping my first visitor, and to all appearance pouring out the woes of my wedded life in her lap,—woes so deep that they drew tears from her as she listened. All this flashed upon me as I started to my feet: but I could give no explanation; I could only make haste to introduce my husband to my cousin Judy.

He behaved, of course, as if he had heard nothing. But I fancy Judy caught a glimpse of the awkward position, for she plunged into the affair at once.

"Here is my cousin, Mr. Percivale, has been abusing my husband to my face, calling him rich and stupid, and I don't know what all. I confess he is so stupid as to be very fond of me, but that's all I know against him."

And her handkerchief went once more to her eyes.

"Dear Judy!" I expostulated, "you know I didn't say one word about him."

"Of course I do, you silly coz!" she cried, and burst out laughing. "But I won't forgive you except you make amends by dining with us to-morrow."

Thus for the time she carried it off; but I believe, and have since had good reason for believing, that she had really mistaken me at first, and been much annoyed.

She and Percivale got on very well. He showed her the portrait he was still working at,—even accepted one or two trifling hints as to the likeness, and they parted the best friends in the world. Glad as I had been to see her, how I longed to see the last of her! The moment she was gone, I threw myself into his arms, and told him how it came about. He laughed heartily.

"I *was* a little puzzled," he said, "to hear you informing a lady I had never seen that I was so very stupid."

"But I wasn't telling a story, either, for you know you are ve-e-e-ry stupid, Percivale. You don't know a leg from a shoulder of mutton, and you can't carve a bit. How ever you can draw as you do, is a marvel to me, when you know nothing about the shapes of things. It was very wrong to say it, even for the sake of covering poor Mrs. Morley's husband; but it was quite true you know."

"Perfectly true, my love," he said, with something else where I've only put commas; "and I mean to remain so, in order that you may always have something to fall back upon when you get yourself into a scrape by forgetting that other people have husbands as well as you."

# CHAPTER V.

## "GOOD SOCIETY."

We had agreed, rather against the inclination of both of us, to dine the next evening with the Morleys. We should have preferred our own society, but we could not refuse.

"They will be talking to me about my pictures," said my husband, "and that is just what I hate. People that know nothing of art, that can't distinguish purple from black, will yet parade their ignorance, and expect me to be pleased."

"Mr. Morley is a well-bred man, Percivale," I said.

"That's the worst of it,—they do it for good manners; I know the kind of people perfectly. I hate to have my pictures praised. It is as bad as talking to one's face about the nose upon it."

I wonder if all ladies keep their husbands waiting. I did that night, I know, and, I am afraid, a good many times after,—not, however, since Percivale told me very seriously that being late for dinner was the only fault of mine the blame of which he would not take on his own shoulders. The fact on this occasion was, that I could not get my hair right. It was the first time I missed what I had been used to, and longed for the deft fingers of my mother's maid to help me. When I told him the cause, he said he would do my hair for me next time, if I would teach him how. But I have managed very well since without either him or a lady's-maid.

When we reached Bolivar Square, we found the company waiting; and, as if for a rebuke to us, the butler announced dinner the moment we entered. I was seated between Mr. Morley and a friend of his who took me down, Mr. Baddeley, a portly gentleman, with an expanse of snowy shirt from which flashed three diamond studs. A huge gold chain reposed upon his front, and on his finger shone a brilliant of great size. Every thing about him seemed to say, "Look how real I am! No shoddy about me!" His hands were plump and white, and looked as if they did not know what dust was. His talk sounded very rich, and yet there was no pretence in it. His wife looked less of a lady than he of a gentleman, for she betrayed conscious importance. I found afterwards that he was the only son of a railway contractor, who had himself handled the spade, but at last died enormously rich. He spoke blandly, but with a certain quiet authority which I disliked.

"Are you fond of the opera, Mrs. Percivale?" he asked me in order to make talk.

"I have never been to the opera," I answered.

"Never been to the opera? Ain't you fond of music?"

"Did you ever know a lady that wasn't?"

"Then you must go to the opera."

"But it is just because I fancy myself fond of music that I don't think I should like the opera."

"You can't hear such music anywhere else."

"But the antics of the singers, pretending to be in such furies of passion, yet modulating every note with the cunning of a carver in ivory, seems to me so preposterous! For surely song springs from a brooding over past feeling,—I do not mean lost feeling; never from present emotion."

"Ah! you would change your mind after having once been. I should strongly advise you to go, if only for once. You ought now, really."

"An artist's wife must do without such expensive amusements,—except her husband's pictures be very popular indeed. I might as well cry for the moon. The cost of a box at the opera for a single night would keep my little household for a fortnight."

"Ah, well! but you should see 'The Barber,'" he said.

"Perhaps if I could hear without seeing, I should like it better," I answered.

He fell silent, busying himself with his fish, and when he spoke again turned to the lady on his left. I went on with my dinner. I knew that our host had heard what I said, for I saw him turn rather hastily to his butler.

Mr. Morley is a man difficult to describe, stiff in the back, and long and loose in the neck, reminding me of those toy-birds that bob head and tail up and down alternately. When he agrees with any thing you say, down comes his head with a rectangular nod; when he does not agree with you, he is so silent and motionless that he leaves you in doubt whether he has heard a word of what you have been saying. His face is hard, and was to me then inscrutable, while what he said always seemed to have little or nothing to do with what he was thinking; and I had not then learned whether he had a heart or not. His features were well formed, but they and his head and face too small for his body. He seldom smiled except when in doubt. He had, I understood, been very successful in business, and always looked full of schemes.

"Have you been to the Academy yet?" he asked.

"No; this is only the first day of it."

"Are your husband's pictures well hung?"

"As high as Haman," I answered; "skied, in fact. That is the right word, I believe."

"I would advise you to avoid slang, my dear cousin,—*professional* slang especially; and to remember that in London there are no professions after six o clock."

"Indeed!" I returned. "As we came along in the carriage,—cabbage, I mean,—I saw no end of shops open."

"I mean in society,—at dinner,—amongst friends, you know."

"My dear Mr. Morley, you have just done asking me about my husband's pictures; and, if you will listen a moment, you will hear that lady next my husband talking to him about Leslie and Turner, and I don't know who more,—all in the trade."

"Hush! hush! I beg," he almost whispered, looking agonized. "That's Mrs. Baddeley. Her husband, next to you, is a great picture-buyer. That's why I asked him to meet you."

"I thought there were no professions in London after six o'clock."

"I am afraid I have not made my meaning quite clear to you."

"Not quite. Yet I think I understand you."

"We'll have a talk about it another time."

"With pleasure."

It irritated me rather that he should talk to me, a married woman, as to a little girl who did not know how to behave herself; but his patronage of my husband displeased me far more, and I was on the point of committing the terrible blunder of asking Mr. Baddeley if he had any poor relations; but I checked myself in time, and prayed to know whether he was a member of Parliament. He answered that he was not in the house at present, and asked in return why I had wished to know. I answered that I wanted a bill brought in for the punishment of fraudulent milkmen; for I couldn't get a decent pennyworth of milk in all Camden Town. He laughed, and said it would be a very desirable measure, only too great an interference with the liberty of the subject. I told him that kind of liberty was just what law in general owed its existence to, and was there on purpose to interfere with; but he did not seem to see it.

The fact is, I was very silly. Proud of being the wife of an artist, I resented the social injustice which I thought gave artists no place but one of sufferance. Proud also of being poor for Percivale's sake, I made a show of my poverty before people whom I supposed, rightly enough in many cases, to be proud of their riches. But I knew nothing of what poverty really meant, and was as yet only playing at being poor; cherishing a foolish, though unacknowledged notion of protecting my husband's poverty with the ægis of my position as the daughter of a man of consequence in his county. I was thus wronging the dignity of my husband's position, and complimenting wealth by making so much of its absence. Poverty or wealth ought to have been in my eyes such a trifle that I never thought of publishing whether I was rich or poor. I ought to have taken my position without wasting a thought on what it might appear in the eyes of those about me, meeting them on the mere level of humanity, and leaving them to settle with themselves how they were to think of me, and where they were to place me. I suspect also, now that I think of it, that I looked down upon my cousin Judy because she had a mere man of business for her husband; forgetting that our Lord had found a collector of conquered taxes,—a man, I presume, with little enough of the artistic about him,—one of the fittest in his nation to bear the message of his redemption to the hearts of his countrymen. It is his loves and his hopes, not his visions and intentions, by which a man is to be judged. My father had taught me all this; but I did not understand it then, nor until years after I had left him.

"Is Mrs. Percivale a lady of fortune?" asked Mr. Baddeley of my cousin Judy when we were gone, for we were the first to leave.

"Certainly not. Why do you ask?" she returned.

"Because, from her talk, I thought she must be," he answered.

Cousin Judy told me this the next day, and I could see she thought I had been bragging of my family. So I recounted all the conversation I had had with him, as nearly as I could recollect, and set down the question to an impertinent irony. But I have since changed my mind: I now judge that he could not believe any poor person would joke about poverty. I never found one of those people who go about begging for charities believe me when I told him the simple truth that I could not afford to subscribe. None but a rich person, they seem to think, would dare such an excuse, and that only in the just expectation that its very assertion must render it incredible.

# CHAPTER VI.

## A REFUGE FROM THE HEAT.

There was a little garden, one side enclosed by the house, another by the studio, and the remaining two by walls, evidently built for the nightly convenience of promenading cats. There was one pear-tree in the grass-plot which occupied the centre, and a few small fruit-trees, which, I may now safely say, never bore any thing, upon the walls. But the last occupant had cared for his garden; and, when I came to the cottage, it was, although you would hardly believe it now that my garden is inside the house, a pretty little spot,—only, if you stop thinking about a garden, it begins at once to go to the bad. Used although I had been to great wide lawns and park and gardens and wilderness, the tiny enclosure soon became to me the type of the boundless universe. The streets roared about me with ugly omnibuses and uglier cabs, fine carriages, huge earth-shaking drays, and, worse far, with the cries of all the tribe, of costermongers,—one especially offensive which soon began to haunt me. I almost hated the man who sent it forth to fill the summer air with disgust. He always put his hollowed hand to his jaw, as if it were loose and he had to hold it in its place, before he uttered his hideous howl, which would send me hurrying up the stairs to bury my head under all the pillows of my bed until, coming back across the wilderness of streets and lanes like the cry of a jackal growing fainter and fainter upon the wind, it should pass, and die away in the distance. Suburban London, I say, was roaring about me, and I was confined to a few square yards of grass and gravel-walk and flower-plot; but above was the depth of the sky, and thence at night the hosts of heaven looked in upon me with the same calm assured glance with which they shone upon southern forests, swarming with great butterflies and creatures that go flaming through the tropic darkness; and there the moon would come, and cast her lovely shadows; and there was room enough to feel alone and to try to pray. And what was strange, the room seemed greater, though the loneliness was gone, when my husband walked up and down in it with me. True, the greater part of the walk seemed to be the turnings, for they always came just when you wanted to go on and on; but, even with the scope of the world for your walk, you must turn and come back some time. At first, when he was smoking his great brown meerschaum, he and I would walk in opposite directions, passing each other in the middle, and so make the space double the size, for he had all the garden to himself, and I had it all to myself; and so I had his garden and mine too. That is how by degrees I got able to bear the smoke of tobacco, for I had never been used to it, and found it a small trial at first; but now I have got actually to like it, and greet a stray whiff from the study like a message from my husband. I fancy I could tell the smoke of that old black and red meerschaum from the smoke of any other pipe in creation.

"You *must* cure him of that bad habit," said cousin Judy to me once.

It made me angry. What right had she to call any thing my husband did a bad habit? and to expect me to agree with her was ten times worse. I am saving my money now to buy him a grand new pipe; and I may just mention here, that once I spent ninepence out of my last shilling to get him a packet of Bristol bird's-eye, for he was on the point of giving up smoking altogether because of—well, because of what will appear by and by.

England is getting dreadfully crowded with mean, ugly houses. If they were those of the poor and struggling, and not of the rich and comfortable, one might be consoled. But rich barbarism, in the shape of ugliness, is again pushing us to the sea. There, however, its "control stops;" and since I lived in London the sea has grown more precious to me than it was even in those lovely days at Kilkhaven,—merely because no one can build upon it. Ocean and sky remain as God made them. He must love space for us, though it be needless for himself; seeing that in all the magnificent notions of creation afforded us by astronomers,—shoal upon shoal of suns, each the centre of complicated and infinitely varied systems,—the spaces between are yet more overwhelming in their vast inconceivableness. I thank God for the room he thus gives us, and hence can endure to see the fair face of his England disfigured by the mud-pies of his children.

There was in the garden a little summer-house, of which I was fond, chiefly because, knowing my passion for the flower, Percivale had surrounded it with a multitude of sweet peas, which, as they grew, he had trained over the trellis-work of its sides. Through them filtered the sweet airs of the summer as through an Æolian harp of unheard harmonies. To sit there in a warm evening, when the moth-airs just woke and gave two or three wafts of their wings and ceased, was like sitting in the midst of a small gospel.

The summer had come on, and the days were very hot,—so hot and changeless, with their unclouded skies and their glowing centre, that they seemed to grow stupid with their own heat. It was as if—like a hen brooding over her chickens—the day, brooding over its coming harvests, grew dull and sleepy, living only in what was to come. Notwithstanding the feelings I have just recorded, I began to long for a wider horizon, whence some wind might come and blow upon me, and wake me up, not merely to live, but to know that I lived.

One afternoon I left my little summer-seat, where I had been sitting at work, and went through the house, and down the precipice, into my husband's study.

"It is so hot," I said, "I will try my little grotto: it may be cooler."

He opened the door for me, and, with his palette on his thumb, and a brush in his hand, sat down for a moment beside me.

"This heat is too much for you, darling," he said.

"I do feel it. I wish I could get from the garden into my nest without going up through the house and down the Jacob's ladder," I said. "It is so hot! I never felt heat like it before."

He sat silent for a while, and then said,—

"I've been thinking I must get you into the country for a few weeks. It would do you no end of good."

"I suppose the wind does blow somewhere," I returned. "But"—

"You don't want to leave me?" he said.

"I don't. And I know with that ugly portrait on hand you can't go with me."

"He happened to be painting the portrait of a plain red-faced lady, in a delicate lace cap,—a very unfit subject for art,—much needing to be made over again first, it seemed to me. Only there she was, with a right to have her portrait painted if she wished it; and there was Percivale, with time on his hands, and room in his pockets, and the faith that whatever God had thought worth making could not be unworthy of representation. Hence he had willingly undertaken a likeness of her, to be finished within a certain time, and was now working at it as conscientiously as if it had been the portrait of a lovely young duchess or peasant-girl. I was only afraid he would make it too like to please the lady herself. His time was now getting short, and he could not leave home before fulfilling his engagement.

"But," he returned, "why shouldn't you go to the Hall for a week or two without me? I will take you down, and come and fetch you."

"I'm so stupid you want to get rid of me!" I said.

I did not in the least believe it, and yet was on the edge of crying, which is not a habit with me.

"You know better than that, my Wynnie," he answered gravely. "You want your mother to comfort you. And there must be some air in the country. So tell Sarah to put up your things, and I'll take you down to-morrow morning. When I get this portrait done, I will come and stay a few days, if they will have me, and then take you home."

The thought of seeing my mother and my father, and the old place, came over me with a rush. I felt all at once as if I had been absent for years instead of weeks. I cried in earnest now,—with delight though,—and there is no shame in that. So it was all arranged; and next afternoon I was lying on a couch in the yellow drawing-room, with my mother seated beside me, and Connie in an easy-chair by the open window, through which came every now and then such a sweet wave of air as bathed me with hope, and seemed to wash all the noises, even the loose-jawed man's hateful howl, from my brain.

Yet, glad as I was to be once more at home, I felt, when Percivale left me the next morning to return by a third-class train to his ugly portrait,—for the lady was to sit to him that same afternoon,—that the idea of home was already leaving Oldcastle Hall, and flitting back to the suburban cottage haunted by the bawling voice of the costermonger.

But I soon felt better: for here there was plenty of shadow, and in the hottest days my father could always tell where any wind would be stirring; for he knew every out and in of the place like his own pockets, as Dora said, who took a little after cousin Judy in her way. It will give a notion of his tenderness if I set down just one tiniest instance of his attention to me. The forenoon was oppressive. I was sitting under a tree, trying to read when he came up to me. There was a wooden gate, with open bars near. He went and set it wide, saying,—

"There, my love! You will fancy yourself cooler if I leave the gate open."

Will my reader laugh at me for mentioning such a trifle? I think not, for it went deep to my heart, and I seemed to know God better for it ever after. A father is a great and marvellous truth, and one you can never get at the depth of, try how you may.

Then my mother! She was, if possible, yet more to me than my father. I could tell her any thing and every thing without fear, while I confess to a little dread of my father still. He is too like my own conscience to allow of my being quite confident with him. But Connie is just as comfortable with him as I am with my mother. If in my childhood I was ever tempted to conceal any thing from her, the very thought of it made me miserable until I had told her. And now she would watch me with her gentle, dove-like eyes, and seemed to know at once, without being told, what was the matter with me. She never asked me what I should like, but went and brought something; and, if she saw that I didn't care for it, wouldn't press me, or offer any thing instead, but chat for a minute or two, carry it away, and return with something else. My heart was like to break at times with the swelling of the love that was in it. My eldest child, my Ethelwyn,—for my husband would have her called the same name as me, only I insisted it should be after my mother and not after me,—has her very eyes, and for years has been trying to mother me over again to the best of her sweet ability.

# CHAPTER VII.

## CONNIE.

It is high time, though, that I dropped writing about myself for a while. I don't find my self so interesting as it used to be.

The worst of some kinds especially of small illnesses is, that they make you think a great deal too much about yourself. Connie's, which was a great and terrible one, never made her do so. She was always forgetting herself in her interest about others. I think I was made more selfish to begin with; and yet I have a hope that a too-much-thinking about yourself may not *always* be pure selfishness. It may be something else wrong in you that makes you uncomfortable, and keeps drawing your eyes towards the aching place. I will hope so till I get rid of the whole business, and then I shall not care much how it came or what it was.

Connie was now a thin, pale, delicate-looking—not handsome, but lovely girl. Her eyes, some people said, were too big for her face; but that seemed to me no more to the discredit of her beauty than it would have been a reproach to say that her soul was too big for her body. She had been early ripened by the hot sun of suffering, and the self-restraint which pain had taught her. Patience had mossed her over and made her warm and soft and sweet. She never looked for attention, but accepted all that was offered with a smile which seemed to say, "It is more than I need, but you are so good I mustn't spoil it." She was not confined to her sofa now, though she needed to lie down often, but could walk about pretty well, only you must give her time. You could always make her merry by saying she walked like an old woman; and it was the only way we could get rid of the sadness of seeing it. We betook ourselves to her to laugh *her* sadness away from us.

Once, as I lay on a couch on the lawn, she came towards me carrying a bunch of grapes from the greenhouse,—a great bunch, each individual grape ready to burst with the sunlight it had bottled up in its swollen purple skin.

"They are too heavy for you, old lady," I cried.

"Yes; I *am* an old lady," she answered. "Think what good use of my time I have made compared with you! I have got ever so far before you: I've nearly forgotten how to walk!"

The tears gathered in my eyes as she left me with the bunch; for how could one help being sad to think of the time when she used to bound like a fawn over the grass, her slender figure borne like a feather on its own slight yet firm muscles, which used to knot so much harder than any of ours. She turned to say something, and, perceiving my emotion, came slowly back.

"Dear Wynnie," she said, "you wouldn't have me back with my old foolishness, would you? Believe me, life is ten times more precious than it was before. I feel and enjoy and love so much more! I don't know how often I thank God for what befell me."

I could only smile an answer, unable to speak, not now from pity, but from shame of my own petulant restlessness and impatient helplessness.

I believe she had a special affection for poor Sprite, the pony which threw her,—special, I mean, since the accident,—regarding him as in some sense the angel which had driven her out of paradise into a better world. If ever he got loose, and Connie was anywhere about, he was sure to find her: he was an omnivorous animal, and she had always something he would eat when his favorite apples were unattainable. More than once she had been roused from her sleep on the lawn by the lips and the breath of Sprite upon her face; but, although one painful sign of her weakness was, that she started at the least noise or sudden discovery of a presence, she never started at the most unexpected intrusion of Sprite, any more than at the voice of my father or mother. Need I say there was one more whose voice or presence never startled her?

The relation between them was lovely to see. Turner was a fine, healthy, broad-shouldered fellow, of bold carriage and frank manners, above the middle height, with rather large features, keen black eyes, and great personal strength. Yet to such a man, poor little wan-faced, big-eyed Connie assumed imperious airs, mostly, but perhaps not entirely, for the fun of it; while he looked only enchanted every time she honored him with a little tyranny.

"There! I'm tired," she would say, holding out her arms like a baby. "Carry me in."

And the great strong man would stoop with a worshipping look in his eyes, and, taking her carefully, would carry her in as lightly and gently and steadily as if she had been but the baby whose manners she had for the moment assumed. This began, of course, when she was unable to walk; but it did not stop then, for she would occasionally tell him to carry her after she was quite capable of crawling at least. They had now been engaged for some months; and before me, as a newly-married woman, they did not mind talking a little.

One day she was lying on a rug on the lawn, with him on the grass beside her, leaning on his elbow, and looking down into her sky-like eyes. She lifted her hand, and stroked his mustache with a forefinger, while he kept as still as a statue, or one who fears to scare the bird that is picking up the crumbs at his feet.

"Poor, poor man!" she said; and from the tone I knew the tears had begun to gather in those eyes.

"Why do you pity me, Connie?" he asked.

"Because you will have such a wretched little creature for a wife some day,—or perhaps never,—which would be best after all."

He answered cheerily.

"If you will kindly allow me my choice, I prefer just *such* a wretched little creature to any one else in the world."

"And why, pray? Give a good reason, and I will forgive your bad taste."

"Because she won't be able to hurt me much when she beats me."

"A better reason, or she will."

"Because I can punish her if she isn't good by taking her up in my arms, and carrying her about until she gives in."

"A better reason, or I shall be naughty directly."

"Because I shall always know where to find her."

"Ah, yes! she must leave *you* to find *her*. But that's a silly reason. If you don't give me a better, I'll get up and walk into the house."

"Because there won't be any waste of me. Will that do?"

"What do you mean?" she asked, with mock imperiousness.

"I mean that I shall be able to lay not only my heart but my brute strength at her feet. I shall be allowed to be her beast of burden, to carry her whither she would; and so with my body her to worship more than most husbands have a chance of worshipping their wives."

"There! take me, take me!" she said, stretching up her arms to him. "How good you are! I don't deserve such a great man one bit. But I *will* love him. Take me directly; for there's Wynnie listening to every word we say to each other, and laughing at us. She can laugh without looking like it."

The fact is, I was crying, and the creature knew it. Turner brought her to me, and held her down for me to kiss; then carried her in to her mother.

I believe the county people round considered our family far gone on the inclined plane of degeneracy. First my mother, the heiress, had married a clergyman of no high family; then they had given their eldest daughter to a poor artist, something of the same standing as—well, I will be rude to no order of humanity, and therefore avoid comparisons; and now it was generally known that Connie was engaged to a country practitioner, a man who made up his own prescriptions. We talked and laughed over certain remarks of the kind that reached us, and compared our two with the gentlemen about us,—in no way to the advantage of any of the latter, you may be sure. It was silly work; but we were only two loving girls, with the best possible reasons for being proud of the men who had honored us with their love.

# CHAPTER VIII.

## CONNIE'S BABY.

It is time I told my readers something about the little Theodora. She was now nearly four years old I think,—a dark-skinned, lithe-limbed, wild little creature, very pretty,—at least most people said so, while others insisted that she had a common look. I admit she was not like a lady's child—only one has seen ladies' children look common enough; neither did she look like the child of working people—though amongst such, again, one sees sometimes a child the oldest family in England might be proud of. The fact is, she had a certain tinge of the savage about her, specially manifest in a certain furtive look of her black eyes, with which she seemed now and then to be measuring you, and her prospects in relation to you. I have seen the child of cultivated parents sit and stare at a stranger from her stool in the most persistent manner, never withdrawing her eyes, as if she would pierce to his soul, and understand by very force of insight whether he was or was not one to be honored with her confidence; and I have often seen the side-long glance of sly merriment, or loving shyness, or small coquetry; but I have never, in any other child, seen *that* look of self-protective speculation; and it used to make me uneasy, for of course, like every one else in the house, I loved the child. She was a wayward, often unmanageable creature, but affectionate,—sometimes after an insane, or, at least, very ape-like fashion. Every now and then she would take an unaccountable preference for some one of the family or household, at one time for the old housekeeper, at another for the stable-boy, at another for one of us; in which fits of partiality she would always turn a blind and deaf side upon every one else, actually seeming to imagine she showed the strength of her love to the one by the paraded exclusion of the others. I cannot tell how much of this was natural to her, and how much the result of the foolish and injurious jealousy of the servants. I say *servants*, because I know such an influencing was all but impossible in the family itself. If my father heard any one utter such a phrase as "Don't you love me best?"—or, "better than" such a one? or, "Ain't I your favorite?"—well, you all know my father, and know him really, for he never wrote a word he did not believe—but you would have been astonished, I venture to think, and perhaps at first bewildered as well, by the look of indignation flashed from his eyes. He was not the gentle, all-excusing man some readers, I know, fancy him from his writings. He was gentle even to tenderness when he had time to think a moment, and in any quiet judgment he always took as much the side of the offender as was possible with any likelihood of justice; but in the first moments of contact with what he thought bad in principle, and that in the smallest trifle, he would speak words that made even those who were not included in the condemnation tremble with sympathetic fear. "There, Harry, you take it—quick, or Charley will have it," said the nurse one day, little thinking who overheard her. "Woman!" cried a voice of wrath from the corridor, "do you know what you are doing? Would you make him twofold more the child of hell than yourself?" An hour after, she was sent for to the study; and when she came out her eyes were very red. My father was unusually silent at dinner; and, after the younger ones were gone, he turned to my mother, and said, "Ethel, I spoke the truth. All *that* is of the Devil,—horribly bad; and yet I am more to blame in my condemnation of them than she for the words themselves. The thought of so polluting the mind of a child makes me fierce, and the wrath of man worketh not the righteousness of God. The old Adam is only too glad to get a word in, if even in behalf of his supplanting successor." Then he rose, and, taking my mother by the arm, walked away with her. I confess I honored him for his self-condemnation the most. I must add that the offending nurse had been ten years in the family, and ought to have known better.

But to return to Theodora. She was subject to attacks of the most furious passion, especially when any thing occurred to thwart the indulgence of the ephemeral partiality I have just described. Then, wherever she was, she would throw herself down at once,—on the floor, on the walk or lawn, or, as happened on one occasion, in the water,—and kick and scream. At such times she cared nothing even for my father, of whom generally she stood in considerable awe,—a feeling he rather encouraged. "She has plenty of people about her to represent the gospel," he said once. "I will keep the department of the law, without which she will never appreciate the gospel. My part will, I trust, vanish in due time, and the law turn out to have been, after all, only the imperfect gospel, just as the leaf is the imperfect flower. But the gospel is no gospel till it gets into the heart, and it sometimes wants a torpedo to blow the gates of that open." For no torpedo or Krupp gun, however, did Theodora care at such times; and, after repeated experience of the inefficacy of coaxing, my father gave orders, that, when a fit occurred, every one, without exception, should not merely leave her alone, but go out of sight, and if possible out of hearing,—at least out of her hearing—that she might know she had driven her friends far from her, and be brought to a sense of loneliness and need. I am pretty sure that if she had been one of us, that is, one of his own, he would have taken sharper measures with her; but he said we must never attempt to treat other people's children as our own, for they are not our own. We did not love them enough, he said, to make severity safe either for them or for us.

The plan worked so far well, that after a time, varied in length according to causes inscrutable, she would always re-appear smiling; but, as to any conscience of wrong, she seemed to have no more than Nature herself, who looks out with *her* smiling face after hours of thunder, lightning, and rain;

and, although this treatment brought her out of them sooner, the fits themselves came quite as frequently as before.

But she had another habit, more alarming, and more troublesome as well: she would not unfrequently vanish, and have to be long sought, for in such case she never reappeared of herself. What made it so alarming was that there were dangerous places about our house; but she would generally be found seated, perfectly quiet, in some out-of-the-way nook where she had never been before, playing, not with any of her toys, but with something she had picked up and appropriated, finding in it some shadowy amusement which no one understood but herself.

She was very fond of bright colors, especially in dress; and, if she found a brilliant or gorgeous fragment of any substance, would be sure to hide it away in some hole or corner, perhaps known only to herself. Her love of approbation was strong, and her affection demonstrative; but she had not yet learned to speak the truth. In a word, she must, we thought, have come of wild parentage, so many of her ways were like those of a forest animal.

In our design of training her for a maid to Connie, we seemed already likely enough to be frustrated; at all events, there was nothing to encourage the attempt, seeing she had some sort of aversion to Connie, amounting almost to dread. We could rarely persuade her to go near her. Perhaps it was a dislike to her helplessness,—some vague impression that her lying all day on the sofa indicated an unnatural condition of being, with which she could have no sympathy. Those of us who had the highest spirits, the greatest exuberance of animal life, were evidently those whose society was most attractive to her. Connie tried all she could to conquer her dislike, and entice the wayward thing to her heart; but nothing would do. Sometimes she would seem to soften for a moment; but all at once, with a wriggle and a backward spasm in the arms of the person who carried her, she would manifest such a fresh access of repulsion, that, for fear of an outburst of fierce and objurgatory wailing which might upset poor Connie altogether, she would be borne off hurriedly,—sometimes, I confess, rather ungently as well. I have seen Connie cry because of the child's treatment of her.

You could not interest her so much in any story, but that if the buzzing of a fly, the flutter of a bird, reached eye or ear, away she would dart on the instant, leaving the discomfited narrator in lonely disgrace. External nature, and almost nothing else, had free access to her mind: at the suddenest sight or sound, she was alive on the instant. She was a most amusing and sometimes almost bewitching little companion; but the delight in her would be not unfrequently quenched by some altogether unforeseen outbreak of heartless petulance or turbulent rebellion. Indeed, her resistance to authority grew as she grew older, and occasioned my father and mother, and indeed all of us, no little anxiety. Even Charley and Harry would stand with open mouths, contemplating aghast the unheard-of atrocity of resistance to the will of the unquestioned authorities. It was what they could not understand, being to them an impossibility. Such resistance was almost always accompanied by storm and tempest; and the treatment which carried away the latter, generally carried away the former with it; after the passion had come and gone, she would obey. Had it been otherwise,—had she been sullen and obstinate as well,—I do not know what would have come of it, or how we could have got on at all. Miss Bowdler, I am afraid, would have had a very satisfactory crow over papa. I have seen him sit for minutes in silent contemplation of the little puzzle, trying, no doubt, to fit her into his theories, or, as my mother said, to find her a three-legged stool and a corner somewhere in the kingdom of heaven; and we were certain something or other would come out of that pondering, though whether the same night or a twelvemonth after, no one could tell. I believe the main result of his thinking was, that he did less and less with her.

"Why do you take so little notice of the child?" my mother said to him one evening. "It is all your doing that she is here, you know. You mustn't cast her off now."

"Cast her off!" exclaimed my father: "what *do* you mean, Ethel?"

"You never speak to her now."

"Oh, yes I do, sometimes!"

"Why only sometimes?"

"Because—I believe because I am a little afraid of her. I don't know how to attack the small enemy. She seems to be bomb-proof, and generally impregnable."

"But you mustn't therefore make *her* afraid of *you*."

"I don't know that. I suspect it is my only chance with her. She wants a little of Mount Sinai, in order that she may know where the manna comes from. But indeed I am laying myself out only to catch the little soul. I am but watching and pondering how to reach her. I am biding my time to come in with my small stone for the building up of this temple of the Holy Ghost."

At that very moment—in the last fold of the twilight, with the moon rising above the wooded brow of Gorman Slope—the nurse came through the darkening air, her figure hardly distinguishable from the dusk, saying,—

"Please, ma'am, have you seen Miss Theodora?"

"I don't want you to call her *Miss*," said my father.

"I beg your pardon, sir," said the nurse; "I forgot."

"I have not seen her for an hour or more," said my mother.

"I declare," said my father, "I'll get a retriever pup, and train him to find Theodora. He will be capable in a few months, and she will be foolish for years."

Upon this occasion the truant was found in the apple-loft, sitting in a corner upon a heap of straw, quite in the dark. She was discovered only by the munching of her little teeth; for she had found some wizened apples, and was busy devouring them. But my father actually did what he had said: a favorite spaniel had pups a few days after, and he took one of them in hand. In an incredibly short space of time, the long-drawn nose of Wagtail, as the children had named him, in which, doubtless, was gathered the experience of many thoughtful generations, had learned to track Theodora to whatever retreat she might have chosen; and very amusing it was to watch the course of the proceedings. Some one would come running to my father with the news that Theo was in hiding. Then my father would give a peculiar whistle, and Wagtail, who (I must say *who*) very seldom failed to respond, would come bounding to his side. It was necessary that my father should *lay him on* (is that the phrase?); for he would heed no directions from any one else. It was not necessary to follow him, however, which would have involved a tortuous and fatiguing pursuit; but in a little while a joyous barking would be heard, always kept up until the ready pursuers were guided by the sound to the place. There Theo was certain to be found, hugging the animal, without the least notion of the traitorous character of his blandishments: it was long before she began to discover that there was danger in that dog's nose. Thus Wagtail became a very important member of the family,—a bond of union, in fact, between its parts. Theo's disappearances, however, became less and less frequent,—not that she made fewer attempts to abscond, but that, every one knowing how likely she was to vanish, whoever she was with had come to feel the necessity of keeping both eyes upon her.

# CHAPTER IX.

## THE FOUNDLING RE-FOUND.

One evening, during this my first visit to my home, we had gone to take tea with the widow of an old servant, who lived in a cottage on the outskirts of the home farm,—Connie and I in the pony carriage, and my father and mother on foot. It was quite dark when we returned, for the moon was late. Connie and I got home first, though we had a good round to make, and the path across the fields was but a third of the distance; for my father and mother were lovers, and sure to be late when left out by themselves. When we arrived, there was no one to take the pony; and when I rung the bell, no one answered. I could not leave Connie in the carriage to go and look; so we waited and waited till we were getting very tired, and glad indeed we were to hear the voices of my father and mother as they came through the shrubbery. My mother went to the rear to make inquiry, and came back with the news that Theo was missing, and that they had been searching for her in vain for nearly an hour. My father instantly called Wagtail, and sent him after her. We then got Connie in, and laid her on the sofa, where I kept her company while the rest went in different directions, listening from what quarter would come the welcome voice of the dog. This was so long delayed, however, that my father began to get alarmed. At last he whistled very loud; and in a little while Wagtail came creeping to his feet, with his tail between his legs,—no wag left in it,—clearly ashamed of himself. My father was now thoroughly frightened, and began questioning the household as to the latest knowledge of the child. It then occurred to one of the servants to mention that a strange-looking woman had been seen about the place in the morning,—a tall, dark woman, with a gypsy look. She had come begging; but my father's orders were so strict concerning such cases, that nothing had been given her, and she had gone away in anger. As soon as he heard this, my father ordered his horse, and told two of the men to get ready to accompany him. In the mean time, he came to us in the little drawing-room, trying to look calm, but evidently in much perturbation. He said he had little doubt the woman had taken her.

"Could it be her mother?" said my mother.

"Who can tell?" returned my father. "It is the less likely that the deed seems to have been prompted by revenge."

"If she be a gypsy's child,"—said my mother.

"The gypsies," interrupted my father, "have always been more given to taking other people's children than forsaking their own. But one of them might have had reason for being ashamed of her child, and, dreading the severity of her family, might have abandoned it, with the intention of repossessing herself of it, and passing it off as the child of gentlefolks she had picked up. I don't know their habits and ways sufficiently; but, from what I have heard, that seems possible. However, it is not so easy as it might have been once to succeed in such an attempt. If we should fail in finding her to-night, the police all over the country can be apprised of the fact in a few hours, and the thief can hardly escape."

"But if she *should* be the mother?" suggested my mother.

"She will have to *prove* that."

"And then?"

"What then?" returned my father, and began pacing up and down the room, stopping now and then to listen for the horses' hoofs.

"Would you give her up?" persisted my mother.

Still my father made no reply. He was evidently much agitated,—more, I fancied, by my mother's question than by the present trouble. He left the room, and presently his whistle for Wagtail pierced the still air. A moment more, and we heard them all ride out of the paved yard. I had never known him leave my mother without an answer before.

We who were left behind were in evil plight. There was not a dry eye amongst the women, I am certain; while Harry was in floods of tears, and Charley was howling. We could not send them to bed in such a state; so we kept them with us in the drawing-room, where they soon fell fast asleep, one in an easy-chair, the other on a sheepskin mat. Connie lay quite still, and my mother talked so sweetly and gently that she soon made me quiet too. But I was haunted with the idea somehow,—I think I must have been wandering a little, for I was not well,—that it was a child of my own that was lost out in the dark night, and that I could not anyhow reach her. I cannot explain the odd kind of feeling it was,—as if a dream had wandered out of the region of sleep, and half-possessed my waking brain. Every now and then my mother's voice would bring me back to my senses, and I would understand it all perfectly; but in a few moments I would be involved once more in a mazy search after my child. Perhaps, however, as it was by that time late, sleep had, if such a thing be possible, invaded a part of my brain, leaving another part able to receive the impressions of the external about me. I can recall some of the things my mother said,—one in particular.

"It is more absurd," she said, "to trust God by halves, than it is not to believe in him at all. Your papa taught me that before one of you was born."

When my mother said any thing in the way of teaching us, which was not often, she would generally add, "Your papa taught me that," as if she would take refuge from the assumption of teaching even her own girls. But we set a good deal of such assertion down to her modesty, and the evidently inextricable blending of the thought of my father with every movement of her mental life.

"I remember quite well," she went on, "how he made that truth dawn upon me one night as we sat together beside the old mill. Ah, you don't remember the old mill! it was pulled down while Wynnie was a mere baby."

"No, mamma; I remember it perfectly," I said.

"Do you really?—Well, we were sitting beside the mill one Sunday evening after service; for we always had a walk before going home from church. You would hardly think it now; but after preaching he was then always depressed, and the more eloquently he had spoken, the more he felt as if he had made an utter failure. At first I thought it came only from fatigue, and wanted him to go home and rest; but he would say he liked Nature to come before supper, for Nature restored him by telling him that it was not of the slightest consequence if he had failed, whereas his supper only made him feel that he would do better next time. Well, that night, you will easily believe he startled me when he said, after sitting for some time silent, 'Ethel, if that yellow-hammer were to drop down dead now, and God not care, God would not be God any longer.' Doubtless I showed myself something between puzzled and shocked, for he proceeded with some haste to explain to me how what he had said was true. 'Whatever belongs to God is essential to God,' he said. 'He is one pure, clean essence of being, to use our poor words to describe the indescribable. Nothing hangs about him that does not belong to him,—that he could part with and be nothing the worse. Still less is there any thing he could part with and be the worse. Whatever belongs to him is of his own kind, is part of himself, so to speak. Therefore there is nothing indifferent to his character to be found in him; and therefore when our Lord says not a sparrow falls to the ground without our Father, that, being a fact with regard to God, must be an essential fact,—one, namely, without which he could be no God.' I understood him, I thought; but many a time since, when a fresh light has broken in upon me, I have thought I understood him then only for the first time. I told him so once; and he said he thought that would be the way forever with all truth,—we should never get to the bottom of any truth, because it was a vital portion of the all of truth, which is God."

I had never heard so much philosophy from my mother before. I believe she was led into it by her fear of the effect our anxiety about the child might have upon us: with what had quieted her heart in the old time she sought now to quiet ours, helping us to trust in the great love that never ceases to watch. And she did make us quiet. But the time glided so slowly past that it seemed immovable.

When twelve struck, we heard in the stillness every clock in the house, and it seemed as if they would never have done. My mother left the room, and came back with three shawls, with which, having first laid Harry on the rug, she covered the boys and Dora, who also was by this time fast asleep, curled up at Connie's feet.

Still the time went on; and there was no sound of horses or any thing to break the silence, except the faint murmur which now and then the trees will make in the quietest night, as if they were dreaming, and talked in their sleep; for the motion does not seem to pass beyond them, but to swell up and die again in the heart of them. This and the occasional cry of an owl was all that broke the silent flow of the undivided moments,—glacier-like flowing none can tell how. We seldom spoke, and at length the house within seemed possessed by the silence from without; but we were all ear,—one hungry ear, whose famine was silence,—listening intently.

We were not so far from the high road, but that on a night like this the penetrating sound of a horse's hoofs might reach us. Hence, when my mother, who was keener of hearing than any of her daughters, at length started up, saying, "I hear them! They're coming!" the doubt remained whether it might not be the sound of some night-traveller hurrying along that high road that she had heard. But when *we* also heard the sound of horses, we knew they must belong to our company; for, except the riders were within the gates, their noises could not have come nearer to the house. My mother hurried down to the hall. I would have staid with Connie; but she begged me to go too, and come back as soon as I knew the result; so I followed my mother. As I descended the stairs, notwithstanding my anxiety, I could not help seeing what a picture lay before me, for I had learned already to regard things from the picturesque point of view,—the dim light of the low-burning lamp on the forward-bent heads of the listening, anxious group of women, my mother at the open door with the housekeeper and her maid, and the men-servants visible through the door in the moonlight beyond.

The first news that reached me was my father's shout the moment he rounded the sweep that brought him in sight of the house.

"All right! Here she is!" he cried.

And, ere I could reach the stair to run up to Connie, Wagtail was jumping upon me and barking furiously. He rushed up before me with the scramble of twenty feet, licked Connie's face all over in spite of her efforts at self-defence, then rushed at Dora and the boys one after the other, and woke them all up. He was satisfied enough with himself now; his tail was doing the wagging of forty; there was no tucking of it away now,—no drooping of the head in mute confession of conscious worthlessness; he was a dog self-satisfied because his master was well pleased with him.

But here I am talking about the dog, and forgetting what was going on below.

My father cantered up to the door, followed by the two men. My mother hurried to meet him, and then only saw the little lost lamb asleep in his bosom. He gave her up, and my mother ran in with her; while he dismounted, and walked merrily but wearily up the stair after her. The first thing he did was to quiet the dog; the next to sit down beside Connie; the third to say, "Thank God!" and the next, "God bless Wagtail!" My mother was already undressing the little darling, and her maid was gone to fetch her night things. Tumbled hither and thither, she did not wake, but was carried off stone-sleeping to her crib.

Then my father,—for whom some supper, of which he was in great need, had been brought,—as soon as he had had a glass of wine and a mouthful or two of cold chicken, began to tell us the whole story.

# CHAPTER X.

## WAGTAIL COMES TO HONOR.

As they rode out of the gate, one of the men, a trustworthy man, who cared for his horses like his children, and knew all their individualities as few men know those of their children, rode up along side of my father, and told him that there was an encampment of gypsies on the moor about five miles away, just over Gorman Slope, remarking, that if the woman had taken the child, and belonged to them, she would certainly carry her thither. My father thought, in the absence of other indication, they ought to follow the suggestion, and told Burton to guide them to the place as rapidly as possible. After half an hour's sharp riding, they came in view of the camp,—or rather of a rising ground behind which it lay in the hollow. The other servant was an old man, who had been whipper-in to a baronet in the next county, and knew as much of the ways of wild animals as Burton did of those of his horses; it was his turn now to address my father, who had halted for a moment to think what ought to be done next.

"She can't well have got here before us, sir, with that child to carry. But it's wonderful what the likes of her can do. I think I had better have a peep over the brow first. She may be there already, or she may not; but, if we find out, we shall know better what to do."

"I'll go with you," said my father.

"No, sir; excuse me; that won't do. You can't creep like a sarpent. I can. They'll never know I'm a stalking of them. No more you couldn't show fight if need was, you know, sir."

"How did you find that out, Sim?" asked my father, a little amused, notwithstanding the weight at his heart.

"Why, sir, they do say a clergyman mustn't show fight."

"Who told you that, Sim?" he persisted.

"Well, I can't say, sir. Only it wouldn't be respectable; would it, sir?"

"There's nothing respectable but what's right, Sim; and what's right always *is* respectable, though it mayn't *look* so one bit."

"Suppose you was to get a black eye, sir?"

"Did you ever hear of the martyrs, Sim?"

"Yes, sir. I've heerd you talk on 'em in the pulpit, sir."

"Well, they didn't get black eyes only,—they got black all over, you know,—burnt black; and what for, do you think, now?"

"Don't know, sir, except it was for doing right."

"That's just it. Was it any disgrace to them?"

"No, sure, sir."

"Well, if I were to get a black eye for the sake of the child, would that be any disgrace to me, Sim?"

"None that I knows on, sir. Only it'd *look* bad."

"Yes, no doubt. People might think I had got into a row at the Griffin. And yet I shouldn't be ashamed of it. I should count my black eye the more respectable of the two. I should also regard the evil judgment much as another black eye, and wait till they both came round again. Lead on, Sim."

They left their horses with Burton, and went toward the camp. But when they reached the slope behind which it lay, much to Sim's discomfiture, my father, instead of lying down at the foot of it, as he expected, and creeping up the side of it, after the doom of the serpent, walked right up over the brow, and straight into the camp, followed by Wagtail. There was nothing going on,—neither tinkering nor cooking; all seemed asleep; but presently out of two or three of the tents, the dingy squalor of which no moonshine could silver over, came three or four men, half undressed, who demanded of my father, in no gentle tones, what he wanted there.

"I'll tell you all about it," he answered. "I'm the parson of this parish, and therefore you're my own people, you see."

"We don't go to *your* church, parson," said one of them.

"I don't care; you're my own people, for all that, and I want your help."

"Well, what's the matter? Who's cow's dead?" said the same man.

"This evening," returned my father, "one of my children is missing; and a woman who might be one of your clan,—mind, I say *might be*; I don't know, and I mean no offence,—but such a woman was seen about the place. All I want is the child, and if I don't find her, I shall have to raise the county. I should be very sorry to disturb you; but I am afraid, in that case, whether the woman be one of you or not, the place will be too hot for you. I'm no enemy to honest gypsies; but you know there is a set of tramps that call themselves gypsies, who are nothing of the sort,—only thieves. Tell me what I had better do to find my child. You know all about such things."

The men turned to each other, and began talking in undertones, and in a language of which what my father heard he could not understand. At length the spokesman of the party addressed him again.

"We'll give you our word, sir, if that will satisfy you," he said, more respectfully than he had spoken before, "to send the child home directly if any one should bring her to our camp. That's all we can say."

My father saw that his best chance lay in accepting the offer.

"Thank you," he said. "Perhaps I may have an opportunity of serving you some day."

They in their turn thanked him politely enough, and my father and Sim left the camp.

Upon this side the moor was skirted by a plantation which had been gradually creeping up the hill from the more sheltered hollow. It was here bordered by a deep trench, the bottom of which was full of young firs. Through the plantation there was a succession of green rides, by which the outskirts of my father's property could be reached. But, the moon being now up, my father resolved to cross the trench, and halt for a time, watching the moor from the shelter of the firs, on the chance of the woman's making her appearance; for, if she belonged to the camp, she would most probably approach it from the plantation, and might be overtaken before she could cross the moor to reach it.

They had lain ensconced in the firs for about half an hour, when suddenly, without any warning, Wagtail rushed into the underwood and vanished. They listened with all their ears, and in a few moments heard his joyous bark, followed instantly, however, by a howl of pain; and, before they had got many yards in pursuit, he came cowering to my father's feet, who, patting his side, found it bleeding. He bound his handkerchief round him, and, fastening the lash of Sim's whip to his collar that he might not go too fast for them, told him to find Theodora. Instantly he pulled away through the brushwood, giving a little yelp now and then as the stiff remnant of some broken twig or stem hurt his wounded side.

Before we reached the spot for which he was making, however, my father heard a rustling, nearer to the outskirts of the wood, and the same moment Wagtail turned, and tugged fiercely in that direction. The figure of a woman rose up against the sky, and began to run for the open space beyond. Wagtail and my father pursued at speed; my father crying out, that, if she did not stop, he would loose the dog on her. She paid no heed, but ran on.

"Mount and head her, Sim. Mount, Burton. Ride over every thing," cried my father, as he slipped Wagtail, who shot through the underwood like a bird, just as she reached the trench, and in an instant had her by the gown. My father saw something gleam in the moonlight, and again a howl broke from Wagtail, who was evidently once more wounded. But he held on. And now the horsemen, having crossed the trench, were approaching her in front, and my father was hard upon her behind. She gave a peculiar cry, half a shriek, and half a howl, clasped the child to her bosom, and stood rooted like a tree, evidently in the hope that her friends, hearing her signal, would come to her rescue. But it was too late. My father rushed upon her the instant she cried out. The dog was holding her by the poor ragged skirt, and the horses were reined snorting on the bank above her. She heaved up the child over her head, but whether in appeal to Heaven, or about to dash her to the earth in the rage of frustration, she was not allowed time to show; for my father caught both her uplifted arms with his, so that she could not lower them, and Burton, having flung himself from his horse and come behind her, easily took Theodora from them, for from their position they were almost powerless. Then my father called off Wagtail; and the poor creature sunk down in the bottom of the trench amongst the young firs without a sound, and there lay. My father went up to her; but she only stared at him with big blank black eyes, and yet such a lost look on her young, handsome, yet gaunt face, as almost convinced him she was the mother of the child. But, whatever might be her rights, she could not be allowed to recover possession, without those who had saved and tended the child having a word in the matter of her fate.

As he was thinking what he could say to her, Sim's voice reached his ear.

"They're coming over the brow, sir,—five or six from the camp. We'd better be off."

"The child is safe," he said, as he turned to leave her.

"From *me*," she rejoined, in a pitiful tone; and this ambiguous utterance was all that fell from her.

My father mounted hurriedly, took the child from Burton, and rode away, followed by the two men and Wagtail. Through the green rides they galloped in the moonlight, and were soon beyond all danger of pursuit. When they slackened pace, my father instructed Sim to find out all he could about the gypsies,—if possible to learn their names and to what tribe or community they belonged. Sim promised to do what was in his power, but said he did not expect much success.

The children had listened to the story wide awake. Wagtail was lying at my father's feet, licking his wounds, which were not very serious, and had stopped bleeding.

"It is all your doing, Wagtail," said Harry, patting the dog.

"I think he deserves to be called *Mr.* Wagtail," said Charley.

And from that day he was no more called bare Wagtail, but Mr. Wagtail, much to the amusement of visitors, who, hearing the name gravely uttered, as it soon came to be, saw the owner of it approach on all fours, with a tireless pendulum in his rear.

# CHAPTER XI.

## A STUPID CHAPTER.

Before proceeding with my own story, I must mention that my father took every means in his power to find out something about the woman and the gang of gypsies to which she appeared to belong. I believe he had no definite end in view further than the desire to be able at some future time to enter into such relations with her, for her own and her daughter's sake,—if, indeed, Theodora were her daughter,—as might be possible. But, the very next day, he found that they had already vanished from the place; and all the inquiries he set on foot, by means of friends and through the country constabulary, were of no avail. I believe he was dissatisfied with himself in what had occurred, thinking he ought to have laid himself out at the time to discover whether she was indeed the mother, and, in that case, to do for her what he could. Probably, had he done so, he would only have heaped difficulty upon difficulty; but, as it was, if he was saved from trouble, he was not delivered from uneasiness. Clearly, however, the child must not be exposed to the danger of the repetition of the attempt; and the whole household was now so fully alive to the necessity of not losing sight of her for a moment, that her danger was far less than it had been at any time before.

I continued at the Hall for six weeks, during which my husband came several times to see me; and, at the close of that period, took me back with him to my dear little home. The rooms, all but the study, looked very small after those I had left; but I felt, notwithstanding, that the place was my home. I was at first a little ashamed of the feeling; for why should I be anywhere more at home than in the house of such parents as mine? But I presume there is a certain amount of the queenly element in every woman, so that she cannot feel perfectly at ease without something to govern, however small and however troublesome her queendom may be. At my father's, I had every ministration possible, and all comforts in profusion; but I had no responsibilities, and no rule; so that sometimes I could not help feeling as if I was idle, although I knew I was not to blame. Besides, I could not be at all sure that my big bear was properly attended to; and the knowledge that he was the most independent of comforts of all the men I had ever come into any relation with, made me only feel the more anxious that he should not be left to his own neglect. For although my father, for instance, was ready to part with any thing, even to a favorite volume, if the good reason of another's need showed itself, he was not at all indifferent in his own person to being comfortable. One with his intense power of enjoying the gentleness of the universe could not be so. Hence it was always easy to make him a little present; whereas I have still to rack my brains for weeks before my bear's birthday comes round, to think of something that will in itself have a chance of giving him pleasure. Of course, it would be comparatively easy if I had plenty of money to spare, and hadn't "to muddle it all away" in paying butchers and bakers, and such like people.

So home I went, to be queen again. Friends came to see me, but I returned few of their calls. I liked best to sit in my bedroom. I would have preferred sitting in my wonderful little room off the study, and I tried that first; but, the same morning, somebody called on Percivale, and straightway I felt myself a prisoner. The moment I heard the strange voice through the door, I wanted to get out, and could not, of course. Such a risk I would not run again. And when Percivale asked me, the next day, if I would not go down with him, I told him I could not bear the feeling of confinement it gave me.

"I did mean," he said, "to have had a door made into the garden for you, and I consulted an architect friend on the subject; but he soon satisfied me it would make the room much too cold for you, and so I was compelled to give up the thought."

"You dear!" I said. That was all; but it was enough for Percivale, who never bothered me, as I have heard of husbands doing, for demonstrations either of gratitude or affection. Such must be of the mole-eyed sort, who can only read large print. So I betook myself to my chamber, and there sat and worked; for I did a good deal of needle-work now, although I had never been fond of it as a girl. The constant recurrence of similar motions of the fingers, one stitch just the same as another in countless repetition, varied only by the bother when the thread grew short and would slip out of the eye of the needle, and yet not short enough to be exchanged with still more bother for one too long, had been so wearisome to me in former days, that I spent half my pocket-money in getting the needle-work done for me which my mother and sister did for themselves. For this my father praised me, and my mother tried to scold me, and couldn't. But now it was all so different! Instead of toiling at plain stitching and hemming and sewing, I seemed to be working a bit of lovely tapestry all the time,—so many thoughts and so many pictures went weaving themselves into the work; while every little bit finished appeared so much of the labor of the universe actually done,—accomplished, ended: for the first time in my life, I began to feel myself of consequence enough to be taken care of. I remember once laying down the little—what I was working at—but I am growing too communicative and important.

My father used often to say that the commonest things in the world were the loveliest,—sky and water and grass and such; now I found that the commonest feelings of humanity—for what feelings could be commoner than those which now made me blessed amongst women?—are those that are fullest of the divine. Surely this looks as if there were a God of the whole earth,—as if the world existed in the very foundations of its history and continuance by the immediate thought of a causing thought. For simply because the life of the world was moving on towards its unseen goal, and I knew it and had a helpless share in it, I felt as if God was with me. I do not say I always felt like this,—far from it: there were times when life itself seemed vanishing in an abyss of nothingness, when all my consciousness consisted in this, that I knew I was *not*, and when I could not believe that I should ever be restored to the well-being of existence. The worst of it was, that, in such moods, it seemed as if I had hitherto been deluding myself with rainbow fancies as often as I had been aware of blessedness, as there was, in fact, no wine of life apart from its effervescence. But when one day I told Percivale—not while I was thus oppressed, for then I could not speak; but in a happier moment whose happiness I mistrusted—something of what I felt, he said one thing which has comforted me ever since in such circumstances:—

"Don't grumble at the poverty, darling, by which another is made rich."

I confess I did not see all at once what he meant; but I did after thinking over it for a while. And if I have learned any valuable lesson in my life, it is this, that no one's feelings are a measure of eternal facts.

The winter passed slowly away,—fog, rain, frost, snow, thaw, succeeding one another in all the seeming disorder of the season. A good many things happened, I believe; but I don't remember any of them. My mother wrote, offering me Dora for a companion; but somehow I preferred being without her. One great comfort was good news about Connie, who was getting on famously. But even this moved me so little that I began to think I was turning into a crab, utterly incased in the shell of my own selfishness. The thought made me cry. The fact that I could cry consoled me, for how could I be heartless so long as I could cry? But then came the thought it was for myself, my own hard-heartedness I was crying,—not certainly for joy that Connie was getting better. "At least, however," I said to myself, "I am not content to be selfish. I am a little troubled that I am not good." And then I tried to look up, and get my needlework, which always did me good, by helping me to reflect. It is, I can't help thinking, a great pity that needlework is going so much out of fashion; for it tends more to make a woman—one who thinks, that is—acquainted with herself than all the sermons she is ever likely to hear.

My father came to see me several times, and was all himself to me; but I could not feel quite comfortable with him,—I don't in the least know why. I am afraid, much afraid, it indicates something very wrong in me somewhere. But he seemed to understand me; and always, the moment he left me, the tide of confidence began to flow afresh in the ocean that lay about the little island of my troubles. Then I knew he was my own father,—something that even my husband could not be, and would not wish to be to me.

In the month of March, my mother came to see me; and that was all pleasure. My father did not always see when I was not able to listen to him, though he was most considerate when he did; but my mother—why, to be with her was like being with one's own—*mother*, I was actually going to write. There is nothing better than that when a woman is in such trouble, except it be—what my father knows more about than I do: I wish I did know *all* about it.

She brought with her a young woman to take the place of cook, or rather general servant, in our little household. She had been kitchen-maid in a small family of my mother's acquaintance, and had a good character for honesty and plain cooking. Percivale's more experienced ear soon discovered that she was Irish. This fact had not been represented to my mother; for the girl had been in England from childhood, and her mistress seemed either not to have known it, or not to have thought of mentioning it. Certainly, my mother was far too just to have allowed it to influence her choice, notwithstanding the prejudices against Irish women in English families,—prejudices not without a general foundation in reason. For my part, I should have been perfectly satisfied with my mother's choice, even if I had not been so indifferent at the time to all that was going on in the lower regions of the house. But while my mother was there, I knew well enough that nothing could go wrong; and my housekeeping mind had never been so much at ease since we were married. It was very delightful not to be accountable; and, for the present, I felt exonerated from all responsibilities.

# CHAPTER XII.

## AN INTRODUCTION.

I woke one morning, after a sound sleep,—not so sound, however, but that I had been dreaming, and that, when I awoke, I could recall my dream. It was a very odd one. I thought I was a hen, strutting about amongst ricks of corn, picking here and scratching there, followed by a whole brood of chickens, toward which I felt exceedingly benevolent and attentive. Suddenly I heard the scream of a hawk in the air above me, and instantly gave the proper cry to fetch the little creatures under my wings. They came scurrying to me as fast as their legs could carry them,—all but one, which wouldn't mind my cry, although I kept repeating it again and again. Meantime the hawk kept screaming; and I felt as if I didn't care for any of those that were safe under my wings, but only for the solitary creature that kept pecking away as if nothing was the matter. About it I grew so terribly anxious, that at length I woke with a cry of misery and terror.

The moment I opened my eyes, there was my mother standing beside me. The room was so dark that I thought for a moment what a fog there must be; but the next, I forgot every thing at hearing a little cry, which I verily believe, in my stupid dream, I had taken for the voice of the hawk; whereas it was the cry of my first and only chicken, which I had not yet seen, but which my mother now held in her grandmotherly arms, ready to hand her to me. I dared not speak; for I felt very weak, and was afraid of crying from delight. I looked in my mother's face; and she folded back the clothes, and laid the baby down beside me, with its little head resting on my arm.

"Draw back the curtain a little bit, mother dear," I whispered, "and let me see what it is like."

I believe I said *it*, for I was not quite a mother yet. My mother did as I requested; a ray of clear spring light fell upon the face of the little white thing by my side,—for white she was, though most babies are red,—and if I dared not speak before, I could not now. My mother went away again, and sat down by the fireside, leaving me with my baby. Never shall I forget the unutterable content of that hour. It was not gladness, nor was it thankfulness, that filled my heart, but a certain absolute contentment,—just on the point, but for my want of strength, of blossoming into unspeakable gladness and thankfulness. Somehow, too, there was mingled with it a sense of dignity, as if I had vindicated for myself a right to a part in the creation; for was I not proved at least a link in the marvellous chain of existence, in carrying on the designs of the great Maker? Not that the thought was there,—only the feeling, which afterwards found the thought, in order to account for its own being. Besides, the state of perfect repose after what had passed was in itself bliss; the very sense of weakness was delightful, for I had earned the right to be weak, to rest as much as I pleased, to be important, and to be congratulated.

Somehow I had got through. The trouble lay behind me; and here, for the sake of any one who will read my poor words, I record the conviction, that, in one way or other, special individual help is given to every creature to endure to the end. I think I have heard my father say, and hitherto it has been my own experience, that always when suffering, whether mental or bodily, approached the point where further endurance appeared impossible, the pulse of it began to ebb, and a lull ensued. I do not venture to found any general assertion upon this: I only state it as a fact of my own experience. He who does not allow any man to be tempted above that he is able to bear, doubtless acts in the same way in all kinds of trials.

I was listening to the gentle talk about me in the darkened room—not listening, indeed, only aware that loving words were spoken. Whether I was dozing, I do not know; but something touched my lips. I did not start. I had been dreadfully given to starting for a long time,—so much so that I was quite ashamed sometimes, for I would even cry out,—I who had always been so sharp on feminine affectations before; but now it seemed as if nothing could startle me. I only opened my eyes; and there was my great big huge bear looking down on me, with something in his eyes I had never seen there before. But even his presence could not ripple the waters of my deep rest. I gave him half a smile,—I knew it was but half a smile, but I thought it would do,—closed my eyes, and sunk again, not into sleep, but into that same blessed repose. I remember wondering if I should feel any thing like that for the first hour or two after I was dead. May there not one day be such a repose for all,—only the heavenly counterpart, coming of perfect activity instead of weary success?

This was all but the beginning of endlessly varied pleasures. I dare say the mothers would let me go on for a good while in this direction,—perhaps even some of the fathers could stand a little more of it; but I must remember, that, if anybody reads this at all, it will have multitudes of readers in whom the chord which could alone respond to such experiences hangs loose over the sounding-board of their being.

By slow degrees the daylight, the light of work, that is, began to penetrate me, or rather to rise in my being from its own hidden sun. First I began to wash and dress my baby myself. One who has not tried that kind of amusement cannot know what endless pleasure it affords. I do not doubt that to the paternal spectator it appears monotonous, unproductive, unprogressive; but then he, looking upon it from the outside, and regarding the process with a speculative compassion, and not with sympathy, so cannot know the communion into which it brings you with the baby. I remember well enough what my father has written about it in "The Seaboard Parish;" but he is all wrong—I mean him to confess that before this is printed. If things were done as he proposes, the tenderness of mothers would be far less developed, and the moral training of children would be postponed to an indefinite period. There, papa! that's something in your own style!

Next I began to order the dinners; and the very day on which I first ordered the dinner, I took my place at the head of the table. A happier little party—well, of course, I saw it all through the rose-mists of my motherhood, but I am nevertheless bold to assert that my husband was happy, and that my mother was happy; and if there was one more guest at the table concerning whom I am not prepared to assert that he was happy, I can confidently affirm that he was merry and gracious and talkative, originating three parts of the laughter of the evening. To watch him with the baby was a pleasure even to the heart of a mother, anxious as she must be when any one, especially a gentleman, more especially a bachelor, and most especially a young bachelor, takes her precious little wax-doll in his arms, and pretends to know all about the management of such. It was he indeed who introduced her to the dining-room; for, leaving the table during dessert, he returned bearing her in his arms, to my astonishment, and even mild maternal indignation at the liberty. Resuming his seat, and pouring out for his charge, as he pretended, a glass of old port, he said in the soberest voice:—

"Charles Percivale, with all the solemnity suitable to the occasion, I, the old moon, with the new moon in my arms, propose the health of Miss Percivale on her first visit to this boring bullet of a world. By the way, what a mercy it is that she carries her atmosphere with her!"

Here I, stupidly thinking he reflected on the atmosphere of baby, rose to take her from him with suppressed indignation; for why should a man, who assumes a baby unbidden, be so very much nicer than a woman who accepts her as given, and makes the best of it? But he declined giving her up.

"I'm not pinching her," he said.

"No; but I am afraid you find her disagreeable."

"On the contrary, she is the nicest of little ladies; for she lets you talk all the nonsense you like, and never takes the least offence."

I sat down again directly.

"I propose her health," he repeated, "coupled with that of her mother, to whom I, for one, am more obliged than I can explain, for at length convincing me that I belong no more to the youth of my country, but am an uncle with a homuncle in his arms."

"Wifie, your health! Baby, yours too!" said my husband; and the ladies drank the toast in silence.

It is time I explained who this fourth—or should I say fifth?—person in our family party was. He was the younger brother of my Percivale, by name Roger,—still more unsuccessful than he; of similar trustworthiness, but less equanimity; for he was subject to sudden elevations and depressions of the inner barometer. I shall have more to tell about him by and by. Meantime it is enough to mention that my daughter—how grand I thought it when I first said *my daughter*!—now began her acquaintance with him. Before long he was her chief favorite next to her mother and—I am sorry I cannot conscientiously add *father*; for, at a certain early period of her history, the child showed a decided preference for her uncle over her father.

But it is time I put a stop to this ooze of maternal memories. Having thus introduced my baby and her Uncle Roger, I close the chapter.

# CHAPTER XIII.

## MY FIRST DINNER-PARTY. A NEGATIVED PROPOSAL.

It may well be believed that we had not yet seen much company in our little house. To parties my husband had a great dislike; evening parties he eschewed utterly, and never accepted an invitation to dinner, except it were to the house of a friend, or to that of one of my few relatives in London, whom, for my sake, he would not displease. There were not many, even among his artist-acquaintances, whom he cared to visit; and, altogether, I fear he passed for an unsociable man. I am certain he would have sold more pictures if he had accepted what invitations came in his way. But to hint at such a thing would, I knew, crystallize his dislike into a resolve.

One day, after I had got quite strong again, as I was sitting by him in the study, with my baby on my knee, I proposed that we should ask some friends to dinner. Instead of objecting to the procedure upon general principles, which I confess I had half anticipated, he only asked me whom I thought of inviting. When I mentioned the Morleys, he made no reply, but went on with his painting as if he had not heard me; whence I knew, of course, that the proposal was disagreeable to him.

"You see, we have been twice to dine with them," I said.

"Well, don't you think that enough for a while?"

"I'm talking of asking them here now."

"Couldn't you go and see your cousin some morning instead?"

"It's not that I want to see my cousin particularly. I want to ask them to dinner."

"Oh!" he said, as if he couldn't in the least make out what I was after, "I thought people asked people because they desired their company."

"But, you see, we owe them a dinner."

"Owe them a dinner! Did you borrow one, then?"

"Percivale, why will you pretend to be so stupid?"

"Perhaps I'm only pretending to be the other thing."

"Do you consider yourself under no obligation to people who ask you to dinner?"

"None in the least—if I accept the invitation. That is the natural acknowledgment of their kindness. Surely my company is worth my dinner. It is far more trouble to me to put on black clothes and a white choker and go to their house, than it is for them to ask me, or, in a house like theirs, to have the necessary preparations made for receiving me in a manner befitting their dignity. I do violence to my own feelings in going: is not that enough? You know how much I prefer a chop with my wife alone to the grandest dinner the grandest of her grand relations could give me."

"Now, don't you make game of my grand relations. I'm not sure that you haven't far grander relations yourself, only you say so little about them, they might all have been transported for housebreaking. Tell me honestly, don't you think it natural, if a friend asks you to dinner, that you should ask him again?"

"Yes, if it would give him any pleasure. But just imagine your Cousin Morley dining at our table. Do you think he would enjoy it?"

"Of course we must have somebody in to help Jemima."

"And somebody to wait, I suppose?"

"Yes, of course, Percivale."

"And what Thackeray calls cold balls handed about?"

"Well, I wouldn't have them cold."

"But they would be."

I was by this time so nearly crying, that I said nothing here.

"My love," he resumed, "I object to the whole thing. It's all false together. I have not the least disinclination to asking a few friends who would enjoy being received in the same style as your father or my brother; namely, to one of our better dinners, and perhaps something better to drink than I can afford every day; but just think with what uneasy compassion Mr. Morley would regard our poor ambitions, even if you had an occasional cook and an undertaker's man. And what would he do without his glass of dry sherry after his soup, and his hock and champagne later, not to mention his fine claret or tawny port afterwards? I don't know how to get these things good enough for him without laying in a stock; and, that you know, would be as absurd as it is impossible."

"Oh, you gentlemen always think so much of the wine!"

"Believe me, it is as necessary to Mr. Morley's comfort as the dainties you would provide him with. Indeed, it would be a cruelty to ask him. He would not, could not, enjoy it."

"If he didn't like it, he needn't come again," I said, cross with the objections of which I could not but see the justice.

"Well, I must say you have an odd notion of hospitality," said my bear. "You may be certain," he resumed, after a moment's pause, "that a man so well aware of his own importance will take it far more as a compliment that you do not presume to invite him to your house, but are content to enjoy his society when he asks you to his."

"I don't choose to take such an inferior position," I said.

"You can't help it, my dear," he returned. "Socially considered, you *are* his inferior. You cannot give dinners he would regard with any thing better than a friendly contempt, combined with a certain mild indignation at your having presumed to ask *him*, used to such different ways. It is far more graceful to accept the small fact, and let him have his whim, which is not a subversive one or at all dangerous to the community, being of a sort easy to cure. Ha! ha! ha!"

"May I ask what you are laughing at?" I said with severity.

"I was only fancying how such a man must feel,—if what your blessed father believes be true,—when he is stripped all at once of every possible source of consequence,—stripped of position, funds, house, including cellar, clothes, body, including stomach"—

"There, there! don't be vulgar. It is not like you, Percivale."

"My love, there is far greater vulgarity in refusing to acknowledge the inevitable, either in society or in physiology. Just ask my brother his experience in regard of the word to which you object."

"I will leave that to you."

"Don't be vexed with me, my wife," he said.

"I don't like not to be allowed to pay my debts."

"Back to the starting-point, like a hunted hare! A woman's way," he said merrily, hoping to make me laugh; for he could not doubt I should see the absurdity of my position with a moment's reflection. But I was out of temper, and chose to pounce upon the liberty taken with my sex, and regard it as an insult. Without a word I rose, pressed my baby to my bosom as if her mother had been left a widow, and swept away. Percivale started to his feet. I did not see, but I knew he gazed after me for a moment; then I heard him sit down to his painting as if nothing had happened, but, I knew, with a sharp pain inside his great chest. For me, I found the precipice, or Jacob's ladder, I had to climb, very subversive of my dignity; for when a woman has to hold a baby in one arm, and with the hand of the other lift the front of her skirt in order to walk up an almost perpendicular staircase, it is quite impossible for her to *sweep* any more.

When I reached the top, I don't know how it was, but the picture he had made of me, with the sunset-shine coming through the window, flashed upon my memory. All dignity forgotten, I bolted through the door at the top, flung my baby into the arms of her nurse, turned, almost tumbled headlong down the precipice, and altogether tumbled down at my husband's chair. I couldn't speak; I could only lay my head on his knees.

"Darling," he said, "you shall ask the great Pan Jan with his button atop, if you like. I'll do my best for him."

Between crying and laughing, I nearly did what I have never really done yet,—I nearly *went off*. There! I am sure that phrase is quite as objectionable as the word I wrote a little while ago; and there it shall stand, as a penance for having called any word my husband used *vulgar*.

"I was very naughty, Percivale," I said. "I will give a dinner-party, and it shall be such as you shall enjoy, and I won't ask Mr. Morley."

"Thank you, my love," he said; "and the next time Mr. Morley asks us I will go without a grumble, and make myself as agreeable as I can."

* * * * *

It may have seemed, to some of my readers, occasion for surprise that the mistress of a household should have got so far in the construction of a book without saying a word about her own or other people's servants in general. Such occasion shall no longer be afforded them; for now I am going to say several things about one of mine, and thereby introduce a few results of much experience and some thought. I do not pretend to have made a single discovery, but only to have achieved what I count a certain measure of success; which, however, I owe largely to my own poverty, and the stupidity of my cook.

I have had a good many servants since, but Jemima seems a fixture. How this has come about, it would be impossible to say in ever so many words. Over and over I have felt, and may feel again before the day is ended, a profound sympathy with Sindbad the sailor, when the Old Man of the Sea was on his back, and the hope of ever getting him off it had not yet begun to dawn. She has by turns every fault under the sun,—I say *fault* only; will struggle with one for a day, and succumb to it for a month; while the smallest amount of praise is sufficient to render her incapable of deserving a word of commendation for a week. She is intensely stupid, with a remarkable genius—yes, genius—for cooking. My father says that all stupidity is caused, or at least maintained, by conceit. I cannot quite accompany him to his conclusions; but I have seen plainly enough that the stupidest people are the most conceited, which in some degree favors them. It was long an impossibility to make her see, or at least own, that she was to blame for any thing. If the dish she had last time cooked to perfection made its appearance the next time uneatable, she would lay it all to the *silly* oven, which was too hot or too cold; or the silly pepper-pot, the top of which fell off as she was using it. She had no sense of the value of proportion,—would insist, for instance, that she had made the cake precisely as she had been told, but suddenly betray that she had not weighed the flour, which *could* be of no consequence, seeing she had weighed every thing else.

"Please, 'm, could you eat your dinner now? for it's all ready," she came saying an hour before dinner-time, the very first day after my mother left. Even now her desire to be punctual is chiefly evidenced by absurd precipitancy, to the danger of doing every thing either to a pulp or a cinder. Yet here she is, and here she is likely to remain, so far as I see, till death, or some other catastrophe, us do part. The reason of it is, that, with all her faults—and they are innumerable—she has some heart; yes, after deducting all that can be laid to the account of a certain cunning perception that she is well off, she has yet a good deal of genuine attachment left; and after setting down the half of her possessions to the blarney which is the natural weapon of the weak-witted Celt, there seems yet left in her of the vanishing clan instinct enough to render her a jealous partisan of her master and mistress.

Those who care only for being well-served will of course feel contemptuous towards any one who would put up with such a woman for a single moment after she could find another; but both I and my husband have a strong preference for living in a family, rather than in a hotel. I know many houses in which the master and mistress are far more like the lodgers, on sufferance of their own servants. I have seen a worthy lady go about wringing her hands because she could not get her orders attended to in the emergency of a slight accident, not daring to go down to her own kitchen, as her love prompted, and expedite the ministration. I am at least mistress in my own house; my servants are, if not yet so much members of the family as I could wish, gradually becoming more so; there is a circulation of common life through the household, rendering us an organization, although as yet perhaps a low one; I am sure of being obeyed, and there are no underhand out-of-door connections. When I go to the houses of my rich relations, and hear what they say concerning their servants, I feel as if they were living over a mine, which might any day be sprung, and blow them into a state of utter helplessness; and I return to my house blessed in the knowledge that my little kingdom is my own, and that, although it is not free from internal upheavings and stormy commotions, these are such as to be within the control and restraint of the general family influences; while the blunders of the cook seem such trifles beside the evil customs established in most kitchens of which I know any thing, that they are turned even into sources of congratulation as securing her services for ourselves. More than once my husband has insisted on raising her wages, on the ground of the endless good he gets in his painting from the merriment her oddities afford him,—namely, the clear insight, which, he asserts, is the invariable consequence. I must in honesty say, however, that I have seen him something else than merry with her behavior, many a time.

But I find the things I have to say so crowd upon me, that I must either proceed to arrange them under heads,—which would immediately deprive them of any right to a place in my story,—or keep them till they are naturally swept from the bank of my material by the slow wearing of the current of my narrative. I prefer the latter, because I think my readers will.

What with one thing and another, this thing to be done and that thing to be avoided, there was nothing more said about the dinner-party, until my father came to see us in the month of July. I was to have paid them a visit before then; but things had come in the way of that also, and now my father was commissioned by my mother to arrange for my going the next month.

As soon as I had shown my father to his little room, I ran down to Percivale.

"Papa is come," I said.

"I am delighted to hear it," he answered, laying down his palette and brushes. "Where is he?"

"Gone up stairs," I answered. "I wouldn't disturb you till he came down again."

He answered with that world-wide English phrase, so suggestive of a hopeful disposition, "All right!" And with all its grumbling, and the *tristesse* which the French consider its chief characteristic, I think my father is right, who says, that, more than any other nation, England has been, is, and will be, saved by hope. Resuming his implements, my husband added,—

"I haven't quite finished my pipe,—I will go on till he comes down."

Although he laid it on his pipe, I knew well enough it was just that little bit of paint he wanted to finish, and not the residue of tobacco in the black and red bowl.

"And now we'll have our dinner party," I said.

I do believe, that, for all the nonsense I had talked about returning invitations, the real thing at my heart even then was an impulse towards hospitable entertainment, and the desire to see my husband merry with his friends, under—shall I say it?—the protecting wing of his wife. For, as mother of the family, the wife has to mother her husband also; to consider him as her first-born, and look out for what will not only give him pleasure but be good for him. And I may just add here, that for a long time my bear has fully given in to this.

"And who are you going to ask?" he said. "Mr. and Mrs. Morley to begin with, and"—

"No, no," I answered. "We are going to have a jolly evening of it, with nobody present who will make you either anxious or annoyed. Mr. Blackstone,"—he wasn't married then,—"Miss Clare, I think,—and"—

"What do you ask her for?"

"I won't if you don't like her, but"—

"I haven't had a chance of liking or disliking her yet."

"That is partly why I want to ask her,—I am so sure you would like her if you knew her."

"Where did you tell me you had met her?"

"At Cousin Judy's. I must have one lady to keep me in countenance with so many gentlemen, you know. I have another reason for asking her, which I would rather you should find out than I tell you. Do you mind?"

"Not in the least, if you don't think she will spoil the fun."

"I am sure she won't. Then there's your brother Roger."

"Of course. Who more?"

"I think that will do. There will be six of us then,—quite a large enough party for our little dining-room."

"Why shouldn't we dine here? It wouldn't be so hot, and we should have more room."

I liked the idea. The night before, Percivale arranged every thing, so that not only his paintings, of which he had far too many, and which were huddled about the room, but all his *properties* as well, should be accessory to a picturesque effect. And when the table was covered with the glass and plate,—of which latter my mother had taken care I should not be destitute,—and adorned with the flowers which Roger brought me from Covent Garden, assisted by a few of our own, I thought the bird's-eye view from the top of Jacob's ladder a very pretty one indeed.

Resolved that Percivale should have no cause of complaint as regarded the simplicity of my arrangements, I gave orders that our little Ethel, who at that time of the evening was always asleep, should be laid on the couch in my room off the study, with the door ajar, so that Sarah, who was now her nurse, might wait with an easy mind. The dinner was brought in by the outer door of the study, to avoid the awkwardness and possible disaster of the private precipice.

The principal dish, a small sirloin of beef, was at the foot of the table, and a couple of boiled fowls, as I thought, before me. But when the covers were removed, to my surprise I found they were roasted.

"What have you got there, Percivale?" I asked. "Isn't it sirloin?"

"I'm not an adept in such matters," he replied. "I should say it was."

My father gave a glance at the joint. Something seemed to be wrong. I rose and went to my husband's side. Powers of cuisine! Jemima had roasted the fowls, and boiled the sirloin. My exclamation was the signal for an outbreak of laughter, led by my father. I was trembling in the balance between mortification on my own account and sympathy with the evident amusement of my father and Mr. Blackstone. But the thought that Mr. Morley might have been and was not of the party came with such a pang and such a relief, that it settled the point, and I burst out laughing.

"I dare say it's all right," said Roger. "Why shouldn't a sirloin be boiled as well as roasted? I venture to assert that it is all a whim, and we are on the verge of a new discovery to swell the number of those which already owe their being to blunders."

"Let us all try a slice, then," said Mr. Blackstone, "and compare results."

This was agreed to; and a solemn silence followed, during which each sought acquaintance with the new dish.

"I am sorry to say," remarked my father, speaking first, "that Roger is all wrong, and we have only made the discovery that custom is right. It is plain enough why sirloin is always roasted."

"I yield myself convinced," said Roger.

"And I am certain," said Mr. Blackstone, "that if the loin set before the king, whoever he was, had been boiled, he would never have knighted it."

Thanks to the loin, the last possible touch of constraint had vanished, and the party grew a very merry one. The apple-pudding which followed was declared perfect, and eaten up. Percivale produced some good wine from somewhere, which evidently added to the enjoyment of the gentlemen, my father included, who likes a good glass of wine as well as anybody. But a tiny little whimper called me away, and Miss Clare accompanied me; the gentlemen insisting that we should return as soon as possible, and bring the homuncle, as Roger called the baby, with us.

When we returned, the two clergymen were in close conversation, and the other two gentlemen were chiefly listening. My father was saying,—

"My dear sir, I don't see how any man can do his duty as a clergyman who doesn't visit his parishioners."

"In London it is simply impossible," returned Mr. Blackstone. "In the country you are welcome wherever you go; any visit I might pay would most likely be regarded either as an intrusion, or as giving the right to pecuniary aid, of which evils the latter is the worse. There are portions of every London parish which clergymen and their coadjutors have so degraded by the practical teaching of beggary, that they have blocked up every door to a healthy spiritual relation between them and pastor possible."

"Would you not give alms at all, then?"

"One thing, at least, I have made up my mind upon,—that alms from any but the hand of personal friendship tend to evil, and will, in the long run, increase misery."

"What, then, do you suppose the proper relation between a London clergyman and his parishioners?"

"One, I am afraid, which does not at present exist,—one which it is his first business perhaps to bring about. I confess I regard with a repulsion amounting to horror the idea of walking into a poor man's house, except either I have business with him, or desire his personal acquaintance."

"But if our office"—

"Makes it my business to serve—not to assume authority over them especially to the degree of forcing service upon them. I will not say how far intimacy may not justify you in immediate assault upon a man's conscience; but I shrink from any plan that seems to take it for granted that the poor are more wicked than the rich. Why don't we send missionaries to Belgravia? The outside of the cup and platter may sometimes be dirtier than the inside."

"Your missionary could hardly force his way through the servants to the boudoir or drawing-room."

"And the poor have no servants to defend them."

I have recorded this much of the conversation chiefly for the sake of introducing Miss Clare, who now spoke.

"Don't you think, sir," she asked, addressing my father, "that the help one can give to another must always depend on the measure in which one is free one's self?"

My father was silent—thinking. We were all silent. I said to myself, "There, papa! that is something after your own heart." With marked deference and solemnity he answered at length,—

"I have little doubt you are right, Miss Clare. That puts the question upon its own eternal foundation. The mode used must be of infinitely less importance than the person who uses it."

As he spoke, he looked at her with a far more attentive regard than hitherto. Indeed, the eyes of all the company seemed to be scanning the small woman; but she bore the scrutiny well, if indeed she was not unconscious of it; and my husband began to find out one of my reasons for asking her, which was simply that he might see her face. At this moment it was in one of its higher phases. It was, at its best, a grand face,—at its worst, a suffering face; a little too large, perhaps, for the small body which it crowned with a flame of soul; but while you saw her face you never thought of the rest of her; and her attire seemed to court an escape from all observation.

"But," my father went on, looking at Mr. Blackstone, "I am anxious from the clergyman's point of view, to know what my friend here thinks he must try to do in his very difficult position."

"I think the best thing I could do," returned Mr. Blackstone, laughing, "would be to go to school to Miss Clare."

"I shouldn't wonder," my father responded.

"But, in the mean time, I should prefer the chaplaincy of a suburban cemetery."

"Certainly your charge would be a less troublesome one. Your congregation would be quiet enough, at least," said Roger.

"'Then are they glad because they be quiet,'" said my father, as if unconsciously uttering his own reflections. But he was a little cunning, and would say things like that when, fearful of irreverence, he wanted to turn the current of the conversation.

"But, surely," said Miss Clare, "a more active congregation would be quite as desirable."

She had one fault—no, defect: she was slow to enter into the humor of a thing. It seemed almost as if the first aspect of any bit of fun presented to her was that of something wrong. A moment's reflection, however, almost always ended in a sunny laugh, partly at her own stupidity, as she called it.

"You mistake my meaning," said Mr. Blackstone. "My chief, almost sole, attraction to the regions of the grave is the sexton, and not the placidity of the inhabitants; though perhaps Miss Clare might value that more highly if she had more experience of how noisy human nature can be."

Miss Clare gave a little smile, which after-knowledge enabled me to interpret as meaning, "Perhaps I do know a trifle about it;" but she said nothing.

"My first inquiry," he went on, "before accepting such an appointment, would be as to the character and mental habits of the sexton. If I found him a man capable of regarding human nature from a stand-point of his own, I should close with the offer at once. If, on the contrary, he was a common-place man, who made faultless responses, and cherished the friendship of the undertaker, I should decline. In fact, I should regard the sexton as my proposed master; and whether I should accept the place or not would depend altogether on whether I liked him or not. Think what revelations of human nature a real man in such a position could give me: 'Hand me the shovel. You stop a bit,—you're out of breath. Sit down on that stone there, and light your pipe; here's some tobacco. Now tell me the rest of the story. How did the old fellow get on after he had buried his termagant wife?' That's how I should treat him; and I should get, in return, such a succession of peeps into human life and intent and aspirations, as, in the course of a few years, would send me to the next vicarage that turned up a sadder and wiser man, Mr. Walton."

"I don't doubt it," said my father; but whether in sympathy with Mr. Blackstone, or in latent disapproval of a tone judged unbecoming to a clergyman, I cannot tell. Sometimes, I confess, I could not help suspecting the source of the deficiency in humor which he often complained of in me; but I always came to the conclusion that what seemed such a deficiency in him was only occasioned by the presence of a deeper feeling.

Miss Clare was the first to leave.

"What a lovely countenance that is!" said my husband, the moment she was out of hearing.

"She is a very remarkable woman," said my father.

"I suspect she knows a good deal more than most of us," said Mr. Blackstone. "Did you see how her face lighted up always before she said any thing? You can never come nearer to seeing a thought than in her face just before she speaks."

"What is she?" asked Roger.

"Can't you see what she is?" returned his brother. "She's a saint,—Saint Clare."

"If you had been a Scotchman, now," said Roger "that fine name would have sunk to *Sinkler* in your mouth."

"Not a more vulgar corruption, however, than is common in the mouths of English lords and ladies, when they turn *St. John* into *Singen*, reminding one of nothing but the French for an ape," said my father.

"But what does she do?" persisted Roger.

"Why should you think she does any thing?" I asked.

"She looks as if she had to earn her own living."

"She does. She teaches music."

"Why didn't you ask her to play?"

"Because this is the first time she has been to the house."

"Does she go to church, do you suppose?"

"I have no doubt of it; but why do you ask?"

"Because she looks as if she didn't want it. I never saw such an angelic expression upon a countenance."

"You must take me to call upon her," said my father.

"I will with pleasure," I answered.

I found, however, that this was easier promised than performed; for I had asked her by word of mouth at Cousin Judy's, and had not the slightest idea where she lived. Of course I applied to Judy; but she had mislaid her address, and, promising to ask her for it, forgot more than once. My father had to return home without seeing her again.

# CHAPTER XIV.

## A PICTURE.

Things went on very quietly for some time. Of course I was fully occupied, as well I might be, with a life to tend and cultivate which must blossom at length into the human flowers of love and obedience and faith. The smallest service I did the wonderful thing that lay in my lap seemed a something in itself so well worth doing, that it was worth living to do it. As I gazed on the new creation, so far beyond my understanding, yet so dependent upon me while asserting an absolute and divine right to all I did for her, I marvelled that God should intrust me with such a charge, that he did not keep the lovely creature in his own arms, and refuse her to any others. Then I would bethink myself that in giving her into mine, he had not sent her out of his own; for I, too, was a child in his arms, holding and tending my live doll, until it should grow something like me, only ever so much better. Was she not given to me that she might learn what I had begun to learn, namely, that a willing childhood was the flower of life? How can any mother sit with her child on her lap and not know that there is a God over all,—know it by the rising of her own heart in prayer to him? But so few have had parents like mine! If my mother felt thus when I lay in her arms, it was no wonder I should feel thus when my child lay in mine.

Before I had children of my own, I did not care about children, and therefore did not understand them; but I had read somewhere,—and it clung to me although I did not understand it,—that it was in laying hold of the heart of his mother that Jesus laid his first hold on the world to redeem it; and now at length I began to understand it. What a divine way of saving us it was,—to let her bear him, carry him in her bosom, wash him and dress him and nurse him and sing him to sleep,—offer him the adoration of mother's love, misunderstand him, chide him, forgive him even for fancied wrong! Such a love might well save a world in which were mothers enough. It was as if he had said, "Ye shall no more offer vain sacrifices to one who needs them not, and cannot use them. I will need them, so require them at your hands. I will hunger and thirst and be naked and cold, and ye shall minister to me. Sacrifice shall be no more a symbol, but a real giving unto God; and when I return to the Father, inasmuch as ye do it to one of the least of these, ye do it unto me." So all the world is henceforth the temple of God; its worship is ministration; the commonest service is divine service.

I feared at first that the new strange love I felt in my heart came only of the fact that the child was Percivale's and mine; but I soon found it had a far deeper source,—that it sprung from the very humanity of the infant woman, yea, from her relation in virtue of that humanity to the Father of all. The fountain *appeared* in my heart: it arose from an infinite store in the unseen.

Soon, however, came jealousy of my love for my baby. I feared lest it should make me—nay, was making me—neglect my husband. The fear first arose in me one morning as I sat with her half dressed on my knees. I was dawdling over her in my fondness, as I used to dawdle over the dressing of my doll, when suddenly I became aware that never once since her arrival had I sat with my husband in his study. A pang of dismay shot through me. "Is this to be a wife?" I said to myself,—"to play with a live love like a dead doll, and forget her husband!" I caught up a blanket from the cradle,—I am not going to throw away that good old word for the ugly outlandish name they give it now, reminding one only of a helmet,—I caught up a blanket from the cradle, I say, wrapped it round the treasure, which was shooting its arms and legs in every direction like a polypus feeling after its food,—and rushed down stairs, and down the precipice into the study. Percivale started up in terror, thinking something fearful had happened, and I was bringing him all that was left of the child.

"What—what—what's the matter?" he gasped.

I could not while he was thus frightened explain to him what had driven me to him in such alarming haste.

"I've brought you the baby to kiss," I said, unfolding the blanket, and holding up the sprawling little goddess towards the face that towered above me.

"Was it dying for a kiss then?" he said, taking her, blanket and all, from my arms.

The end of the blanket swept across his easel, and smeared the face of the baby in a picture of the *Three Kings*, at which he was working.

"O Percivale!" I cried, "you've smeared your baby!"

"But this is a real live baby; she may smear any thing she likes."

"Except her own face and hands, please, then, Percivale."

"Or her blessed frock," said Percivale. "She hasn't got one, though. Why hasn't the little angel got her feathers on yet?"

"I was in such a hurry to bring her."

"To be kissed?"

"No, not exactly. It wasn't her I was in a hurry to bring; it was myself."

"Ah! you wanted to be kissed, did you?"

"No, sir. I didn't want to be kissed; but I did so want to kiss you, Percivale."

"Isn't it all the same, though, darling?" he said. "It seems so to me."

"Sometimes, Percivale, you are so very stupid! It's not the same at all. There's a world of difference between the two; and you ought to know it, or be told it, if you don't."

"I shall think it over as soon as you leave me," he said.

"But I'm not going to leave you for a long time. I haven't seen you paint for weeks and weeks,—not since this little troublesome thing came poking in between us."

"But she's not dressed yet."

"That doesn't signify. She's well wrapped up, and quite warm."

He put me a chair where I could see his picture without catching the shine of the paint. I took the baby from him, and he went on with his work.

"You don't think I am going to sacrifice all my privileges to this little tyrant, do you?" I said.

"It would be rather hard for me, at least," he rejoined.

"You did think I was neglecting you, then, Percivale?"

"Not for a moment."

"Then you didn't miss me?"

"I did, very much."

"And you didn't grumble?"

"No."

"Do I disturb you?" I asked, after a little pause. "Can you paint just as well when I am here as when you are alone?"

"Better. I feel warmer to my work somehow."

I was satisfied, and held my peace. When I am best pleased I don't want to talk. But Percivale, perhaps not having found this out yet, looked anxiously in my face; and, as at the moment my eyes were fixed on his picture, I thought he wanted to find out whether I liked the design.

"I see it now!" I cried. "I could not make out where the Magi were."

He had taken for the scene of his picture an old farm kitchen, or yeoman's hall, with its rich brown rafters, its fire on the hearth, and its red brick floor.

A tub half full of bright water, stood on one side; and the mother was bending over her baby, which, undressed for the bath, she was holding out for the admiration of the Magi. Immediately behind the mother stood, in the garb of a shepherd, my father, leaning on the ordinary shepherd's crook; my mother, like a peasant-woman in her Sunday-best, with a white handkerchief crossed upon her bosom, stood beside him, and both were gazing with a chastened yet profound pleasure on the lovely child.

In front stood two boys and a girl,—between the ages of five and nine,—gazing each with a peculiar wondering delight on the baby. The youngest boy, with a great spotted wooden horse in his hand, was approaching to embrace the infant in such fashion as made the toy look dangerous, and the left hand of the mother was lifted with a motion of warning and defence. The little girl, the next youngest, had, in her absorption, dropped her gaudily dressed doll at her feet, and stood sucking her thumb, her big blue eyes wide with contemplation. The eldest boy had brought his white rabbit to give the baby, but had forgotten all about it, so full was his heart of his new brother. An expression of mingled love and wonder and perplexity had already begun to dawn upon the face, but it was as yet far from finished. He stood behind the other two peeping over their heads.

"Were you thinking of that Titian in the Louvre, with the white rabbit in it?" I asked Percivale.

"I did not think of it until after I had put in the rabbit," he replied. "And it shall remain; for it suits my purpose, and Titian would not claim all the white rabbits because of that one."

"Did you think of the black lamb in it, then, when you laid that black pussy on the hearth?" I asked.

"Black lamb?" he returned.

"Yes," I insisted; "a black lamb, in the dark background—such a very black lamb, and in such a dark background, that it seems you never discovered it."

"Are you sure?" he persisted.

"Absolutely certain," I replied. "I pointed it out to papa in the picture itself in the Louvre; he had not observed it before either."

"I am very glad to know there is such a thing there. I need not answer your question, you see. It is odd enough I should have put in the black puss. Upon some grounds I might argue that my puss is better than Titian's lamb."

"What grounds? tell me."

"If the painter wanted a contrast, a lamb, be he as black as ever paint could make him, must still be a more Christian animal than a cat as white as snow. Under what pretence could a cat be used for a Christian symbol?"

"What do you make of her playfulness?"

"I should count that a virtue, were it not for the fatal objection that it is always exercised at the expense of other creatures."

"A ball of string, or a reel, or a bit of paper, is enough for an uncorrupted kitten."

"But you must not forget that it serves only in virtue of the creature's imagination representing it as alive. If you do not make it move, she will herself set it in motion as the initiative of the game. If she cannot do that, she will take no notice of it."

"Yes, I see. I give in."

All this time he had been painting diligently. He could now combine talking and painting far better than he used. But a knock came to the study door; and, remembering baby's unpresentable condition, I huddled her up, climbed the stair again, and finished the fledging of my little angel in a very happy frame of mind.

# CHAPTER XV.

## RUMORS.

Hardly was it completed, when Cousin Judy called, and I went down to see her, carrying my baby with me. As I went, something put me in mind that I must ask her for Miss Clare's address. Lest I should again forget, as soon as she had kissed and admired the baby, I said,—

"Have you found out yet where Miss Clare lives, Judy?"

"I don't choose to find out," she answered. "I am sorry to say I have had to give her up. It is a disappointment, I confess."

"What do you mean?" I said. "I thought you considered her a very good teacher."

"I have no fault to find with her on that score. She was always punctual, and I must allow both played well and taught the children delightfully. But I have heard such questionable things about her!—very strange things indeed!"

"What are they?"

"I can't say I've been able to fix on more than one thing directly against her character, but"—

"Against her character!" I exclaimed.

"Yes, indeed. She lives by herself in lodgings, and the house is not at all a respectable one."

"But have you made no further inquiry?"

"I consider that quite enough. I had already met more than one person, however, who seemed to think it very odd that I should have her to teach music in my family."

"Did they give any reason for thinking her unfit?"

"I did not choose to ask them. One was Miss Clarke—you know her. She smiled in her usual supercilious manner, but in her case I believe it was only because Miss Clare looks so dowdy. But nobody knows any thing about her except what I've just told you."

"And who told you that?"

"Mrs. Jeffreson."

"But you once told me that she was a great gossip."

"Else she wouldn't have heard it. But that doesn't make it untrue. In fact, she convinced me of its truth, for she knows the place she lives in, and assured me it was at great risk of infection to the children that I allowed her to enter the house; and so, of course, I felt compelled to let her know that I didn't require her services any longer."

"There must be some mistake, surely!" I said.

"Oh, no! not the least, I am sorry to say."

"How did she take it?"

"Very sweetly indeed. She didn't even ask me why, which was just as well, seeing I should have found it awkward to tell her. But I suppose she knew too many grounds herself to dare the question."

I was dreadfully sorry, but I could not say much more then. I ventured only to express my conviction that there could not be any charge to bring against Miss Clare herself; for that one who looked and spoke as she did could have nothing to be ashamed of. Judy, however, insisted that what she had heard was reason enough for at least ending the engagement; indeed, that no one was fit for such a situation of whom such things could be said, whether they were true or not.

When she left me, I gave baby to her nurse, and went straight to the study, peeping in to see if Percivale was alone.

He caught sight of me, and called to me to come down.

"It's only Roger," he said.

I was always pleased to see Roger. He was a strange creature,—one of those gifted men who are capable of any thing, if not of every thing, and yet carry nothing within sight of proficiency. He whistled like a starling, and accompanied his whistling on the piano; but never played. He could copy a drawing to a hair's-breadth, but never drew. He could engrave well on wood; but although he had often been employed in that way, he had always got tired of it after a few weeks. He was forever wanting to do something other than what he was at; and the moment he got tired of a thing, he would work at it no longer; for he had never learned to *make* himself. He would come every day to the study for a week to paint in backgrounds, or make a duplicate; and then, perhaps, we wouldn't see him for a fortnight. At other times he would work, say for a month, modelling, or carving marble, for a sculptor friend, from whom he might have had constant employment if he had pleased. He had given lessons in various branches, for he was an excellent scholar, and had the finest ear for verse, as well as the keenest appreciation of the loveliness of poetry, that I have ever known. He had stuck to this longer than to any thing else, strange to say; for one would have thought it the least attractive of employments to one of his volatile disposition. For some time indeed he had supported himself comfortably in this way; for through friends of his family he had had good introductions, and, although he wasted a good deal of money in buying nick-nacks that promised to be useful and seldom were, he had no objectionable habits except inordinate smoking. But it happened that a pupil—a girl of imaginative disposition, I presume—fell so much in love with him that she betrayed her feelings to her countess-mother, and the lessons were of course put an end to. I suspect he did not escape heart-whole himself; for he immediately dropped all his other lessons, and took to writing poetry for a new magazine, which proved of ephemeral constitution, and vanished after a few months of hectic existence.

It was remarkable that with such instability his moral nature should continue uncorrupted; but this I believe he owed chiefly to his love and admiration of his brother. For my part, I could not help liking him much. There was a half-plaintive playfulness about him, alternated with gloom, and occasionally with wild merriment, which made him interesting even when one felt most inclined to quarrel with him. The worst of him was that he considered himself a generally misunderstood, if not ill-used man, who could not only distinguish himself, but render valuable service to society, if only society would do him the justice to give him a chance. Were it only, however, for his love to my baby, I could not but be ready to take up his defence. When I mentioned what I had just heard about Miss Clare, Percivale looked both astonished and troubled; but before he could speak, Roger, with the air of a man of the world whom experience enabled to come at once to a decision, said,—

"Depend upon it, Wynnie, there is falsehood there somewhere. You will always be nearer the truth if you believe nothing, than if you believe the half of what you hear."

"That's very much what papa says," I answered. "He affirms that he never searched into an injurious report in his own parish without finding it so nearly false as to deprive it of all right to go about."

"Besides," said Roger, "look at that face! How I should like to model it. She's a good woman that, depend upon it."

I was delighted with his enthusiasm.

"I wish you would ask her again, as soon as you can," said Percivale, who always tended to embody his conclusions in acts rather than in words. "Your cousin Judy is a jolly good creature, but from your father's description of her as a girl, she must have grown a good deal more worldly since her marriage. Respectability is an awful snare."

"Yes," said Roger; "one ought to be very thankful to be a Bohemian, and have nothing expected of him, for respectability is a most fruitful mother of stupidity and injustice."

I could not help thinking that *he* might, however, have a little more and be none the worse.

"I should be very glad to do as you desire, husband," I said, "but how can I? I haven't learned where she lives. It was asking Judy for her address once more that brought it all out. I certainly didn't insist, as I might have done, notwithstanding what she told me; but, if she didn't remember it before, you may be sure she could not have given it me then."

"It's very odd," said Roger, stroking his long mustache, the sole ornament of the kind he wore. "It's very odd," he repeated thoughtfully, and then paused again.

"What's so very odd, Roger?" asked Percivale.

"The other evening," answered Roger, after yet a short pause, "happening to be in Tottenham Court Road, I walked for some distance behind a young woman carrying a brown beer-jug in her hand—for I sometimes amuse myself in the street by walking persistently behind some one, devising the unseen face in my mind, until the recognition of the same step following causes the person to look round at me, and give me the opportunity of comparing the two—I mean the one I had devised and the real one. When the young woman at length turned her head, it was only my astonishment that kept me from addressing her as Miss Clare. My surprise, however, gave me time to see how absurd it would have been. Presently she turned down a yard and disappeared."

"Don't tell my cousin Judy," I said. "She would believe it *was* Miss Clare."

"There isn't much danger," he returned. "Even if I knew your cousin, I should not be likely to mention such an incident in her hearing."

"Could it have been she?" said Percivale thoughtfully.

"Absurd!" said Roger. "Miss Clare is a lady, wherever she may live."

"I don't know," said his brother thoughtfully; "who can tell? It mightn't have been beer she was carrying."

"I didn't say it was beer," returned Roger. "I only said it was a beer-jug,—one of those brown, squat, stone jugs,—the best for beer that I know, after all,—brown, you know, with a dash of gray."

"Brown jug or not, I wish I could get a few sittings from her. She would make a lovely St. Cecilia," said my husband.

"Brown jug and all?" asked Roger.

"If only she were a little taller," I objected.

"And had an aureole," said my husband. "But I might succeed in omitting the jug as well as in adding the aureole and another half-foot of stature, if only I could get that lovely countenance on the canvas,—so full of life and yet of repose."

"Don't you think it a little hard?" I ventured to say.

"I think so," said Roger.

"I don't," said my husband. "I know what in it looks like hardness; but I think it comes of the repression of feeling."

"You have studied her well for your opportunities," I said.

"I have; and I am sure, whatever Mrs. Morley may say, that, if there be any truth at all in those reports, there is some satisfactory explanation of whatever has given rise to them. I wish we knew anybody else that knew her. Do try to find some one that does, Wynnie."

"I don't know how to set about it," I said. "I should be only too glad."

"I will try," said Roger. "Does she sing?"

"I have heard Judy say she sang divinely; but the only occasion on which I met her—at their house, that time you couldn't go, Percivale—she was never asked to sing."

"I suspect," remarked Roger, "it will turn out to be only that she's something of a Bohemian, like ourselves."

"Thank you, Roger; but for my part, I don't consider myself a Bohemian at all," I said.

"I am afraid you must rank with your husband, wifie," said *mine*, as the wives of the working people of London often call their husbands.

"Then you do count yourself a Bohemian: pray, what significance do you attach to the epithet?" I asked.

"I don't know, except it signifies our resemblance to the gypsies," he answered.

"I don't understand you quite."

"I believe the gypsies used to be considered Bohemians," interposed Roger, "though they are doubtless of Indian origin. Their usages being quite different from those amongst which they live, the name Bohemian came to be applied to painters, musicians, and such like generally, to whom, save by courtesy, no position has yet been accorded by society—so called."

"But why have they not yet vindicated for themselves a social position," I asked, "and that a high one?"

"Because they are generally poor, I suppose," he answered; "and society is generally stupid."

"May it not be because they are so often, like the gypsies, lawless in their behavior, as well as peculiar in their habits?" I suggested.

"I understand you perfectly, Mrs. Percivale," rejoined Roger with mock offence. "But how would that apply to Charlie?"

"Not so well as to you, I confess," I answered. "But there is ground for it with him too."

"I have thought it all over many a time," said Percivale; "and I suppose it comes in part from inability to understand the worth of our calling, and in part from the difficulty of knowing where to put us."

"I suspect," I said, "one thing is that so many of them are content to be received as merely painters, or whatever they may be by profession. Many, you have told me, for instance, accept invitations which do not include their wives."

"They often go to parties, of course, where there are no ladies," said Roger.

"That is not what I mean," I replied. "They go to dinner-parties where there are ladies, and evening parties, too, without their wives."

"Whoever does that," said Percivale, "has at least no right to complain that he is regarded as a Bohemian; for in accepting such invitations, he accepts insult, and himself insults his wife."

Nothing irritated my bear so much as to be asked to dinner without me. He would not even offer the shadow of a reason for declining the invitation. "For," he would say, "if I give the real reason, namely, that I do not choose to go where my wife is excluded, they will set it down to her jealous ambition of entering a sphere beyond her reach; I will not give a false reason, and indeed have no objection to their seeing that I am offended; therefore, I assign none. If they have any chivalry in them, they may find out my reason readily enough."

I don't think I ever displeased him so much as once when I entreated him to accept an invitation to dine with the Earl of H——. The fact was, I had been fancying it my duty to persuade him to get over his offence at the omission of my name, for the sake of the advantage it would be to him in his profession. I laid it before him as gently and coaxingly as I could, representing how expenses increased, and how the children would be requiring education by and by,—reminding him that the reputation of more than one of the most popular painters had been brought about in some measure by their social qualities and the friendships they made.

"Is it likely your children will be ladies and gentlemen," he said, "if you prevail on their father to play the part of a sneaking parasite?"

I was frightened. He had never spoken to me in such a tone, but I saw too well how deeply he was hurt to take offence at his roughness. I could only beg him to forgive me, and promise never to say such a word again, assuring him that I believed as strongly as himself that the best heritage of children was their father's honor.

Free from any such clogs as the possession of a wife encumbers a husband withal, Roger could of course accept what invitations his connection with an old and honorable family procured him. One evening he came in late from a dinner at Lady Bernard's.

"Whom do you think I took down to dinner?" he asked, almost before he was seated.

"Lady Bernard?" I said, flying high.

"Her dowager aunt?" said Percivale.

"No, no; Miss Clare."

"Miss Clare!" we both repeated, with mingled question and exclamation.

"Yes, Miss Clare, incredible as it may appear," he answered.

"Did you ask her if it was she you saw carrying the jug of beer in Tottenham Court Road?" said Percivale.

"Did you ask her address?" I said. "That is a question more worthy of an answer."

"Yes, I did. I believe I did. I think I did."

"What is it, then?"

"Upon my word, I haven't the slightest idea."

"So, Mr. Roger! You have had a perfect opportunity, and have let it slip! You are a man to be trusted indeed!"

"I don't know how it could have been. I distinctly remember approaching the subject more than once or twice; and now first I discover that I never asked the question. Or if I did, I am certain I got no answer."

"Bewitched!"

"Yes, I suppose so."

"Or," suggested Percivale, "she did not choose to tell you; saw the question coming, and led you away from it; never let you ask it."

"I have heard that ladies can keep one from saying what they don't want to hear. But she sha'n't escape me so a second time."

"Indeed, you don't deserve another chance," I said. "You're not half so clever as I took you to be, Roger."

"When I think of it, though, it wasn't a question so easy to ask, or one you would like to be overheard asking."

"Clearly bewitched," I said. "But for that I forgive you. Did she sing?"

"No. I don't suppose any one there ever thought of asking such a dingy-feathered bird to sing."

"You had some music?"

"Oh, yes! Pretty good, and very bad. Miss Clare's forehead was crossed by no end of flickering shadows as she listened."

"It wasn't for want of interest in her you forgot to find out where she lived! You had better take care, Master Roger."

"Take care of what?"

"Why, you don't know her address."

"What has that to do with taking care?"

"That you won't know where to find your heart if you should happen to want it."

"Oh! I am past that kind of thing long ago. You've made an uncle of me."

And so on, with a good deal more nonsense, but no news of Miss Clare's retreat.

I had before this remarked to my husband that it was odd she had never called since dining with us; but he made little of it, saying that people who gained their own livelihood ought to be excused from attending to rules which had their origin with another class; and I had thought no more about it, save in disappointment that she had not given me that opportunity of improving my acquaintance with her.

# CHAPTER XVI.

## A DISCOVERY.

One Saturday night, my husband happening to be out, an event of rare occurrence, Roger called; and as there were some things I had not been able to get during the day, I asked him to go with me to Tottenham Court Road. It was not far from the region where we lived, and I did a great part of my small shopping there. The early closing had, if I remember rightly, begun to show itself; anyhow, several of the shops were shut, and we walked a long way down the street, looking for some place likely to supply what I required.

"It was just here I came up with the girl and the brown jug," said Roger, as we reached the large dissenting chapel.

"That adventure seems to have taken a great hold of you, Roger," I said.

"She *was* so like Miss Clare!" he returned. "I can't get the one face clear of the other. When I met her at Lady Bernard's, the first thing I thought of was the brown jug."

"Were you as much pleased with her conversation as at our house?" I asked.

"Even more," he answered. "I found her ideas of art so wide, as well as just and accurate, that I was puzzled to think where she had had opportunity of developing them. I questioned her about it, and found she was in the habit of going, as often as she could spare time, to the National Gallery, where her custom was, she said, not to pass from picture to picture, but keep to one until it formed itself in her mind,—that is the expression she used, explaining herself to mean, until she seemed to know what the painter had set himself to do, and why this was and that was which she could not at first understand. Clearly, without ever having taken a pencil in her hand, she has educated herself to a keen perception of what is demanded of a true picture. Of course the root of it lies in her musical development.—There," he cried suddenly, as we came opposite a paved passage, "that is the place I saw her go down."

"Then you do think the girl with the beer-jug was Miss Clare, after all?"

"Not in the least. I told you I could not separate them in my mind."

"Well, I must say, it seems odd. A girl like that and Miss Clare! Why, as often as you speak of the one, you seem to think of the other."

"In fact," he returned, "I am, as I say, unable to dissociate them. But if you had seen the girl, you would not wonder. The likeness was absolutely complete."

"I believe you do consider them one and the same; and I am more than half inclined to think so myself, remembering what Judy said."

"Isn't it possible some one who knows Miss Clare may have seen this girl, and been misled by the likeness?"

"But where, then, does Miss Clare live? Nobody seems to know."

"You have never asked any one but Mrs. Morley."

"You have yourself, however, given me reason to think she avoids the subject. If she did live anywhere hereabout, she would have some cause to avoid it."

I had stopped to look down the passage.

"Suppose," said Roger, "some one were to come past now and see Mrs. Percivale, the wife of the celebrated painter, standing in Tottenham Court Road beside the swing-door of a corner public-house, talking to a young man."

"Yes; it might have given occasion for scandal," I said. "To avoid it, let us go down the court and see what it is like."

"It's not a fit place for you to go into."

"If it were in my father's parish, I should have known everybody in it."

"You haven't the slightest idea what you are saying."

"Come, anyhow, and let us see what the place is like," I insisted.

Without another word he gave me his arm, and down the court we went, past the flaring gin-shop, and into the gloom beyond. It was one of those places of which, while the general effect remains vivid in one's mind, the salient points are so few that it is difficult to say much by way of description. The houses had once been occupied by people in better circumstances than its present inhabitants; and indeed they looked all decent enough until, turning two right angles, we came upon another sort. They were still as large, and had plenty of windows; but, in the light of a single lamp at the corner, they looked very dirty and wretched and dreary. A little shop, with dried herrings and bull's-eyes in the window, was lighted by a tallow candle set in a ginger-beer bottle, with a card of "Kinahan's LL Whiskey" for a reflector.

"They can't have many customers to the extent of a bottle," said Roger. "But no doubt they have some privileges from the public-house at the corner for hanging up the card."

The houses had sunk areas, just wide enough for a stair, and the basements seemed full of tenants. There was a little wind blowing, so that the atmosphere was tolerable, notwithstanding a few stray leaves of cabbage, suggestive of others in a more objectionable condition not far off.

A confused noise of loud voices, calling and scolding, hitherto drowned by the tumult of the street, now reached our ears. The place took one turn more, and then the origin of it became apparent. At the farther end of the passage was another lamp, the light of which shone upon a group of men and women, in altercation, which had not yet come to blows. It might, including children, have numbered twenty, of which some seemed drunk, and all more or less excited. Roger turned to go back the moment he caught sight of them; but I felt inclined, I hardly knew why, to linger a little. Should any danger offer, it would be easy to gain the open thoroughfare.

"It's not at all a fit place for a lady," he said.

"Certainly not," I answered; "it hardly seems a fit place for human beings. These are human beings, though. Let us go through it."

He still hesitated; but as I went on, he could but follow me. I wanted to see what the attracting centre of the little crowd was; and that it must be occupied with some affair of more than ordinary interest, I judged from the fact that a good many superterrestrial spectators looked down from the windows at various elevations upon the disputants, whose voices now and then lulled for a moment only to break out in fresh objurgation and dispute.

Drawing a little nearer, a slight parting of the crowd revealed its core to us. It was a little woman, without bonnet or shawl, whose back was towards us. She turned from side to side, now talking to one, and now to another of the surrounding circle. At first I thought she was setting forth her grievances, in the hope of sympathy, or perhaps of justice; but I soon perceived that her motions were too calm for that. Sometimes the crowd would speak altogether, sometimes keep silent for a full minute while she went on talking. When she turned her face towards us, Roger and I turned ours, and stared at each other. The face was disfigured by a swollen eye, evidently from a blow; but clearly enough, if it was not Miss Clare, it was the young woman of the beer-jug. Neither of us spoke, but turned once more to watch the result of what seemed to have at length settled down into an almost amicable conference. After a few more grumbles and protestations, the group began to break up into twos and threes. These the young woman seemed to set herself to break up again. Here, however, an ill-looking fellow like a costermonger, with a broken nose, came up to us, and with a strong Irish accent and offensive manner, but still with a touch of Irish breeding, requested to know what our business was. Roger asked if the place wasn't a thoroughfare.

"Not for the likes o' you," he answered, "as comes pryin' after the likes of us. We manage our own affairs down here—*we* do. You'd better be off, my lady."

I have my doubts what sort of reply Roger might have returned if he had been alone, but he certainly spoke in a very conciliatory manner, which, however, the man did not seem to appreciate, for he called it blarney; but the young woman, catching sight of our little group, and supposing, I presume, that it also required dispersion, approached us. She had come within a yard of us, when suddenly her face brightened, and she exclaimed, in a tone of surprise,—

"Mrs. Percivale! You here?"

It was indeed Miss Clare. Without the least embarrassment, she held out her hand to me, but I am afraid I did not take it very cordially. Roger, however, behaved to her as if they stood in a drawing-room, and this brought me to a sense of propriety.

"I don't look very respectable, I fear," she said, putting her hand over her eye. "The fact is, I have had a blow, and it will look worse to-morrow. Were you coming to find me?"

I forget what lame answer either of us gave.

"Will you come in?" she said.

On the spur of the moment, I declined. For all my fine talk to Roger, I shrunk from the idea of entering one of those houses. I can only say, in excuse, that my whole mind was in a condition of bewilderment.

"Can I do any thing for you, then?" she asked, in a tone slightly marked with disappointment, I thought.

"Thank you, no," I answered, hardly knowing what my words were.

"Then good-night," she said, and, nodding kindly, turned, and entered one of the houses.

We also turned in silence, and walked out of the court.

"Why didn't you go with her?" said Roger, as soon as we were in the street.

"I'm sorry I didn't if you wanted to go, Roger; but"—

"I think you might have gone, seeing I was with you," he said.

"I don't think it would have been at all a proper thing to do, without knowing more about her," I answered, a little hurt. "You can't tell what sort of a place it may be."

"It's a good place, wherever she is, or I am much mistaken," he returned.

"You may be much mistaken, Roger."

"True. I have been mistaken more than once in my life. I am not mistaken this time, though."

"I presume you would have gone if I hadn't been with you?"

"Certainly, if she had asked me, which is not very likely."

"And you lay the disappointment of missing a glimpse into the sweet privacy of such a home to my charge?"

It was a spiteful speech; and Roger's silence made me feel it was, which, with the rather patronizing opinion I had of Roger, I found not a little galling. So I, too, kept silence, and nothing beyond a platitude had passed between us when I found myself at my own door, my shopping utterly forgotten, and something acid on my mind.

"Don't you mean to come in?" I said, for he held out his hand at the top of the stairs to bid me good-night. "My husband will be home soon, if he has not come already. You needn't be bored with my company—you can sit in the study."

"I think I had better not," he answered.

"I am very sorry, Roger, if I was rude to you," I said; "but how could you wish me to be hand-and-glove with a woman who visits people who she is well aware would not think of inviting her if they had a notion of her surroundings. That can't be right, I am certain. I protest I feel just as if I had been reading an ill-invented story,—an unnatural fiction. I cannot get these things together in my mind at all, do what I will."

"There must be some way of accounting for it," said Roger.

"No doubt," I returned; "but who knows what that way may be?"

"You may be wrong in supposing that the people at whose houses she visits know nothing about her habits."

"Is it at all likely they do, Roger? Do you think it is? I know at least that my cousin dispensed with her services as soon as she came to the knowledge of certain facts concerning these very points."

"Excuse me—certain rumors—very uncertain facts."

When you are cross, the slightest play upon words is an offence. I knocked at the door in dudgeon, then turned and said,—

"My cousin Judy, Mr. Roger"—

But here I paused, for I had nothing ready. Anger makes some people cleverer for the moment, but when I am angry I am always stupid. Roger finished the sentence for me.

—"Your cousin Judy is, you must allow, a very conventional woman," he said.

"She is very good-natured, anyhow. And what do you say to Lady Bernard?"

"She hasn't repudiated Miss Clare's acquaintance, so far as I know."

"But, answer me,—do you believe Lady Bernard would invite her to meet her friends if she knew all?"

"Depend upon it, Lady Bernard knows what she is about. People of her rank can afford to be unconventional."

This irritated me yet more, for it implied that I was influenced by the conventionality which both he and my husband despised; and Sarah opening the door that instant, I stepped in, without even saying good-night to him. Before she closed it, however, I heard my husband's voice, and ran out again to welcome him.

He and Roger had already met in the little front garden. They did not shake hands—they never did—they always met as if they had parted only an hour ago.

"What were you and my wife quarrelling about, Rodge?" I heard Percivale ask, and paused on the middle of the stair to hear his answer.

"How do you know we were quarrelling?" returned Roger gloomily.

"I heard you from the very end of the street," said my husband.

"That's not so far," said Roger; for indeed one house, with, I confess, a good space of garden on each side of it, and the end of another house, finished the street. But notwithstanding the shortness of the distance it stung me to the quick. Here had I been regarding, not even with contempt, only with disgust, the quarrel in which Miss Clare was mixed up; and half an hour after, my own voice was heard in dispute with my husband's brother from the end of the street in which we lived! I felt humiliated, and did not rush down the remaining half of the steps to implore my husband's protection against Roger's crossness.

"Too far to hear a wife and a brother, though," returned Percivale jocosely.

"Go on," said Roger; "pray go on. *Let dogs delight* comes next. I beg Mrs. Percivale's pardon. I will amend the quotation: 'Let dogs delight to worry'"—

"Cats," I exclaimed; and rushing down the steps, I kissed Roger before I kissed my husband.

"I meant—I mean—I was going to say *lambs*."

"Now, Roger, don't add to your vices flattery and"—

"And fibbing," he subjoined.

"I didn't say so."

"You only meant it."

"Don't begin again," interposed Percivale: "Come in, and refer the cause in dispute to me."

We did go in, and we did refer the matter to him. By the time we had between us told him the facts of the case, however, the point in dispute between us appeared to have grown hazy, the fact being that neither of us cared to say any thing more about it. Percivale insisted that there was no question before the court. At length Roger, turning from me to his brother, said,—

"It's not worth mentioning, Charley; but what led to our irreconcilable quarrel was this: I thought Wynnie might have accepted Miss Clare's invitation to walk in and pay her a visit; and Wynnie thought me, I suppose, too ready to sacrifice her dignity to the pleasure of seeing a little more of the object of our altercation. There!"

My husband turned to me and said,—

"Mrs. Percivale, do you accept this as a correct representation of your difference?"

"Well," I answered, hesitating—"yes, on the whole. All I object to is the word *dignity*."

"I retract it," cried Roger, "and accept any substitute you prefer."

"Let it stand," I returned. "It will do as well as a better. I only wish to say that it was not exactly my dignity"—

"No, no; your sense of propriety," said my husband; and then sat silent for a minute or two, pondering like a judge. At length he spoke:—

"Wife," he said, "you might have gone with your brother, I think; but I quite understand your disinclination. At the same time, a more generous judgment of Miss Clare might have prevented any difference of feeling in the matter."

"But," I said, greatly inclined to cry, "I only postponed my judgment concerning her."

And I only postponed my crying, for I was very much ashamed of myself.

# CHAPTER XVII.

## MISS CLARE.

Of course my husband and I talked a good deal more about what I ought to have done; and I saw clearly enough that I ought to have run any risk there might be in accepting her invitation. I had been foolishly taking more care of myself than was necessary. I told him I would write to Roger, and ask him when he could take me there again.

"I will tell you a better plan," he said. "I will go with you myself. And that will get rid of half the awkwardness there would be if you went with Roger, after having with him refused to go in."

"But would that be fair to Roger? She would think I didn't like going with him, and I would go with Roger anywhere. It was I who did not want to go. He did."

"My plan, however, will pave the way for a full explanation—or confession rather, I suppose it will turn out to be. I know you are burning to make it, with your mania for confessing your faults."

I knew he did not like me the worse for that *mania*, though.

"The next time," he added, "you can go with Roger, always supposing you should feel inclined to continue the acquaintance, and then you will be able to set him right in her eyes."

The plan seemed unobjectionable. But just then Percivale was very busy; and I being almost as much occupied with my baby as he was with his, day after day and week after week passed, during which our duty to Miss Clare was, I will not say either forgotten or neglected, but unfulfilled.

One afternoon I was surprised by a visit from my father. He not unfrequently surprised us.

"Why didn't you let us know, papa?" I said. "A surprise is very nice; but an expectation is much nicer, and lasts so much longer."

"I might have disappointed you."

"Even if you had, I should have already enjoyed the expectation. That would be safe."

"There's a good deal to be said in excuse of surprises," he rejoined; "but in the present case, I have a special one to offer. I was taken with a sudden desire to see you. It was very foolish no doubt, and you are quite right in wishing I weren't here, only going to come to-morrow."

"Don't be so cruel, papa. Scarcely a day passes in which *I* do not long to see *you*. My baby makes me think more about my home than ever."

"Then she's a very healthy baby, if one may judge by her influences. But you know, if I had had to give you warning, I could not have been here before to-morrow; and surely you will acknowledge, that, however nice expectation may be, presence is better."

"Yes, papa. We will make a compromise, if you please. Every time you think of coming to me, you must either come at once, or let me know you are coming. Do you agree to that?"

"I agree," he said.

So I have the pleasure of a constant expectation. Any day he may walk in unheralded; or by any post I may receive a letter with the news that he is coming at such a time.

As we sat at dinner that evening, he asked if we had lately seen Miss Clare.

"I've seen her only once, and Percivale not at all, since you were here last, papa," I answered.

"How's that?" he asked again, a little surprised. "Haven't you got her address yet? I want very much to know more of her."

"So do we. I haven't got her address, but I know where she lives."

"What do you mean, Wynnie? Has she taken to dark sayings of late, Percivale?"

I told him the whole story of my adventure with Roger, and the reports Judy had prejudiced my judgment withal. He heard me through in silence, for it was a rule with him never to interrupt a narrator. He used to say, "You will generally get at more, and in a better fashion, if you let any narrative take its own devious course, without the interruption of requested explanations. By the time it is over, you will find the questions you wanted to ask mostly vanished."

"Describe the place to me, Wynnie," he said, when I had ended. "I must go and see her. I have a suspicion, amounting almost to a conviction, that she is one whose acquaintance ought to be cultivated at any cost. There is some grand explanation of all this contradictory strangeness."

"I don't think I could describe the place to you so that you would find it. But if Percivale wouldn't mind my going with you instead of with him, I should be only too happy to accompany you. May I, Percivale?"

"Certainly. It will do just as well to go with your father as with me. I only stipulate, that, if you are both satisfied, you take Roger with you next time."

"Of course I will."

"Then we'll go to-morrow morning," said my father.

"I don't think she is likely to be at home in the morning," I said. "She goes out giving lessons, you know; and the probability is, that at that time we should not find her."

"Then why not to-night?" he rejoined.

"Why not, if you wish it?"

"I do wish it, then."

"If you knew the place, though, I think you would prefer going a little earlier than we can to-night."

"Ah, well! we will go to-morrow evening. We could dine early, couldn't we?"

So it was arranged. My father went about some business in the morning. We dined early, and set out about six o'clock.

My father was getting an old man, and if any protection had been required, he could not have been half so active as Roger; and yet I felt twice as safe with him. I am satisfied that the deepest sense of safety, even in respect of physical dangers, can spring only from moral causes; neither do you half so much fear evil happening to you, as fear evil happening which ought not to happen to you. I believe what made me so courageous was the undeveloped fore-feeling, that, if any evil should overtake me in my father's company, I should not care; it would be all right then, anyhow. The repose was in my father himself, and neither in his strength nor his wisdom. The former might fail, the latter might mistake; but so long as I was with him in what I did, no harm worth counting harm could come to me,—only such as I should neither lament nor feel. Scarcely a shadow of danger, however, showed itself.

It was a cold evening in the middle of November. The light, which had been scanty enough all day, had vanished in a thin penetrating fog. Round every lamp in the street was a colored halo; the gay shops gleamed like jewel-caverns of Aladdin hollowed out of the darkness; and the people that hurried or sauntered along looked inscrutable. Where could they live? Had they anybody to love them? Were their hearts quiet under their dingy cloaks and shabby coats?

"Yes," returned my father, to whom I had said something to this effect, "what would not one give for a peep into the mysteries of all these worlds that go crowding past us. If we could but see through the opaque husk of them, some would glitter and glow like diamond mines; others perhaps would look mere earthy holes; some of them forsaken quarries, with a great pool of stagnant water in the bottom; some like vast coal-pits of gloom, into which you dared not carry a lighted lamp for fear of explosion. Some would be mere lumber-rooms; others ill-arranged libraries, without a poets' corner anywhere. But what a wealth of creation they show, and what infinite room for hope it affords!"

"But don't you think, papa, there may be something of worth lying even in the earth-pit, or at the bottom of the stagnant water in the forsaken quarry?"

"Indeed I do; though I *have* met more than one in my lifetime concerning whom I felt compelled to say that it wanted keener eyes than mine to discover the hidden jewel. But then there *are* keener eyes than mine, for there are more loving eyes. Myself I have been able to see good very clearly where some could see none; and shall I doubt that God can see good where my mole-eyes can see none? Be sure of this, that, as he is keen-eyed for the evil in his creatures to destroy it, he would, if it were possible, be yet keener-eyed for the good to nourish and cherish it. If men would only side with the good that is in them,—will that the seed should grow and bring forth fruit!"

# CHAPTER XVIII.

## MISS CLARE'S HOME.

We had now arrived at the passage. The gin-shop was flaring through the fog. A man in a fustian jacket came out of it, and walked slowly down before us, with the clay of the brick-field clinging to him as high as the leather straps with which his trousers were confined, garter-wise, under the knee. The place was quiet. We and the brickmaker seemed the only people in it. When we turned the last corner, he was walking in at the very door where Miss Clare had disappeared. When I told my father that was the house, he called after the man, who came out again, and, standing on the pavement, waited until we came up.

"Does Miss Clare live in this house?" my father asked.

"She do," answered the man curtly.

"First floor?"

"No. Nor yet the second, nor the third. She live nearer heaven than 'ere another in the house 'cep' myself. I live in the attic, and so do she."

"There is a way of living nearer to heaven than that," said my father, laying his hand, "with a right old man's grace," on his shoulder.

"I dunno, 'cep' you was to go up in a belloon," said the man, with a twinkle in his eye, which my father took to mean that he understood him better than he chose to acknowledge; but he did not pursue the figure.

He was a rough, lumpish young man, with good but dull features—only his blue eye was clear. He looked my father full in the face, and I thought I saw a dim smile about his mouth.

"You know her, then, I suppose?"

"Everybody in the house knows *her*. There ain't many the likes o' her as lives wi' the likes of us. You go right up to the top. I don't know if she's in, but a'most any one'll be able to tell you. I ain't been home yet."

My father thanked him, and we entered the house, and began to ascend. The stair was very much worn and rather dirty, and some of the banisters were broken away, but the walls were tolerably clean. Half-way up we met a little girl with tangled hair and tattered garments, carrying a bottle.

"Do you know, my dear," said my father to her, "whether Miss Clare is at home?"

"I dunno," she answered. "I dunno who you mean. I been mindin' the baby. He ain't well. Mother says his head's bad. She's a-going up to tell grannie, and see if she can't do suthin' for him. You better ast mother.—Mother!" she called out—"here's a lady an' a gen'lem'."

"You go about yer business, and be back direckly," cried a gruff voice from somewhere above.

"That's mother," said the child, and ran down the stair.

When we reached the second floor, there stood a big fat woman on the landing, with her face red, and her hair looking like that of a doll ill stuck on. She did not speak, but stood waiting to see what we wanted.

"I'm told Miss Clare lives here," said my father. "Can you tell me, my good woman, whether she's at home?"

"I'm neither good woman nor bad woman," she returned in an insolent tone.

"I beg your pardon," said my father; "but you see I didn't know your name."

"An' ye don't know it yet. You've no call to know my name. I'll ha' nothing to do wi' the likes o' you as goes about takin' poor folks's childer from 'em. There's my poor Glory's been an' took atwixt you an' grannie, and shet up in a formatory as you calls it; an' I should like to know what right you've got to go about that way arter poor girls as has mothers to help."

"I assure you I had nothing to do with it," said my father. "I'm a country clergyman myself, and have no duty in London."

"Well, that's where they've took her—down in the country. I make no doubt but you've had your finger in that pie. You don't come here to call upon us for the pleasure o' makin' our acquaintance—ha! ha! ha!—You're allus arter somethin' troublesome. I'd adwise you, sir and miss, to let well alone. Sleepin' dogs won't bite; but you'd better let 'em lie—and that I tell you."

"Believe me," said my father quite quietly, "I haven't the least knowledge of your daughter. The country's a bigger place than you seem to think,—far bigger than London itself. All I wanted to trouble you about was to tell us whether Miss Clare was at home or not."

"I don't know no one o' that name. If it's grannie you mean, she's at home, I know—though it's not much reason I've got to care whether she's at home or not."

"It's a young—woman, I mean," said my father.

"'Tain't a young lady, then?—Well, I don't care what you call her. I dare say it'll be all one, come judgment. You'd better go up till you can't go no further, an' knocks yer head agin the tiles, and then you may feel about for a door, and knock at that, and see if the party as opens it is the party you wants."

So saying, she turned in at a door behind her, and shut it. But we could hear her still growling and grumbling.

"It's very odd," said my father, with a bewildered smile. "I think we'd better do as she says, and go up till we knock our heads against the tiles."

We climbed two stairs more,—the last very steep, and so dark that when we reached the top we found it necessary to follow the woman's directions literally, and feel about for a door. But we had not to feel long or far, for there was one close to the top of the stair. My father knocked. There was no reply; but we heard the sound of a chair, and presently some one opened it. The only light being behind her, I could not see her face, but the size and shape were those of Miss Clare.

She did not leave us in doubt, however; for, without a moment's hesitation, she held out her hand to me, saying, "This *is* kind of you, Mrs. Percivale;" then to my father, saying, "I'm very glad to see you, Mr. Walton. Will you walk in?"

We followed her into the room. It was not very small, for it occupied nearly the breadth of the house. On one side the roof sloped so nearly to the floor that there was not height enough to stand erect in. On the other side the sloping part was partitioned off, evidently for a bedroom. But what a change it was from the lower part of the house! By the light of a single mould candle, I saw that the floor was as clean as old boards could be made, and I wondered whether she scrubbed them herself. I know now that she did. The two dormer windows were hung with white dimity curtains. Back in the angle of the roof, between the windows, stood an old bureau. There was little more than room between the top of it and the ceiling for a little plaster statuette with bound hands and a strangely crowned head. A few books on hanging shelves were on the opposite side by the door to the other room; and the walls, which were whitewashed, were a good deal covered with—whether engravings or etchings or lithographs I could not then see—none of them framed, only mounted on card-board. There was a fire cheerfully burning in the gable, and opposite to that stood a tall old-fashioned cabinet piano, in faded red silk. It was open; and on the music-rest lay Handel's "Verdi Prati,"—for I managed to glance at it as we left. A few wooden chairs, and one very old-fashioned easy-chair, covered with striped chintz, from which not glaze only but color almost had disappeared, with an oblong table of deal, completed the furniture of the room. She made my father sit down in the easy-chair, placed me one in front of the fire, and took another at the corner opposite my father. A moment of silence followed, which I, having a guilty conscience, felt awkward. But my father never allowed awkwardness to accumulate.

"I had hoped to have been able to call upon you long ago, Miss Clare, but there was some difficulty in finding out where you lived."

"You are no longer surprised at that difficulty, I presume," she returned with a smile.

"But," said my father, "if you will allow an old man to speak freely"—

"Say what you please, Mr. Walton. I promise to answer *any* question *you* think proper to ask me."

"My dear Miss Clare, I had not the slightest intention of catechising you, though, of course, I shall be grateful for what confidence you please to put in me. What I meant to say might indeed have taken the form of a question, but as such could have been intended only for you to answer to yourself,—whether, namely, it was wise to place yourself at such a disadvantage as living in this quarter must be to you."

"If you were acquainted with my history, you would perhaps hesitate, Mr. Walton, before you said I *placed myself* at such disadvantage."

Here a thought struck me.

"I fancy, papa, it is not for her own sake Miss Clare lives here."

"I hope not," she interposed.

"I believe," I went on, "she has a grandmother, who probably has grown accustomed to the place, and is unwilling to leave it."

She looked puzzled for a moment, then burst into a merry laugh.

"I see," she exclaimed. "How stupid I am! You have heard some of the people in the house talk about *grannie*: that's me! I am known in the house as grannie, and have been for a good many years now—I can hardly, without thinking, tell for how many."

Again she laughed heartily, and my father and I shared her merriment.

"How many grandchildren have you then, pray, Miss Clare?"

"Let me see."

She thought for a minute.

"I could easily tell you if it were only the people in this house I had to reckon up. They are about five and thirty; but unfortunately the name has been caught up in the neighboring houses, and I am very sorry that in consequence I cannot with certainty say how many grandchildren I have. I think I know them all, however; and I fancy that is more than many an English grandmother, with children in America, India, and Australia, can say for herself."

Certainly she was not older than I was; and while hearing her merry laugh, and seeing her young face overflowed with smiles, which appeared to come sparkling out of her eyes as out of two well-springs, one could not help feeling puzzled how, even in the farthest-off jest, she could have got the name of grannie. But I could at the same time, recall expressions of her countenance which would much better agree with the name than that which now shone from it.

"Would you like to hear," she said, when our merriment had a little subsided, "how I have so easily arrived at the honorable name of grannie,—at least all I know about it?"

"I should be delighted," said my father.

"You don't know what you are pledging yourself to when you say so," she rejoined, again laughing. "You will have to hear the whole of my story from the beginning."

"Again I say I shall be delighted," returned my father, confident that her history could be the source of nothing but pleasure to him.

# CHAPTER XIX.

## HER STORY.

Thereupon Miss Clare began. I do not pretend to give her very words, but I must tell her story as if she were telling it herself. I shall be as true as I can to the facts, and hope to catch something of the tone of the narrator as I go on.

"My mother died when I was very young, and I was left alone with my father, for I was his only child. He was a studious and thoughtful man. It *may* be the partiality of a daughter, I know, but I am not necessarily wrong in believing that diffidence in his own powers alone prevented him from distinguishing himself. As it was, he supported himself and me by literary work of, I presume, a secondary order. He would spend all his mornings for many weeks in the library of the British Museum,—reading and making notes; after which he would sit writing at home for as long or longer. I should have found it very dull during the former of these times, had he not early discovered that I had some capacity for music, and provided for me what I now know to have been the best instruction to be had. His feeling alone had guided him right, for he was without musical knowledge. I believe he could not have found me a better teacher in all Europe. Her character was lovely, and her music the natural outcome of its harmony. But I must not forget it is about myself I have to tell you. I went to her, then, almost every day for a time—but how long that was, I can only guess. It must have been several years, I think, else I could not have attained what proficiency I had when my sorrow came upon me.

"What my father wrote I cannot tell. How gladly would I now read the shortest sentence I knew to be his! He never told me for what journals he wrote, or even for what publishers. I fancy it was work in which his brain was more interested than his heart, and which he was always hoping to exchange for something more to his mind. After his death I could discover scarcely a scrap of his writings, and not a hint to guide me to what he had written.

"I believe we went on living from hand to mouth, my father never getting so far ahead of the wolf as to be able to pause and choose his way. But I was very happy, and would have been no whit less happy if he had explained our circumstances, for that would have conveyed to me no hint of danger. Neither has any of the suffering I have had—at least any keen enough to be worth dwelling upon—sprung from personal privation, although I am not unacquainted with hunger and cold.

"My happiest time was when my father asked me to play to him while he wrote, and I sat down to my old cabinet Broadwood,—the one you see there is as like it as I could find,—and played any thing and every thing I liked,—for somehow I never forgot what I had once learned,—while my father sat, as he said, like a mere extension of the instrument, operated upon, rather than listening, as he wrote. What I then *thought*, I cannot tell. I don't believe I thought at all. I only *musicated*, as a little pupil of mine once said to me, when, having found her sitting with her hands on her lap before the piano, I asked her what she was doing: 'I am only musicating,' she answered. But the enjoyment was none the less that there was no conscious thought in it.

"Other branches he taught me himself, and I believe I got on very fairly for my age. We lived then in the neighborhood of the Museum, where I was well known to all the people of the place, for I used often to go there, and would linger about looking at things, sometimes for hours before my father came to me but he always came at the very minute he had said, and always found me at the appointed spot. I gained a great deal by thus haunting the Museum—a great deal more than I supposed at the time. One gain was, that I knew perfectly where in the place any given sort of thing was to be found, if it were there at all: I had unconsciously learned something of classification.

"One afternoon I was waiting as usual, but my father did not come at the time appointed. I waited on and on till it grew dark, and the hour for closing arrived, by which time I was in great uneasiness; but I was forced to go home without him. I must hasten over this part of my history, for even yet I can scarcely bear to speak of it. I found that while I was waiting, he had been seized with some kind of fit in the reading-room, and had been carried home, and that I was alone in the world. The landlady, for we only rented rooms in the house, was very kind to me, at least until she found that my father had left no money. He had then been only reading for a long time; and, when I looked back, I could see that he must have been short of money for some weeks at least. A few bills coming in, all our little effects—for the furniture was our own—were sold, without bringing sufficient to pay them. The things went for less than half their value, in consequence, I believe, of that well-known conspiracy of the brokers which they call *knocking out*. I was especially miserable at losing my father's books, which, although in ignorance, I greatly valued,—more miserable even, I honestly think, than at seeing my loved piano carried off.

"When the sale was over, and every thing removed, I sat down on the floor, amidst the dust and bits of paper and straw and cord, without a single idea in my head as to what was to become of me, or what I was to do next. I didn't cry,—that I am sure of; but I doubt if in all London there was a more wretched child than myself just then. The twilight was darkening down,—the twilight of a November afternoon. Of course there was no fire in the grate, and I had eaten nothing that day; for although the landlady had offered me some dinner, and I had tried to please her by taking some, I found I could not swallow, and had to leave it. While I sat thus on the floor, I heard her come into the room, and some one with her; but I did not look round, and they, not seeing me, and thinking, I suppose, that I was in one of the other rooms, went on talking about me. All I afterwards remembered of their conversation was some severe reflections on my father, and the announcement of the decree that I must go to the workhouse. Though I knew nothing definite as to the import of this doom, it filled me with horror. The moment they left me alone, to look for me, as I supposed, I got up, and, walking as softly as I could, glided down the stairs, and, unbonneted and unwrapped, ran from the house, half-blind with terror.

"I had not gone farther, I fancy, than a few yards, when I ran up against some one, who laid hold of me, and asked me gruffly what I meant by it. I knew the voice: it was that of an old Irishwoman who did all the little charing we wanted,—for I kept the rooms tidy, and the landlady cooked for us. As soon as she saw who it was, her tone changed; and then first I broke out in sobs, and told her I was running away because they were going to send me to the workhouse. She burst into a torrent of Irish indignation, and assured me that such should never be my fate while she lived. I must go back to the house with her, she said, and get my things; and then I should go home with her, until something better should turn up. I told her I would go with her anywhere, except into that house again; and she did not insist, but afterwards went by herself and got my little wardrobe. In the mean time she led me away to a large house in a square, of which she took the key from her pocket to open the door. It looked to me such a huge place!—the largest house I had ever been in; but it was rather desolate, for, except in one little room below, where she had scarcely more than a bed and a chair, a slip of carpet and a frying-pan, there was not an article of furniture in the whole place. She had been put there when the last tenant left, to take care of the place, until another tenant should appear to turn her out. She had her houseroom and a trifle a week besides for her services, beyond which she depended entirely on what she could make by charing. When she had no house to live in on the same terms, she took a room somewhere.

"Here I lived for several months, and was able to be of use; for as Mrs. Conan was bound to be there at certain times to show any one over the house who brought an order from the agent, and this necessarily took up a good part of her working time; and as, moreover, I could open the door and walk about the place as well as another, she willingly left me in charge as often as she had a job elsewhere.

"On such occasions, however, I found it very dreary indeed, for few people called, and she would not unfrequently be absent the whole day. If I had had my piano, I should have cared little; but I had not a single book, except one—and what do you think that was? An odd volume of the Newgate Calendar. I need hardly say that it had not the effect on me which it is said to have on some of its students: it moved me, indeed, to the profoundest sympathy, not with the crimes of the malefactors, only with the malefactors themselves, and their mental condition after the deed was actually done. But it was with the fascination of a hopeless horror, making me feel almost as if I had committed every crime as I perused its tale, that I regarded them. They were to me like living crimes. It was not until long afterwards that I was able to understand that a man's actions are not the man, but may be separated from him; that his character even is not the man, but may be changed while he yet holds the same individuality,—is the man who was blind though he now sees; whence it comes, that, the deeds continuing his, all stain of them may yet be washed out of him. I did not, I say, understand all this until afterwards; but I believe, odd as it may seem, that volume of the Newgate Calendar threw down the first deposit of soil, from which afterwards sprung what grew to be almost a passion in me, for getting the people about me clean,—a passion which might have done as much harm as good, if its companion, patience, had not been sent me to guide and restrain it. In a word, I came at length to understand, in some measure, the last prayer of our Lord for those that crucified him, and the ground on which he begged from his Father their forgiveness,—that they knew not what they did. If the Newgate Calendar was indeed the beginning of this course of education, I need not regret having lost my piano, and having that volume for a while as my only aid to reflection.

"My father had never talked much to me about religion; but when he did, it was with such evident awe in his spirit, and reverence in his demeanor, as had more effect on me, I am certain, from the very paucity of the words in which his meaning found utterance. Another thing which had still more influence upon me was, that, waking one night after I had been asleep for some time, I saw him on his knees by my bedside. I did not move or speak, for fear of disturbing him; and, indeed, such an awe came over me, that it would have required a considerable effort of the will for any bodily movement whatever. When he lifted his head, I caught a glimpse of a pale, tearful face; and it is no wonder that the virtue of the sight should never have passed away.

"On Sundays we went to church in the morning, and in the afternoon, in fine weather, went out for a walk; or, if it were raining or cold, I played to him till he fell asleep on the sofa. Then in the evening, after tea, we had more music, some poetry, which we read alternately, and a chapter of the New Testament, which he always read to me. I mention this, to show you that I did not come all unprepared to the study of the Newgate Calendar. Still, I cannot think, that, under any circumstances, it could have done an innocent child harm. Even familiarity with vice is not necessarily pollution. There cannot be many women of my age as familiar with it in every shape as I am; and I do not find that I grow to regard it with one atom less of absolute abhorrence, although I neither shudder at the mention of it, nor turn with disgust from the person in whom it dwells. But the consolations of religion were not yet consciously mine. I had not yet begun to think of God in any relation to myself.

"The house was in an old square, built, I believe, in the reign of Queen Anne, which, although many of the houses were occupied by well-to-do people, had fallen far from its first high estate. No one would believe, to look at it from the outside, what a great place it was. The whole of the space behind it, corresponding to the small gardens of the other houses, was occupied by a large music-room, under which was a low-pitched room of equal extent, while all under that were cellars, connected with the sunk story in front by a long vaulted passage, corresponding to a wooden gallery above, which formed a communication between the drawing-room floor and the music-room. Most girls of my age, knowing these vast empty spaces about them, would have been terrified at being left alone there, even in mid-day. But I was, I suppose, too miserable to be frightened. Even the horrible facts of the Newgate Calendar did not thus affect me, not even when Mrs. Conan was later than usual, and the night came down, and I had to sit, perhaps for hours, in the dark,—for she would not allow me to have a candle for fear of fire. But you will not wonder that I used to cry a good deal, although I did my best to hide the traces of it, because I knew it would annoy my kind old friend. She showed me a great deal of rough tenderness, which would not have been rough had not the natural grace of her Irish nature been injured by the contact of many years with the dull coarseness of the uneducated Saxon. You may be sure I learned to love her dearly. She shared every thing with me in the way of eating, and would have shared also the tumbler of gin and water with which she generally ended the day, but something, I don't know what, I believe a simple physical dislike, made me refuse that altogether.

"One evening I have particular cause to remember, both for itself, and because of something that followed many years after. I was in the drawing-room on the first floor, a double room with folding doors and a small cabinet behind communicating with a back stair; for the stairs were double all through the house, adding much to the *eeriness* of the place as I look back upon it in my memory. I fear, in describing the place so minutely, I may have been rousing false expectations of an adventure; but I have a reason for being rather minute, though it will not appear until afterwards. I had been looking out of the window all the afternoon upon the silent square, for, as it was no thoroughfare, it was only enlivened by the passing and returning now and then of a tradesman's cart; and, as it was winter, there were no children playing in the garden. It was a rainy afternoon. A gray cloud of fog and soot hung from the whole sky. About a score of yellow leaves yet quivered on the trees, and the statue of Queen Anne stood bleak and disconsolate among the bare branches. I am afraid I am getting long-winded, but somehow that afternoon seems burned into me in enamel. I gazed drearily without interest. I brooded over the past; I never, at this time, so far as I remember, dreamed of looking forward. I had no hope. It never occurred to me that things might grow better. I was dull and wretched. I may just say here in passing, that I think this experience is in a great measure what has enabled me to understand the peculiar misery of the poor in our large towns,—they have no hope, no impulse to look forward, nothing to expect; they live but in the present, and the dreariness of that soon shapes the whole atmosphere of their spirits to its own likeness. Perhaps the first thing one who would help them has to do is to aid the birth of some small vital hope in them; that is better than a thousand gifts, especially those of the ordinary kind, which mostly do harm, tending to keep them what they are,—a prey to present and importunate wants.

"It began to grow dark; and, tired of standing, I sat down upon the floor, for there was nothing to sit upon besides. There I still sat, long after it was quite dark. All at once a surge of self-pity arose in my heart. I burst out wailing and sobbing, and cried aloud, 'God has forgotten me altogether!' The fact was, I had had no dinner that day, for Mrs. Conan had expected to return long before; and the piece of bread she had given me, which was all that was in the house, I had eaten many hours ago. But I was not thinking of my dinner, though the want of it may have had to do with this burst of misery. What I was really thinking of was,—that I could do nothing for anybody. My little ambition had always been to be useful. I knew I was of some use to my father; for I kept the rooms tidy for him, and dusted his pet books—oh, so carefully! for they were like household gods to me. I had also played to him, and I knew he enjoyed that: he said so, many times. And I had begun, though not long before he left me, to think how I should be able to help him better by and by. For I saw that he worked very hard,—so hard that it made him silent; and I knew that my music-mistress made her livelihood, partly at least, by giving lessons; and I thought that I might, by and by, be able to give lessons too, and then papa would not require to work so hard, for I too should bring home money to pay for what we wanted. But now I was of use to nobody, I said, and not likely to become of any. I could not even help poor Mrs. Conan, except by doing what a child might do just as well as I, for I did not earn a penny of our living; I only gave the poor old thing time to work harder, that I might eat up her earnings! What added to the misery was, that I had always thought of myself as a lady; for was not papa a gentleman, let him be ever so poor? Shillings and sovereigns in his pocket could not determine whether a man was a gentleman or not! And if he was a gentleman, his daughter must be a lady. But how could I be a lady if I was content to be a burden to a poor charwoman, instead of earning my own living, and something besides with which to help her? For I had the notion—*how* it came I cannot tell, though I know well enough *whence* it came—that position depended on how much a person was able to help other people; and here I was, useless, worse than useless to anybody! Why did not God remember me, if it was only for my father's sake? He was worth something, if I was not! And I would be worth something, if only I had a chance!—'I am of no use,' I cried, 'and God has forgotten me altogether!' And I went on weeping and moaning in my great misery, until I fell fast asleep on the floor.

"I have no theory about dreams and visions; and I don't know what you, Mr. Walton, may think as to whether these ended with the first ages of the church; but surely if one falls fast asleep without an idea in one's head, and a whole dismal world of misery in one's heart, and wakes up quiet and refreshed, without the misery, and with an idea, there can be no great fanaticism in thinking that the change may have come from somewhere near where the miracles lie,—in fact, that God may have had something—might I not say every thing?—to do with it. For my part, if I were to learn that he had no hand in this experience of mine, I couldn't help losing all interest in it, and wishing that I had died of the misery which it dispelled. Certainly, if it had a physical source, it wasn't that I was more comfortable, for I was hungrier than ever, and, you may well fancy, cold enough, having slept on the bare floor without any thing to cover me on Christmas Eve—for Christmas Eve it was. No doubt my sleep had done me good, but I suspect the sleep came to quiet my mind for the reception of the new idea.

"The way Mrs. Conan kept Christmas Day, as she told me in the morning, was, to comfort her old bones in bed until the afternoon, and then to have a good tea with a chop; after which she said she would have me read the Newgate Calendar to her. So, as soon as I had washed up the few breakfast things, I asked, if, while she lay in bed, I might not go out for a little while to look for work. She laughed at the notion of my being able to do any thing, but did not object to my trying. So I dressed myself as neatly as I could, and set out.

"There were two narrow streets full of small shops, in which those of furniture-brokers predominated, leading from the two lower corners of the square down into Oxford Street; and in a shop in one of these, I was not sure which, I had seen an old piano standing, and a girl of about my own age watching. I found the shop at last, although it was shut up; for I knew the name, and knocked at the door. It was opened by a stout matron, with a not unfriendly expression, who asked me what I wanted. I told her I wanted work. She seemed amused at the idea,—for I was very small for my age then as well as now,—but, apparently willing to have a chat with me, asked what I could do. I told her I could teach her daughter music. She asked me what made me come to her, and I told her. Then she asked me how much I should charge. I told her that some ladies had a guinea a lesson; at which she laughed so heartily, that I had to wait until the first transports of her amusement were over before I could finish by saying, that for my part I should be glad to give an hour's lesson for threepence, only, if she pleased, I should prefer it in silver. But how was she to know, she asked, that I could teach her properly. I told her I would let her hear me play; whereupon she led me into the shop, through a back room in which her husband sat smoking a long pipe, with a tankard at his elbow. Having taken down a shutter, she managed with some difficulty to clear me a passage through a crowd of furniture to the instrument, and with a struggle I squeezed through and reached it; but at the first chord I struck, I gave a cry of dismay. In some alarm she asked what was the matter, calling me *child* very kindly. I told her it was so dreadfully out of tune I couldn't play upon it at all; but, if she would get it tuned, I should not be long in showing her that I could do what I professed. She told me she could not afford to have it tuned; and if I could not teach Bertha on it as it was, she couldn't help it. This, however, I assured her, was utterly impossible; upon which, with some show of offence, she reached over a chest of drawers, and shut down the cover. I believe she doubted whether I could play at all, and had not been merely amusing myself at her expense. Nothing was left but to thank her, bid her good-morning, and walk out of the house, dreadfully disappointed.

"Unwilling to go home at once, I wandered about the neighborhood, through street after street, until I found myself in another square, with a number of business-signs in it,—one of them that of a piano-forte firm, at sight of which, a thought came into my head. The next morning I went in, and requested to see the master. The man to whom I spoke stared, no doubt; but he went, and returning after a little while, during which my heart beat very fast, invited me to walk into the counting-house. Mr. Perkins was amused with the story of my attempt to procure teaching, and its frustration. If I had asked him for money, to which I do not believe hunger itself could have driven me, he would probably have got rid of me quickly enough,—and small blame to him, as Mrs. Conan would have said; but to my request that he would spare a man to tune Mrs. Lampeter's piano, he replied at once that he would, provided I could satisfy him as to my efficiency. Thereupon he asked me a few questions about music, of which some I could answer and some I could not. Next he took me into the shop, set me a stool in front of a grand piano, and told me to play. I could not help trembling a good deal, but I tried my best. In a few moments, however, the tears were dropping on the keys; and, when he asked me what was the matter, I told him it was months since I had touched a piano. The answer did not, however, satisfy him; he asked very kindly how that was, and I had to tell him my whole story. Then he not only promised to have the piano tuned for me at once, but told me that I might go and practise there as often as I pleased, so long as I was a good girl, and did not take up with bad company. Imagine my delight! Then he sent for a tuner, and I suppose told him a little about me, for the man spoke very kindly to me as we went to the broker's.

"Mr. Perkins has been a good friend to me ever since.

"For six months I continued to give Bertha Lampeter lessons. They were broken off only when she went to a dressmaker to learn her business. But her mother had by that time introduced me to several families of her acquaintance, amongst whom I found five or six pupils on the same terms. By this teaching, if I earned little, I learned much; and every day almost I practised at the music-shop.

"When the house was let, Mrs. Conan took a room in the neighborhood, that I might keep up my connection, she said. Then first I was introduced to scenes and experiences with which I am now familiar. Mrs. Percivale might well recoil if I were to tell her half the wretchedness, wickedness, and vulgarity I have seen, and often had to encounter. For two years or so we changed about, at one time in an empty house, at another in a hired room, sometimes better, sometimes worse off, as regarded our neighbors, until, Mrs. Conan having come to the conclusion that it would be better for her to confine herself to charing, we at last settled down here, where I have now lived for many years.

"You may be inclined to ask why I had not kept up my acquaintance with my music-mistress. I believe the shock of losing my father, and the misery that followed, made me feel as if my former world had vanished; at all events, I never thought of going to her until Mr. Perkins one day, after listening to something I was playing, asked me who had taught me; and this brought her back to my mind so vividly that I resolved to go and see her. She welcomed me with more than kindness,—with tenderness,—and told me I had caused her much uneasiness by not letting her know what had become of me. She looked quite aghast when she learned in what sort of place and with whom I lived; but I told her Mrs. Conan had saved me from the workhouse, and was as much of a mother to me as it was possible for her to be, that we loved each other, and that it would be very wrong of me to leave her now, especially that she was not so well as she had been; and I believe she then saw the thing as I saw it. She made me play to her, was pleased,—indeed surprised, until I told her how I had been supporting myself,—and insisted on my resuming my studies with her, which I was only too glad to do. I now, of course, got on much faster; and she expressed satisfaction with my progress, but continued manifestly uneasy at the kind of thing I had to encounter, and become of necessity more and more familiar with.

"When Mrs. Conan fell ill, I had indeed hard work of it. Unlike most of her class, she had laid by a trifle of money; but as soon as she ceased to add to it, it began to dwindle, and was very soon gone. Do what I could for a while, if it had not been for the kindness of the neighbors, I should sometimes have been in want of bread; and when I hear hard things said of the poor, I often think that surely improvidence is not so bad as selfishness. But, of course, there are all sorts amongst them, just as there are all sorts in every class. When I went out to teach, now one, now another of the women in the house would take charge of my friend; and when I came home, except her guardian happened to have got tipsy, I never found she had been neglected. Miss Harper said I must raise my terms; but I told her that would be the loss of my pupils. Then she said she must see what could be done for me, only no one she knew was likely to employ a child like me, if I were able to teach ever so well. One morning, however, within a week, a note came from Lady Bernard, asking me to go and see her.

"I went, and found—a mother. You do not know her, I think? But you must one day. Good people like you must come together. I will not attempt to describe her. She awed me at first, and I could hardly speak to her,—I was not much more than thirteen then; but with the awe came a certain confidence which was far better than ease. The immediate result was, that she engaged me to go and play for an hour, five days a week, at a certain hospital for sick children in the neighborhood, which she partly supported. For she had a strong belief that there was in music a great healing power. Her theory was, that all healing energy operates first on the mind, and from it passes to the body, and that medicines render aid only by removing certain physical obstacles to the healing force. She believes that when music operating on the mind has procured the peace of harmony, the peace in its turn operates outward, reducing the vital powers also into the harmonious action of health. *How much* there may be in it, I cannot tell; but I do think that good has been and is the result of my playing to those children; for I go still, though not quite so often, and it is music to me to watch my music thrown back in light from some of those sweet, pale, suffering faces. She was too wise to pay me much for it at first. She inquired, before making me the offer, how much I was already earning, asked me upon how much I could support Mrs. Conan and myself comfortably, and then made the sum of my weekly earnings up to that amount. At the same time, however, she sent many things to warm and feed the old woman, so that my mind was set at ease about her. She got a good deal better for a while, but continued to suffer so much from rheumatism, that she was quite unfit to go out charing any more; and I would not hear of her again exposing herself to the damps and draughts of empty houses, so long as I was able to provide for her,—of which ability you may be sure I was not a little proud at first.

"I have been talking for a long time, and yet may seem to have said nothing to account for your finding me where she left me; but I will try to come to the point as quickly as possible.

"Before she was entirely laid up, we had removed to this place,—a rough shelter, but far less so than some of the houses in which we had been. I remember one in which I used to dart up and down like a hunted hare at one time; at another to steal along from stair to stair like a well-meaning ghost afraid of frightening people; my mode of procedure depending in part on the time of day, and which of the inhabitants I had reason to dread meeting. It was a good while before the inmates of this house and I began to know each other. The landlord had turned out the former tenant of this garret after she had been long enough in the house for all the rest to know her; and, notwithstanding she had been no great favorite, they all took her part against the landlord; and fancying, perhaps because we kept more to ourselves, that we were his *protégées*, and that he had turned out Muggy Moll, as they called her, to make room for us, regarded us from the first with disapprobation. The little girls would make grimaces at me, and the bigger girls would pull my hair, slap my face, and even occasionally push me down stairs, while the boys made themselves far more terrible in my eyes. But some remark happening to be dropped one day, which led the landlord to disclaim all previous knowledge of us, things began to grow better. And this is not by any means one of the worst parts of London. I could take Mr. Walton to houses in the East End, where the manners are indescribable. We are all earning our bread here. Some have an occasional attack of drunkenness, and idle about; but they are sick of it again after a while. I remember asking a woman once if her husband would be present at a little entertainment to which Lady Bernard had invited them: she answered that he would be there if he was drunk, but if he was sober he couldn't spare the time.

"Very soon they began to ask me after Mrs. Conan; and one day I invited one of them, who seemed a decent though not very tidy woman, to walk up and see her; for I was anxious she should have a visitor now and then when I was out, as she complained a good deal of the loneliness. The woman consented, and ever after was very kind to her. But my main stay and comfort was an old woman who then occupied the room opposite to this. She was such a good creature! Nearly blind, she yet kept her room the very pink of neatness. I never saw a speck of dust on that chest of drawers, which was hers then, and which she valued far more than many a rich man values the house of his ancestors,—not only because it had been her mother's, but because it bore testimony to the respectability of her family. Her floor and her little muslin window-curtain, her bed and every thing about her, were as clean as lady could desire. She objected to move into a better room below, which the landlord kindly offered her,—for she was a favorite from having been his tenant a long time and never having given him any trouble in collecting her rent,—on the ground that there were two windows in it, and therefore too much light for her bits of furniture. They would, she said, look nothing in that room. She was very pleased when I asked her to pay a visit to Mrs.

Conan; and as she belonged to a far higher intellectual grade than my protectress, and as she had a strong practical sense of religion, chiefly manifested in a willing acceptance of the decrees of Providence, I think she did us both good. I wish I could draw you a picture of her coming in at that door, with her all but sightless eyes, the broad borders of her white cap waving, and her hands stretched out before her; for she was more apprehensive than if she had been quite blind, because she could see things without knowing what, or even in what position they were. The most remarkable thing to me was the calmness with which she looked forward to her approaching death, although without the expectation which so many good people seem to have in connection with their departure. I talked to her about it more than once,—not with any presumption of teaching her, for I felt she was far before me, but just to find out how she felt and what she believed. Her answer amounted to this, that she had never known beforehand what lay round the next corner, or what was going to happen to her, for if Providence had meant her to know, it could not be by going to fortune-tellers, as some of the neighbors did; but that she always found things turn out right and good for her, and she did not doubt she would find it so when she came to the last turn.

"By degrees I knew everybody in the house, and of course I was ready to do what I could to help any of them. I had much to lift me into a higher region of mental comfort than was open to them; for I had music, and Lady Bernard lent me books.

"Of course also I kept my rooms as clean and tidy as I could; and indeed, if I had been more carelessly inclined in that way, the sight of the blind woman's would have been a constant reminder to me. By degrees also I was able to get a few more articles of furniture for it, and a bit of carpet to put down before the fire. I whitewashed the walls myself, and after a while began to whitewash the walls of the landing as well, and all down the stair, which was not of much use to the eye, for there is no light. Before long some of the other tenants began to whitewash their rooms also, and contrive to keep things a little tidier. Others declared they had no opinion of such uppish notions; they weren't for the likes of them. These were generally such as would rejoice in wearing finery picked up at the rag-shop; but even some of them began by degrees to cultivate a small measure of order. Soon this one and that began to apply to me for help in various difficulties that arose. But they didn't begin to call me grannie for a long time after this. They used then to call the blind woman grannie, and the name got associated with the top of the house; and I came to be associated with it because I also lived there and we were friends. After her death, it was used from habit, at first with a feeling of mistake, seeing its immediate owner was gone; but by degrees it settled down upon me, and I came to be called grannie by everybody in the house.

Even Mrs. Conan would not unfrequently address me, and speak of me too, as grannie, at first with a laugh, but soon as a matter of course.

"I got by and by a few pupils amongst tradespeople of a class rather superior to that in which I had begun to teach, and from whom I could ask and obtain double my former fee; so that things grew, with fluctuations, gradually better. Lady Bernard continued a true friend to me—but she never was other than that to any. Some of her friends ventured on the experiment whether I could teach their children; and it is no wonder if they were satisfied, seeing I had myself such a teacher.

"Having come once or twice to see Mrs. Conan, she discovered that we were gaining a little influence over the people in the house; and it occurred to her, as she told me afterwards, that the virtue of music might be tried there with a *moral* end in view. Hence it came that I was beyond measure astonished and delighted one evening by the arrival of a piano,—not that one, for it got more worn than I liked, and I was able afterwards to exchange it for a better. I found it an invaluable aid in the endeavor to work out my glowing desire of getting the people about me into a better condition. First I asked some of the children to come and listen while I played. Everybody knows how fond the least educated children are of music; and I feel assured of its elevating power. Whatever the street-organs may be to poets and mathematicians, they are certainly a godsend to the children of our courts and alleys. The music takes possession of them at once, and sets them moving to it with rhythmical grace. I should have been very sorry to make it a condition with those I invited, that they should sit still: to take from them their personal share in it would have been to destroy half the charm of the thing. A far higher development is needful before music can be enjoyed in silence and motionlessness. The only condition I made was, that they should come with clean hands and faces, and with tidy hair. Considerable indignation was at first manifested on the part of those parents whose children I refused to admit because they had neglected the condition. This necessity, however, did not often occur; and the anger passed away, while the condition gathered weight. After a while, guided by what some of the children let fall; I began to invite the mothers to join them; and at length it came to be understood that, every Saturday evening, whoever chose to make herself tidy would be welcome, to an hour or two of my music. Some of the husbands next began to come, but there were never so many of them present. I may just add, that although the manners of some of my audience would be very shocking to cultivated people, and I understand perfectly how they must be so, I am very rarely annoyed on such occasions.

"I must now glance at another point in my history, one on which I cannot dwell. Never since my father's death had I attended public worship. Nothing had drawn me thither; and I hardly know what induced me one evening to step into a chapel of which I knew nothing. There was not even Sunday to account for it. I believe, however, it had to do with this, that all day I had been feeling tired. I think people are often ready to suppose that their bodily condition is the cause of their spiritual discomfort, when it may be only the occasion upon which some inward lack reveals itself. That the spiritual nature should be incapable of meeting and sustaining the body in its troubles is of itself sufficient to show that it is not in a satisfactory condition. For a long time the struggle for mere existence had almost absorbed my energies; but things had been easier for some time, and a re-action had at length come. It was not that I could lay any thing definite to my own charge; I only felt empty all through; I felt that something was not right with me, that something was required of me which I was not rendering. I could not, however, have told you what it was. Possibly the feeling had been for some time growing; but that day, so far as I can tell, I was first aware of it; and I presume it was the dim cause of my turning at the sound of a few singing voices, and entering that chapel. I found about a dozen people present. Something in the air of the place, meagre and waste as it looked, yet induced me to remain. An address followed from a pale-faced, weak-looking man of middle age, who had no gift of person, voice, or utterance, to recommend what he said. But there dwelt a more powerful enforcement in him than any of those,—that of earnestness. I went again, and again; and slowly, I cannot well explain how, the sense of life and its majesty grew upon me. Mr. Walton will, I trust, understand me when I say, that to one hungering for bread, it is of little consequence in what sort of platter it is handed him. This was a dissenting chapel,—of what order, it was long before I knew,—and my predilection was for the Church-services, those to which my father had accustomed me; but any comparison of the two to the prejudice of either, I should still—although a communicant of the Church of England—regard with absolute indifference.

"It will be sufficient for my present purpose to allude to the one practical thought which was the main fruit I gathered from this good man,—the fruit by which I know that he was good. [Footnote: Something like this is the interpretation of the word: "By their fruits ye shall know them" given by Mr. Maurice,—an interpretation which opens much.—G.M.D.] It was this,—that if all the labor of God, as my teacher said, was to bring sons into glory, lifting them out of the abyss of evil bondage up to the rock of his pure freedom, the only worthy end of life must be to work in the same direction,—to be a fellow-worker with God. Might I not, then, do something such, in my small way, and lose no jot of my labor? I thought. The urging, the hope, grew in me. But I was not left to feel blindly after some new and unknown method of labor. My teacher taught me that the way for *me* to help others was not to tell them their duty, but myself to learn of Him who bore our griefs and carried our sorrows. As I learned of him, I should be able to help them. I have never had any theory but just to be their friend,—to do for them the best I can. When I feel I may, I tell them what has done me good, but I never urge any belief of mine upon their acceptance.

"It will now seem no more wonderful to you than to me, that I should remain where I am. I simply have no choice. I was sixteen when Mrs. Conan died. Then my friends, amongst whom Lady Bernard and Miss Harper have ever been first, expected me to remove to lodgings in another neighborhood. Indeed, Lady Bernard came to see me, and said she knew precisely the place for me. When I told her I should remain where I was, she was silent, and soon left me?—I thought offended. I wrote to her at once, explaining why I chose my part here; saying that I would not hastily alter any thing that had been appointed me; that I loved the people; that they called me grannie; that they came to me with their troubles; that there were few changes in the house now; that the sick looked to me for help, and the children for teaching; that they seemed to be steadily rising in the moral scale; that I knew some of them were trying hard to be good; and I put it to her whether, if I were to leave them, in order merely, as servants say, to better myself, I should not be forsaking my post, almost my family; for I knew it would not be to better either myself or my friends: if I was at all necessary to them, I knew they were yet more necessary to me.

"I have a burning desire to help in the making of the world clean,—if it be only by sweeping one little room in it. I want to lead some poor stray sheep home—not home to the church, Mr. Walton—I would not be supposed to curry favor with you. I never think of what they call the church. I only care to lead them home to the bosom of God, where alone man is true man.

"I could talk to you till night about what Lady Bernard has been to me since, and what she has done for me and my grandchildren; but I have said enough to explain how it is that I am in such a questionable position. I fear I have been guilty of much egotism, and have shown my personal feelings with too little reserve. But I cast myself on your mercy."

# CHAPTER XX.

## A REMARKABLE FACT.

A silence followed. I need hardly say we had listened intently. During the story my father had scarcely interrupted the narrator. I had not spoken a word. She had throughout maintained a certain matter-of-fact, almost cold style, no doubt because she was herself the subject of her story; but we could read between the lines, imagine much she did not say, and supply color when she gave only outline; and it moved us both deeply. My father sat perfectly composed, betraying his emotion in silence alone. For myself, I had a great lump in my throat, but in part from the shame which mingled with my admiration. The silence had not lasted more than a few seconds, when I yielded to a struggling impulse, rose, and kneeling before her, put my hands on her knees, said, "Forgive me," and could say no more. She put her hand on my shoulder, whispered. "My dear Mrs. Percivale!" bent down her face, and kissed me on the forehead.

"How could you help being shy of me?" she said. "Perhaps I ought to have come to you and explained it all; but I shrink from self-justification,—at least before a fit opportunity makes it comparatively easy."

"That is the way to give it all its force," remarked my father.

"I suppose it may be," she returned. "But I hate talking about myself: it is an unpleasant subject."

"Most people do not find it such," said my father. "I could not honestly say that I do not enjoy talking of my own experiences of life."

"But there are differences, you see," she rejoined. "My history looks to me such a matter of course, such a something I could not help, or have avoided if I would, that the telling of it is unpleasant, because it implies an importance which does not belong to it."

"St. Paul says something of the same sort,—that a necessity of preaching the gospel was laid upon him," remarked my father; but it seemed to make no impression on Miss Clare, for she went on as if she had not heard him.

"You see, Mr. Walton, it is not in the least as if, living in comfort, I had taken notice of the misery of the poor for the want of such sympathy and help as I could give them, and had therefore gone to live amongst them that I might so help them: it is quite different from that. If I had done so, I might be in danger of magnifying not merely my office but myself. On the contrary, I have been trained to it in such slow and necessitous ways, that it would be a far greater trial to me to forsake my work than it has ever been to continue it."

My father said no more, but I knew he had his own thoughts. I remained kneeling, and felt for the first time as if I understood what had led to saint-worship.

"Won't you sit, Mrs. Percivale?" she said, as if merely expostulating with me for not making myself comfortable.

"Have you forgiven me?" I asked.

"How can I say I have, when I never had any thing to forgive?"

"Well, then, I must go unforgiven, for I cannot forgive myself," I said.

"O Mrs. Percivale! if you think how the world is flooded with forgiveness, you will just dip in your cup, and take what you want."

I felt that I was making too much even of my own shame, rose humbled, and took my former seat.

Narration being over, and my father's theory now permitting him to ask questions, he did so plentifully, bringing out many lights, and elucidating several obscurities. The story grew upon me, until the work to which Miss Clare had given herself seemed more like that of the Son of God than any other I knew. For she was not helping her friends from afar, but as one of themselves,—nor with money, but with herself; she was not condescending to them, but finding her highest life in companionship with them. It seemed at least more like what his life must have been before he was thirty, than any thing else I could think of. I held my peace however; for I felt that to hint at such a thought would have greatly shocked and pained her.

No doubt the narrative I have given is plainer and more coherent for the questions my father put; but it loses much from the omission of one or two parts which she gave dramatically, with evident enjoyment of the fun that was in them. I have also omitted all the interruptions which came from her not unfrequent reference to my father on points that came up. At length I ventured to remind her of something she seemed to have forgotten.

"When you were telling us, Miss Clare," I said, "of the help that came to you that dreary afternoon in the empty house, I think you mentioned that something which happened afterwards made it still more remarkable." "Oh, yes!" she answered: "I forgot about that. I did not carry my history far enough to be reminded of it again.

"Somewhere about five years ago, Lady Bernard, having several schemes on foot for helping such people as I was interested in, asked me if it would not be nice to give an entertainment to my friends, and as many of the neighbors as I pleased, to the number of about a hundred. She wanted to put the thing entirely in my hands, and it should be my entertainment, she claiming only the privilege of defraying expenses. I told her I should be delighted to convey *her* invitation, but that the entertainment must not pretend to be mine; which, besides that it would be a falsehood, and therefore not to be thought of, would perplex my friends, and drive them to the conclusion either that it was not mine, or that I lived amongst them under false appearances. She confessed the force of my arguments, and let me have it my own way.

"She had bought a large house to be a home for young women out of employment, and in it she proposed the entertainment should be given: there were a good many nice young women inmates at the time, who, she said, would be all willing to help us to wait upon our guests. The idea was carried out, and the thing succeeded admirably. We had music and games, the latter such as the children were mostly acquainted with, only producing more merriment and conducted with more propriety than were usual in the court or the streets. I may just remark, in passing, that, had these been children of the poorest sort, we should have had to teach them; for one of the saddest things is that such, in London at least, do not know how to play. We had tea and coffee and biscuits in the lower rooms, for any who pleased; and they were to have a solid supper afterwards. With none of the arrangements, however, had I any thing to do; for my business was to be with them, and help them to enjoy themselves. All went on capitally; the parents entering into the merriment of their children, and helping to keep it up.

"In one of the games, I was seated on the floor with a handkerchief tied over my eyes, waiting, I believe, for some gentle trick to be played upon me, that I might guess at the name of the person who played it. There was a delay—of only a few seconds—long enough, however, for a sudden return of that dreary November afternoon in which I sat on the floor too miserable even to think that I was cold and hungry. Strange to say, it was not the picture of it that came back to me first, but the sound of my own voice calling aloud in the ringing echo of the desolate rooms that I was of no use to anybody, and that God had forgotten me utterly. With the recollection, a doubtful expectation arose which moved me to a scarce controllable degree. I jumped to my feet, and tore the bandage from my eyes.

"Several times during the evening I had had the odd yet well-known feeling of the same thing having happened before; but I was too busy entertaining my friends to try to account for it: perhaps what followed may suggest the theory, that in not a few of such cases the indistinct remembrance of the previous occurrence of some portion of the circumstances may cast the hue of memory over the whole. As—my eyes blinded with the light and straining to recover themselves—I stared about the room, the presentiment grew almost conviction that it was the very room in which I had so sat in desolation and despair. Unable to restrain myself, I hurried into the back room: there was the cabinet beyond! In a few moments more I was absolutely satisfied that this was indeed the house in which I had first found refuge. For a time I could take no further share in what was going on, but sat down in a corner, and cried for joy. Some one went for Lady Bernard, who was superintending the arrangements for supper in the music-room behind. She came in alarm. I told her there was nothing the matter but a little too much happiness, and, if she would come into the cabinet, I would tell her all about it. She did so, and a few words made her a hearty sharer in my pleasure. She insisted that I should tell the company all about it; 'for' she said, 'you do not know how much it may help some poor creature to trust in God.' I promised I would, if I found I could command myself sufficiently. She left me alone for a little while, and after that I was able to join in the games again.

"At supper I found myself quite composed, and, at Lady Bernard's request, stood up, and gave them all a little sketch of grannie's history, of which sketch what had happened that evening was made the central point. Many of the simpler hearts about me received it, without question, as a divine arrangement for my comfort and encouragement,—at least, thus I interpreted their looks to each other, and the remarks that reached my ear; but presently a man stood up,—one who thought more than the rest of them, perhaps because he was blind,—a man at once conceited, honest, and sceptical; and silence having been made for him,—'Ladies and gentlemen,' he began, as if he had been addressing a public meeting, 'you've all heard what grannie has said. It's very kind of her to give us so much of her history. It's a very remarkable one, *I* think, and she deserves to have it. As to what upset her this very night as is,—and I must say for her, I've knowed her now for six years, and I never knowed *her* upset afore,—and as to what upset her, all I can say is, it may or may not ha' been what phylosophers call a coincydence; but at the same time, if it wasn't a coincydence, and if the Almighty had a hand in it, it were no more than you might expect. He would look at it in this light, you see, that maybe she was wrong to fancy herself so down on her luck as all that, but she was a good soul, notwithstandin,' and he would let her know he hadn't forgotten her. And so he set her down in that room there,—wi' her eyes like them here o' mine, as never was no manner o' use to me,—for a minute, jest to put her in mind o' what had been, and what she had said there, an' how it was all so different now. In my opinion, it were no wonder as she broke down, God bless her! I beg leave to propose her health.' So they drank my health in lemonade and ginger-beer; for we were afraid to give some of them stronger drink than that, and therefore had none. Then we had more music and singing; and a clergyman, who knew how to be neighbor to them that had fallen among thieves, read a short chapter and a collect or two, and said a few words to them. Then grannie and her children went home together, all happy, but grannie the happiest of them all."

"Strange and beautiful!" said my father. "But," he added, after a pause, "you must have met with many strange and beautiful things in such a life as yours; for it seems to me that such a life is open to the entrance of all simple wonders. Conventionality and routine and arbitrary law banish their very approach."

"I believe," said Miss Clare, "that every life has its own private experience of the strange and beautiful. But I have sometimes thought that perhaps God took pains to bar out such things of the sort as we should be no better for. The reason why Lazarus was not allowed to visit the brothers of Dives was, that the repentance he would have urged would not have followed, and they would have been only the worse in consequence."

"Admirably said," remarked my father.

Before we took our leave, I had engaged Miss Clare to dine with us while my father was in town.

# CHAPTER XXI.

## LADY BERNARD.

When she came we had no other guest, and so had plenty of talk with her. Before dinner I showed her my husband's pictures; and she was especially pleased with that which hung in the little room off the study, which I called my boudoir,—a very ugly word, by the way, which I am trying to give up,—with a curtain before it. My father has described it in "The Seaboard Parish:" a pauper lies dead, and they are bringing in his coffin. She said it was no wonder it had not been sold, notwithstanding its excellence and force; and asked if I would allow her to bring Lady Bernard to see it. After dinner Percivale had a long talk with her, and succeeded in persuading her to sit to him; not, however, before I had joined my entreaties with his, and my father had insisted that her face was not her own, but belonged to all her kind.

The very next morning she came with Lady Bernard. The latter said she knew my husband well by reputation, and had, before our marriage, asked him to her house, but had not been fortunate enough to possess sufficient attraction. Percivale was much taken with her, notwithstanding a certain coldness, almost sternness of manner, which was considerably repellent,—but only for the first few moments, for, when her eyes lighted up, the whole thing vanished. She was much pleased with some of his pictures, criticising freely, and with evident understanding. The immediate result was, that she bought both the pauper picture and that of the dying knight.

"But I am sorry to deprive your lovely room of such treasures, Mrs. Percivale," she said, with a kind smile.

"Of course I shall miss them," I returned; "but the thought that you have them will console me. Besides, it is good to have a change; and there are only too many lying in the study, from which he will let me choose to supply their place."

"Will you let me come and see which you have chosen?" she asked.

"With the greatest pleasure," I answered.

"And will you come and see me? Do you think you could persuade your husband to bring you to dine with me?"

I told her I could promise the one with more than pleasure, and had little doubt of being able to do the other, now that my husband had seen her.

A reference to my husband's dislike to fashionable society followed, and I had occasion to mention his feeling about being asked without me. Of the latter, Lady Bernard expressed the warmest approval; and of the former, said that it would have no force in respect of her parties, for they were not at all fashionable.

This was the commencement of a friendship for which we have much cause to thank God. Nor did we forget that it came through Miss Clare.

I confess I felt glorious over my cousin Judy; but I would bide my time. Now that I am wiser, and I hope a little better, I see that I was rather spiteful; but I thought then I was only jealous for my new and beautiful friend. Perhaps, having wronged her myself, I was the more ready to take vengeance on her wrongs from the hands of another; which was just the opposite feeling to that I ought to have had.

In the mean time, our intimacy with Miss Clare grew. She interested me in many of her schemes for helping the poor; some of which were for providing them with work in hard times, but more for giving them an interest in life itself, without which, she said, no one would begin to inquire into its relations and duties. One of her positive convictions was, that you ought not to give them any thing they *ought* to provide for themselves, such as food or clothing or shelter. In such circumstances as rendered it impossible for them to do so, the *ought* was in abeyance. But she heartily approved of making them an occasional present of something they could not be expected to procure for themselves,—flowers, for instance. "You would not imagine," I have heard her say, "how they delight in flowers. All the finer instincts of their being are drawn to the surface at the sight of them. I am sure they prize and enjoy them far more, not merely than most people with gardens and greenhouses do, but far more even than they would if they were deprived of them. A gift of that sort can only do them good. But I would rather give a workman a gold watch than a leg of mutton. By a present you mean a compliment; and none feel more grateful for such an acknowledgment of your human relation to them, than those who look up to you as their superior."

Once, when she was talking thus, I ventured to object, for the sake of hearing her further.

"But," I said, "sometimes the most precious thing you can give a man is just that compassion which you seem to think destroys the value of a gift."

"When compassion itself is precious to a man," she answered, "it must be because he loves you, and believes you love him. When that is the case, you may give him any thing you like, and it will do neither you nor him harm. But the man of independent feeling, except he be thus your friend, will not unlikely resent your compassion, while the beggar will accept it chiefly as a pledge for something more to be got from you; and so it will tend to keep him in beggary."

"Would you never, then, give money, or any of the necessaries of life, except in extreme, and, on the part of the receiver, unavoidable necessity?" I asked.

"I would not," she answered; "but in the case where a man *cannot* help himself, the very suffering makes a way for the love which is more than compassion to manifest itself. In every other case, the true way is to provide them with work, which is itself a good thing, besides what they gain by it. If a man will not work, neither should he eat. It must be work with an object in it, however: it must not be mere labor, such as digging a hole and filling it up again, of which I have heard. No man could help resentment at being set to such work. You ought to let him feel that he is giving something of value to you for the money you give to him. But I have known a whole district so corrupted and degraded by clerical alms-giving, that one of the former recipients of it declared, as spokesman for the rest; that threepence given was far more acceptable than five shillings earned."

A good part of the little time I could spare from my own family was now spent with Miss Clare in her work, through which it was chiefly that we became by degrees intimate with Lady Bernard. If ever there was a woman who lived this outer life for the sake of others, it was she. Her inner life was, as it were, sufficient for herself, and found its natural outward expression in blessing others. She was like a fountain of living water that could find no vent but into the lives of her fellows. She had suffered more than falls to the ordinary lot of women, in those who were related to her most nearly, and for many years had looked for no personal blessing from without. She said to me once, that she could not think of any thing that could happen to herself to make her very happy now, except a loved grandson, who was leading a strange, wild life, were to turn out a Harry the Fifth,—a consummation which, however devoutly wished, was not granted her; for the young man died shortly after. I believe no one, not even Miss Clare, knew half the munificent things she did, or what an immense proportion of her large income she spent upon other people. But, as she said herself, no one understood the worth of money better; and no one liked better to have the worth of it: therefore she always administered her charity with some view to the value of the probable return,—with some regard, that is, to the amount of good likely to result to others from the aid given to one. She always took into consideration whether the good was likely to be propagated, or to die with the receiver. She confessed to frequent mistakes; but such, she said, was the principle upon which she sought to regulate that part of her stewardship.

I wish I could give a photograph of her. She was slight, and appeared taller than she was, being rather stately than graceful, with a commanding forehead and still blue eyes. She gave at first the impression of coldness, with a touch of haughtiness. But this was, I think, chiefly the result of her inherited physique; for the moment her individuality appeared, when her being, that is, came into contact with that of another, all this impression vanished in the light that flashed into her eyes, and the smile that illumined her face. Never did woman of rank step more triumphantly over the barriers which the cumulated custom of ages has built between the classes of society. She laid great stress on good manners, little on what is called good birth; although to the latter, in its deep and true sense, she attributed the greatest *à priori* value, as the ground of obligation in the possessor, and of expectation on the part of others. But I shall have an opportunity of showing more of what she thought on this subject presently; for I bethink me that it occupied a great part of our conversation at a certain little gathering, of which I am now going to give an account.

# CHAPTER XXII.

## MY SECOND DINNER-PARTY.

For I judged that I might now give another little dinner: I thought, that, as Percivale had been doing so well lately, he might afford, with his knowing brother's help, to provide, for his part of the entertainment, what might be good enough to offer even to Mr. Morley; and I now knew Lady Bernard sufficiently well to know also that she would willingly accept an invitation from me, and would be pleased to meet Miss Clare, or, indeed, would more likely bring her with her.

I proposed the dinner, and Percivale consented to it. My main object being the glorification of Miss Clare, who had more engagements of one kind and another than anybody I knew, I first invited her, asking her to fix her own day, at some considerable remove. Next I invited Mr. and Mrs. Morley, and next Lady Bernard, who went out very little. Then I invited Mr. Blackstone, and last of all Roger—though I was almost as much interested in his meeting Miss Clare as in any thing else connected with the gathering. For he had been absent from London for some time on a visit to an artist friend at the Hague, and had never seen Miss Clare since the evening on which he and I quarrelled—or rather, to be honest, I quarrelled with him. All accepted, and I looked forward to the day with some triumph.

I had better calm the dread of my wifely reader by at once assuring her that I shall not harrow her feelings with any account of culinary blunders. The moon was in the beginning of her second quarter, and my cook's brain tolerably undisturbed. Lady Bernard offered me her cook for the occasion; but I convinced her that my wisdom would be to decline the offer, seeing such external influence would probably tend to disintegration. I went over with her every item of every dish and every sauce many times,—without any resulting sense of security, I confess; but I had found, that, odd as it may seem, she always did better the more she had to do. I believe that her love of approbation, excited by the difficulty before her, in its turn excited her intellect, which then arose to meet the necessities of the case.

Roger arrived first, then Mr. Blackstone; Lady Bernard brought Miss Clare; and Mr. and Mrs. Morley came last. There were several introductions to be gone through,—a ceremony in which Percivale, being awkward, would give me no assistance; whence I failed to observe how the presence of Miss Clare affected Mr. and Mrs. Morley; but my husband told me that Judy turned red, and that Mr. Morley bowed to her with studied politeness. I took care that Mr. Blackstone should take her down to dinner, which was served in the study as before.

The conversation was broken and desultory at first, as is generally the case at a dinner-party—and perhaps ought to be; but one after another began to listen to what was passing between Lady Bernard and my husband at the foot of the table, until by degrees every one became interested, and took a greater or less part in the discussion. The first of it I heard was as next follows.

"Then you do believe," my husband was saying, "in the importance of what some of the Devonshire people call *havage*?"

"Allow me to ask what they mean by the word," Lady Bernard returned.

"Birth, descent,—the people you come of," he answered.

"Of course I believe that descent involves very important considerations."

"No one," interposed Mr. Morley, "can have a better right than your ladyship to believe that."

"One cannot have a better right than another to believe a fact, Mr. Morley," she answered with a smile. "It is but a fact that you start better or worse according to the position of your starting-point."

"Undeniably," said Mr. Morley. "And for all that is feared from the growth of levelling notions in this country, it will be many generations before a profound respect for birth is eradicated from the feelings of the English people."

He drew in his chin with a jerk, and devoted himself again to his plate, with the air of a "Dixi." He was not permitted to eat in peace, however.

"If you allow," said Mr. Blackstone, "that the feeling can wear out, and is wearing out, it matters little how long it may take to prove itself of a false, because corruptible nature. No growth of notions will blot love, honesty, kindness, out of the human heart."

"Then," said Lady Bernard archly, "am I to understand, Mr. Blackstone, that you don't believe it of the least importance to come of decent people?"

"Your ladyship puts it well," said Mr. Morley, laughing mildly, "and with authority. The longer the descent"—

"The more doubtful," interrupted Lady Bernard, laughing. "One can hardly have come of decent people all through, you know. Let us only hope, without inquiring too closely, that their number preponderates in our own individual cases."

Mr. Morley stared for a moment, and then tried to laugh, but unable to determine whereabout he was in respect of the question, betook himself to his glass of sherry.

Mr. Blackstone considered it the best policy in general not to explain any remark he had made, but to say the right thing better next time instead. I suppose he believed, with another friend of mine, that "when explanations become necessary, they become impossible," a paradox well worth the consideration of those who write letters to newspapers. But Lady Bernard understood him well enough, and was only unwinding the clew of her idea.

"On the contrary, it must be a most serious fact," he rejoined, "to any one who like myself believes that the sins of the fathers are visited on the children."

"Mr. Blackstone," objected Roger, "I can't imagine you believing such a manifest injustice."

"It has been believed in all ages by the best of people," he returned.

"To whom possibly the injustice of it never suggested itself. For my part, I must either disbelieve that, or disbelieve in a God."

"But, my dear fellow, don't you see it is a fact? Don't you see children born with the sins of their parents nestling in their very bodies? You see on which horn of your own dilemma you would impale yourself."

"Wouldn't you rather not believe in a God than believe in an unjust one?"

"An unjust god," said Mr. Blackstone, with the honest evasion of one who will not answer an awful question hastily, "must be a false god, that is, no god. Therefore I presume there is some higher truth involved in every fact that appears unjust, the perception of which would nullify the appearance."

"I see none in the present case," said Roger.

"I will go farther than assert the mere opposite," returned Mr. Blackstone. "I will assert that it is an honor to us to have the sins of our fathers laid upon us. For thus it is given into our power to put a stop to them, so that they shall descend no farther. If I thought my father had committed any sins for which I might suffer, I should be unspeakably glad to suffer for them, and so have the privilege of taking a share in his burden, and some of the weight of it off his mind. You see the whole idea is that of a family, in which we are so grandly bound together, that we must suffer with and for each other. Destroy this consequence, and you destroy the lovely idea itself, with all its thousand fold results of loveliness."

"You anticipate what I was going to say, Mr. Blackstone," said Lady Bernard. "I would differ from you only in one thing. The chain of descent is linked after such a complicated pattern, that the non-conducting condition of one link, or of many links even, cannot break the transmission of qualities. I may inherit from my great-great-grandfather or mother, or some one ever so much farther back. That which was active wrong in some one or other of my ancestors, may appear in me as an impulse to that same wrong, which of course I have to overcome; and if I succeed, then it is so far checked. But it may have passed, or may yet pass, to others of his descendants, who have, or will have, to do the same—for who knows how many generations to come?—before it shall cease. Married people, you see, Mrs. Percivale, have an awful responsibility in regard of the future of the world. You cannot tell to how many millions you may transmit your failures or your victories."

"If I understand you right, Lady Bernard," said Roger, "it is the personal character of your ancestors, and not their social position, you regard as of importance."

"It was of their personal character alone I was thinking. But of course I do not pretend to believe that there are not many valuable gifts more likely to show themselves in what is called a long descent; for doubtless a continuity of education does much to develop the race."

"But if it is personal character you chiefly regard, we may say we are all equally far descended," I remarked; "for we have each had about the same number of ancestors with a character of some sort or other, whose faults and virtues have to do with ours, and for both of which we are, according to Mr. Blackstone, in a most real and important sense accountable."

"Certainly," returned Lady Bernard; "and it is impossible to say in whose descent the good or the bad may predominate. I cannot tell, for instance, how much of the property I inherit has been honestly come by, or is the spoil of rapacity and injustice."

"You are doing the best you can to atone for such a possible fact, then, by its redistribution," said my husband.

"I confess," she answered, "the doubt has had some share in determining my feeling with regard to the management of my property. I have no right to throw up my stewardship, for that was none of my seeking, and I do not know any one who has a better claim to it; but I count it only a stewardship. I am not at liberty to throw my orchard open, for that would result not only in its destruction, but in a renewal of the fight of centuries ago for its possession; but I will try to distribute my apples properly. That is, I have not the same right to give away foolishly that I have to keep wisely."

"Then," resumed Roger, who had evidently been pondering what Lady Bernard had previously said, "you would consider what is called kleptomania as the impulse to steal transmitted by a thief-ancestor?"

"Nothing seems to me more likely. I know a nobleman whose servant has to search his pockets for spoons or forks every night as soon as he is in bed."

"I should find it very hard to define the difference between that and stealing," said Miss Clare, now first taking a part in the conversation. "I have sometimes wondered whether kleptomania was not merely the fashionable name for stealing."

"The distinction is a difficult one, and no doubt the word is occasionally misapplied. But I think there is a difference. The nobleman to whom I referred makes no objection to being thus deprived of his booty; which, for one thing, appears to show that the temptation is intermittent, and partakes at least of the character of a disease."

"But are there not diseases which are only so much the worse diseases that they are not intermittent?" said Miss Clare. "Is it not hard that the privileges of kleptomania should be confined to the rich? You never hear the word applied to a poor child, even if his father was, habit and repute, a thief. Surely, when hunger and cold aggravate the attacks of inherited temptation, they cannot at the same time aggravate the culpability of yielding to them?"

"On the contrary," said Roger, "one would naturally suppose they added immeasurable excuse."

"Only," said Mr. Blackstone, "there comes in our ignorance, and consequent inability to judge. The very fact of the presence of motives of a most powerful kind renders it impossible to be certain of the presence of the disease; whereas other motives being apparently absent, we presume disease as the readiest way of accounting for the propensity; I do not therefore think it is the only way. I believe there are cases in which it comes of pure greed, and is of the same kind as any other injustice the capability of exercising which is more generally distributed. Why should a thief be unknown in a class, a proportion of the members of which is capable of wrong, chicanery, oppression, indeed any form of absolute selfishness?"

"At all events," said Lady Bernard, "so long as we do our best to help them to grow better, we cannot make too much allowance for such as have not only been born with evil impulses, but have had every animal necessity to urge them in the same direction; while, on the other hand, they have not had one of those restraining influences which a good home and education would have afforded. Such must, so far as development goes, be but a little above the beasts."

"You open a very difficult question," said Mr. Morley: "What are we to do with them? Supposing they *are* wild beasts, we can't shoot them; though that would, no doubt, be the readiest way to put an end to the breed."

"Even that would not suffice," said Lady Bernard. "There would always be a deposit from the higher classes sufficient to keep up the breed. But, Mr.

Morley, I did not say *wild* beasts: I only said *beasts*. There is a great difference between a tiger and a sheep-dog."

"There is nearly as much between a Seven-Dialsrough and a sheep-dog."

"In moral attainment, I grant you," said Mr. Blackstone; "but in moral capacity, no. Besides, you must remember, both what a descent the sheep-dog has, and what pains have been taken with his individual education, as well as that of his ancestors."

"Granted all that," said Mr. Morley, "there the fact remains. For my part, I confess I don't see what is to be done. The class to which you refer goes on increasing. There's this garrotting now. I spent a winter at Algiers lately, and found even the suburbs of that city immeasurably safer than any part of London is now, to judge from the police-reports. Yet I am accused of inhumanity and selfishness if I decline to write a check for every shabby fellow who calls upon me pretending to be a clergyman, and to represent this or that charity in the East End!"

"Things are bad enough in the West End, within a few hundred yards of Portland Place, for instance," murmured Miss Clare.

"It seems to me highly unreasonable," Mr. Morley went on. "Why should I spend my money to perpetuate such a condition of things?"

"That would in all likelihood be the tendency of your subscription," said Mr. Blackstone.

"Then why should I?" repeated Mr. Morley with a smile of triumph.

"But," said Miss Clare, in an apologetic tone, "it seems to me you make a mistake in regarding the poor as if their poverty were the only distinction by which they could be classified. The poor are not *all* thieves and garroters, nor even all unthankful and unholy. There are just as strong and as delicate distinctions too, in that stratum of social existence as in the upper strata. I should imagine Mr. Morley knows a few, belonging to the same social grade with himself, with whom, however, he would be sorry to be on any terms of intimacy."

"Not a few," responded Mr. Morley with a righteous frown.

"Then I, who know the poor as well at least as you can know the rich, having lived amongst them almost from childhood, assert that I am acquainted with not a few, who, in all the essentials of human life and character, would be an honor to any circle."

"I should be sorry to seem to imply that there may not be very worthy people amongst them, Miss Clare; but it is not such who draw our attention to the class."

"Not such who force themselves upon your attention certainly," said Miss Clare; "but the existence of such may be an additional reason for bestowing some attention on the class to which they belong. Is there not such a mighty fact as the body of Christ? Is there no connection between the head and the feet?"

"I had not the slightest purpose of disputing the matter with you, Miss Clare," said Mr. Morley—I thought rudely, for who would use the word *disputing* at a dinner-table? "On the contrary, being a practical man, I want to know what is to be done. It is doubtless a great misfortune to the community that there should be such sinks in our cities; but who is to blame for it?—that is the question."

"Every man who says, Am I my brother's keeper? Why, just consider, Mr. Morley: suppose in a family there were one less gifted than the others, and that in consequence they all withdrew from him, and took no interest in his affairs: what would become of him? Must he not sink?"

"Difference of rank is a divine appointment,—you must allow that. If there were not a variety of grades, the social machine would soon come to a stand-still."

"A strong argument for taking care of the smallest wheel, for all the parts are interdependent. That there should be different classes is undoubtedly a divine intention, and not to be turned aside. But suppose the less-gifted boy is fit for some manual labor; suppose he takes to carpentering, and works well, and keeps the house tidy, and every thing in good repair, while his brothers pursue their studies and prepare for professions beyond his reach: is the inferior boy degraded by doing the best he can? Is there any reason in the nature of things why he should sink? But he will most likely sink, sooner or later, if his brothers take no interest in his work, and treat him as a being of nature inferior to their own."

"I beg your pardon," said Mr. Morley, "but is he not on the very supposition inferior to them?"

"Intellectually, yes; morally, no; for he is doing his work, possibly better than they, and therefore taking a higher place in the eternal scale. But granting all kinds of inferiority, his *nature* remains the same with their own; and the question is, whether they treat him as one to be helped up, or one to be kept down; as one unworthy of sympathy, or one to be honored for filling his part: in a word, as one belonging to them, or one whom they put up with only because his work is necessary to them."

"What do you mean by being 'helped up'?" asked Mr. Morley.

"I do not mean helped out of his trade, but helped to make the best of it, and of the intellect that finds its development in that way."

"Very good. But yet I don't see how you apply your supposition."

"For an instance of application, then: How many respectable people know or care a jot about their servants, except as creatures necessary to their comfort?"

"Well, Miss Clare," said Judy, addressing her for the first time, "if you had had the half to do with servants I have had, you would alter your opinion of them."

"I have expressed no opinion," returned Miss Clare. "I have only said that masters and mistresses know and care next to nothing about them."

"They are a very ungrateful class, do what you will for them."

"I am afraid they are at present growing more and more corrupt as a class," rejoined Miss Clare; "but gratitude is a high virtue, therefore in any case I don't see how you could look for much of it from the common sort of them. And yet while some mistresses do not get so much of it as they deserve, I fear most mistresses expect far more of it than they have any right to."

"You *can't* get them to speak the truth."

"That I am afraid is a fact."

"I have never known one on whose word I could depend," insisted Judy.

"My father says he *has* known one," I interjected.

"A sad confirmation of Mrs. Morley," said Miss Clare. "But for my part I know very few persons in any rank on whose representation of things I could absolutely depend. Truth is the highest virtue, and seldom grows wild. It is difficult to speak the truth, and those who have tried it longest best know how difficult it is. Servants need to be taught that as well as everybody else."

"There is nothing they resent so much as being taught," said Judy.

"Perhaps: they are very far from docile; and I believe it is of little use to attempt giving them direct lessons."

"How, then, are you to teach them?"

"By making it very plain to them, but without calling their attention to it, that *you* speak the truth. In the course of a few years they may come to tell a lie or two the less for that."

"Not a very hopeful prospect," said Judy.

"Not a very rapid improvement," said her husband.

"I look for no rapid improvement, so early in a history as the supposition implies," said Miss Clare.

"But would you not tell them how wicked it is?" I asked.

"They know already that it is wicked to tell lies; but they do not feel that *they* are wicked in making the assertions they do. The less said about the abstract truth, and the more shown of practical truth, the better for those whom any one would teach to forsake lying. So, at least, it appears to me. I despair of teaching others, except by learning myself."

"If you do no more than that, you will hardly produce an appreciable effect in a lifetime."

"Why should it be appreciated?" rejoined Miss Clare.

"I should have said, on the contrary," interposed Mr. Blackstone, addressing Mr. Morley, "if you do less—for more you cannot do—you will produce no effect whatever."

"We have no right to make it a condition of our obedience, that we shall see its reflex in the obedience of others," said Miss Clare. "We have to pull out the beam, not the mote."

"Are you not, then, to pull the mote out of your brother's eye?" said Judy.

"In no case and on no pretence, *until* you have pulled the beam out of your own eye," said Mr. Blackstone; "which I fancy will make the duty of finding fault with one's neighbor a rare one; for who will venture to say he has qualified himself for the task?"

It was no wonder that a silence followed upon this; for the talk had got to be very serious for a dinner-table. Lady Bernard was the first to speak. It was easier to take up the dropped thread of the conversation than to begin a new reel.

"It cannot be denied," she said, "whoever may be to blame for it, that the separation between the rich and the poor has either been greatly widened of late, or, which involves the same practical necessity, we have become more aware of the breadth and depth of a gulf which, however it may distinguish their circumstances, ought not to divide them from each other. Certainly the rich withdraw themselves from the poor. Instead, for instance, of helping them to bear their burdens, they leave the still struggling poor of whole parishes to sink into hopeless want, under the weight of those who have already sunk beyond recovery. I am not sure that to shoot them would not involve less injustice. At all events, he that hates his brother is a murderer."

"But there is no question of hating here," objected Mr. Morley.

"I am not certain that absolute indifference to one's neighbor is not as bad. It came pretty nearly to the same thing in the case of the priest and the Levite, who passed by on the other side," said Mr. Blackstone.

"Still," said Mr. Morley, in all the self-importance of one who prided himself on the practical, "I do not see that Miss Clare has proposed any remedy for the state of things concerning the evil of which we are all agreed. What is to be *done*? What can *I* do now? Come, Miss Clare."

Miss Clare was silent.

"Marion, my child," said Lady Bernard, turning to her, "will you answer Mr. Morley?"

"Not, certainly, as to what *he* can do: that question I dare not undertake to answer. I can only speak of what principles I may seem to have discovered. But until a man begins to behave to those with whom he comes into personal contact as partakers of the same nature, to recognize, for instance, between himself and his trades-people a bond superior to that of supply and demand, I cannot imagine how he is to do any thing towards the drawing together of the edges of the gaping wound in the social body."

"But," persisted Mr. Morley, who, I began to think, showed some real desire to come at a practical conclusion, "suppose a man finds himself incapable of that sort of thing—for it seems to me to want some rare qualification or other to be able to converse with an uneducated person"—

"There are many such, especially amongst those who follow handicrafts," interposed Mr. Blackstone, "who think a great deal more than most of the so-called educated. There is a truer education to be got in the pursuit of a handicraft than in the life of a mere scholar. But I beg your pardon, Mr. Morley."

"Suppose," resumed Mr. Morley, accepting the apology without disclaimer,—"Suppose I find I can do nothing of that sort; is there nothing of any sort I can do?"

"Nothing of the best sort, I firmly believe," answered Miss Clare; "for the genuine recognition of the human relationship can alone give value to whatever else you may do, and indeed can alone guide you to what ought to be done. I had a rather painful illustration of this the other day. A gentleman of wealth and position offered me the use of his grounds for some of my poor friends, whom I wanted to take out for a half-holiday. In the neighborhood of London, that is a great boon. But unfortunately, whether from his mistake or mine, I was left with the impression that he would provide some little entertainment for them; I am certain that at least milk was mentioned. It was a lovely day; every thing looked beautiful; and although they were in no great spirits, poor things, no doubt the shade and the grass and the green trees wrought some good in them. Unhappily, two of the men had got drunk on the way; and, fearful of giving offence, I had to take them back to the station.—for their poor helpless wives could only cry,—and send them home by train. I should have done better to risk the offence, and take them into the grounds, where they might soon have slept it off under a tree. I had some distance to go, and some difficulty in getting them along; and when I got back I found things in an unhappy condition, for nothing had been given them to eat or drink,—indeed, no attention, had been paid them whatever. There was company at dinner in the house, and I could not find any one with authority. I hurried into the neighboring village, and bought the contents of two bakers' shops, with which I returned in time to give each a piece of bread before the company came out to *look at* them. A gayly-dressed group, they stood by themselves languidly regarding the equally languid but rather indignant groups of ill-clad and hungry men and women upon the lawn. They made no attempt to mingle with them, or arrive at a notion of what was moving in any of their minds. The nearest approach to communion I saw was a poke or two given to a child with the point of a parasol. Were my poor friends likely to return to their dingy homes with any great feeling of regard for the givers of such cold welcome?"

"But that was an exceptional case," said Mr. Morley.

"Chiefly in this," returned Miss Clare, "that it was a case at all—that they were thus presented with a little more room on the face of the earth for a few hours."

"But you think the fresh air may have done them good?"

"Yes; but we were speaking, I thought, of what might serve towards the filling up of the gulf between the classes."

"Well, will not all kindness shown to the poor by persons in a superior station tend in that direction?"

"I maintain that you can do nothing for them in the way of kindness that shall not result in more harm than good, except you do it from and with genuine charity of soul; with some of that love, in short, which is the heart of religion. Except what is done for them is so done as to draw out their trust and affection, and so raise them consciously in the human scale, it can only tend either to hurt their feelings and generate indignation, or to encourage fawning and beggary. But"—

"I am entirely of your mind," said Mr. Blackstone. "But do go on."

"I was going to add," said Miss Clare, "that while no other charity than this can touch the sore, a good deal might yet be effected by bare justice. It seems to me high time that we dropped talking about charity, and took up the cry of justice. There, now, is a ground on which a man of your influence, Mr. Morley, might do much."

"I don't know what you mean, Miss Clare. So long as I pay the market value for the labor I employ, I do not see how more can be demanded of me—as a right, that is."

"We will not enter on that question, Marion, if you please," said Lady Bernard.

Miss Clare nodded, and went on.

"Is it just in the nation," she said, "to abandon those who can do nothing to help themselves, to be preyed upon by bad landlords, railway-companies, and dishonest trades-people with their false weights, balances, and measures, and adulterations to boot,—from all of whom their more wealthy brethren are comparatively safe? Does not a nation exist for the protection of its parts? Have these no claims on the nation? Would you call it just in a family to abandon its less gifted to any moral or physical spoiler who might be bred within it? To say a citizen must take care of himself *may* be just where he *can* take care of himself, but cannot be just where that is impossible. A thousand causes, originating mainly in the neglect of their neighbors, have combined to sink the poor into a state of moral paralysis: are we to say the paralyzed may be run over in our streets with impunity? *Must* they take care of themselves? Have we not to awake them to the very sense that life is worth caring for? I cannot but feel that the bond between such a neglected class, and any nation in which it is to be found, is very little stronger than, if indeed as strong as, that between slaves and their masters. Who could preach to them their duty to the nation, except on grounds which such a nation acknowledges only with the lips?"

"You have to prove, Miss Clare," said Mr. Morley, in a tone that seemed intended to imply that he was not in the least affected by mistimed eloquence, "that the relation is that of a family."

"I believe," she returned, "that it is closer than the mere human relation of the parts of any family. But, at all events, until we *are* their friends it is worse than useless to pretend to be such, and until they feel that we are their friends it is worse than useless to talk to them about God and religion. They will none of it from our lips."

"Will they from any lips? Are they not already too far sunk towards the brutes to be capable of receiving any such rousing influence?" suggested Mr. Blackstone with a smile, evidently wishing to draw Miss Clare out yet further.

"You turn me aside, Mr. Blackstone. I wanted to urge Mr. Morley to go into parliament as spiritual member for the poor of our large towns. Besides, I know you don't think as your question would imply. As far as my experience guides me, I am bound to believe that there is a spot of soil in every heart sufficient for the growth of a gospel seed. And I believe, moreover, that not only is he a fellow-worker with God who sows that seed, but that he also is one who opens a way for that seed to enter the soil. If such preparation were not necessary, the Saviour would have come the moment Adam and Eve fell, and would have required no Baptist to precede him."

A good deal followed which I would gladly record, enabled as I now am to assist my memory by a more thorough acquaintance with the views of Miss Clare. But I fear I have already given too much conversation at once.

# CHAPTER XXIII.

## THE END OF THE EVENING.

What specially delighted me during the evening, was the marked attention, and the serious look in the eyes, with which Roger listened. It was not often that he did look serious. He preferred, if possible, to get a joke out of a thing; but when he did enter into an argument, he was always fair. Although prone to take the side of objection to any religious remark, he yet never said any thing against religion itself. But his principles, and indeed his nature, seemed as yet in a state of solution,—uncrystallized, as my father would say. Mr. Morley, on the other hand, seemed an insoluble mass, incapable of receiving impressions from other minds. Any suggestion of his own mind, as to a course of action or a mode of thinking, had a good chance of being without question regarded as reasonable and right: he was more than ordinarily prejudiced in his own favor. The day after they thus met at our house, Miss Clare had a letter from him, in which he took the high hand with her, rebuking her solemnly for her presumption in saying, as he represented it, that no good could be done except after the fashion she laid down, and assuring her that she would thus alienate the most valuable assistance from any scheme she might cherish for the amelioration of the condition of the lower classes. It ended with the offer of a yearly subscription of five pounds to any project of the wisdom of which she would take the trouble to convince him. She replied, thanking him both, for his advice and his offer, but saying that, as she had no scheme on foot requiring such assistance, she could not at present accept the latter; should, however, any thing show itself for which that sort of help was desirable, she would take the liberty of reminding him of it.

When the ladies rose, Judy took me aside, and said,—

"What does it all mean, Wynnie?"

"Just what you hear," I answered.

"You asked us, to have a triumph over me, you naughty thing!"

"Well—partly—if I am to be honest; but far more to make you do justice to Miss Clare. You being my cousin, she had a right to that at my hands."

"Does Lady Bernard know as much about her as she seems?"

"She knows every thing about her, and visits her, too, in her very questionable abode. You see, Judy, a report may be a fact, and yet be untrue."

"I'm not going to be lectured by a chit like you. But I should like to have a little talk with Miss Clare."

"I will make you an opportunity."

I did so, and could not help overhearing a very pretty apology; to which Miss Clare replied, that she feared she only was to blame, inasmuch as she ought to have explained the peculiarity of her circumstances before accepting the engagement. At the time, it had not appeared to her necessary, she said; but now she would make a point of explaining before she accepted any fresh duty of the kind, for she saw it would be fairer to both parties. It was no wonder such an answer should entirely disarm cousin Judy, who forthwith begged she would, if she had no objection, resume her lessons with the children at the commencement of the next quarter.

"But I understand from Mrs. Percivale," objected Miss Clare, "that the office is filled to your thorough satisfaction."

"Yes; the lady I have is an excellent teacher; but the engagement was only for a quarter."

"If you have no other reason for parting with her, I could not think of stepping into her place. It would be a great disappointment to her, and my want of openness with you would be the cause of it. If you should part with her for any other reason, I should be very glad to serve you again."

Judy tried to argue with her, but Miss Clare was immovable.

"Will you let me come and see you, then?" said Judy.

"With all my heart," she answered. "You had better come with Mrs. Percivale, though, for it would not be easy for you to find the place."

We went up to the drawing-room to tea, passing through the study, and taking the gentlemen with us. Miss Clare played to us, and sang several songs,—the last a ballad of Schiller's, "The Pilgrim," setting forth the constant striving of the soul after something of which it never lays hold. The last verse of it I managed to remember. It was this:—

Thither, ah! no footpath bendeth;
  Ah! the heaven above, so clear,
Never, earth to touch, descendeth;
  And the There is never Here!"

"That is a beautiful song, and beautifully sung," said Mr. Blackstone; "but I am a little surprised at your choosing to sing it, for you cannot call it a Christian song."

"Don't you find St. Paul saying something very like it again and again?" Miss Clare returned with a smile, as if she perfectly knew what he objected to. "You find him striving, journeying, pressing on, reaching out to lay hold, but never having attained,—ever conscious of failure."

"That is true; but there is this huge difference,—that St. Paul expects to attain,—is confident of one day attaining; while Schiller, in that lyric at least, seems—I only say seems—hopeless of any satisfaction: *Das Dort ist niemals Hier.*"

"It may have been only a mood," said Miss Clare. "St. Paul had his moods also, from which he had to rouse himself to fresh faith and hope and effort."

"But St. Paul writes only in his hopeful moods. Such alone he counts worthy of sharing with his fellows. If there is no hope, why, upon any theory, take the trouble to say so? It is pure weakness to desire sympathy in hopelessness. Hope alone justifies as well as excites either utterance or effort."

"I admit all you say, Mr. Blackstone; and yet I think such a poem invaluable; for is not Schiller therein the mouth of the whole creation groaning and travailling and inarticulately crying out for the sonship?"

"Unconsciously, then. He does not know what he wants."

"*Apparently*, not. Neither does the creation. Neither do we. We do know it is oneness with God we want; but of what that means we have only vague, though glowing hints."

I saw Mr. Morley scratch his left ear like a young calf, only more impatiently.

"But," Miss Clare went on, "is it not invaluable as the confession of one of the noblest of spirits, that he had found neither repose nor sense of attainment?"

"But," said Roger, "did you ever know any one of those you call Christians who professed to have reached satisfaction; or, if so, whose life would justify you in believing him?"

"I have never known a satisfied Christian, I confess," answered Miss Clare. "Indeed, I should take satisfaction as a poor voucher for Christianity. But I have known several contented Christians. I might, in respect of one or two of them, use a stronger word,—certainly not *satisfied.* I believe there is a grand, essential unsatisfaction,—I do not mean dissatisfaction,—which adds the delight of expectation to the peace of attainment; and that, I presume, is the very consciousness of heaven. But where faith may not have produced even contentment, it will yet sustain hope: which, if we may judge from the ballad, no mere aspiration can. We must believe in a living ideal, before we can have a tireless heart; an ideal which draws our poor vague ideal to itself, to fill it full and make it alive."

I should have been amazed to hear Miss Clare talk like this, had I not often heard my father say that aspiration and obedience were the two mightiest forces for development. Her own needs and her own deeds had been her tutors; and the light by which she had read their lessons was the candle of the Lord within her.

When my husband would have put her into Lady Bernard's carriage, as they were leaving, she said she should prefer walking home; and, as Lady Bernard did not press her to the contrary, Percivale could not remonstrate. "I am sorry I cannot walk with you, Miss Clare," he said. "*I* must not leave my duties, but"—

"There's not the slightest occasion," she interrupted. "I know every yard of the way. Good-night."

The carriage drove off in one direction, and Miss Clare tripped lightly along in the other. Percivale darted into the house, and told Roger, who snatched up his hat, and bounded after her. Already she was out of sight; but he, following light-footed, overtook her in the crescent. It was, however, only after persistent entreaty that he prevailed on her to allow him to accompany her.

"You do not know, Mr. Roger," she said pleasantly, "what you may be exposing yourself to, in going with me. I may have to do something you wouldn't like to have a share in."

"I shall be only too glad to have the humblest share in any thing you draw me into," said Roger.

As it fell out, they had not gone far before they came upon a little crowd, chiefly of boys, who ought to have been in bed long before, gathered about a man and woman. The man was forcing his company on a woman who was evidently annoyed that she could not get rid of him.

"Is he your husband?" asked Miss Clare, making her way through the crowd.

"No, miss," the woman answered. "I never saw him afore. I'm only just come in from the country."

She looked more angry than frightened. Roger said her black eyes flashed dangerously, and she felt about the bosom of her dress—for a knife, he was certain.

"You leave her alone," he said to the man, getting between him and her.

"Mind your own business," returned the man, in a voice that showed he was drunk.

For a moment Roger was undecided what to do; for he feared involving Miss Clare in a *row*, as he called it. But when the fellow, pushing suddenly past him, laid his hand on Miss Clare, and shoved her away, he gave him a blow that sent him staggering into the street; whereupon, to his astonishment, Miss

Clare, leaving the woman, followed the man, and as soon as he had recovered his equilibrium, laid her hand on his arm and spoke to him, but in a voice so low and gentle that Roger, who had followed her, could not hear a word she said. For a moment or two the man seemed to try to listen, but his condition was too much for him; and, turning from her, he began again to follow the woman, who was now walking wearily away. Roger again interposed.

"Don't strike him, Mr. Roger," cried Miss Clare: "he's too drunk for that. But keep him back if you can, while I take the woman away. If I see a policeman, I will send him."

The man heard her last words, and they roused him to fury. He rushed at Roger, who, implicitly obedient, only dodged to let him pass, and again confronted him, engaging his attention until help arrived. He was, however, by this time so fierce and violent, that Roger felt bound to assist the policeman.

As soon as the man was locked up, he went to Lime Court. The moon was shining, and the narrow passage lay bright beneath her. Along the street, people were going and coming, though it was past midnight, but the court was very still. He walked into it as far as the spot where we had together seen Miss Clare. The door at which she had entered was open; but he knew nothing of the house or its people, and feared to compromise her by making inquiries. He walked several times up and down, somewhat anxious, but gradually persuading himself that in all probability no further annoyance had befallen her; until at last he felt able to leave the place.

He came back to our house, where, finding his brother at his final pipe in the study, he told him all about their adventure.

# CHAPTER XXIV.

## MY FIRST TERROR.

One of the main discomforts in writing a book is, that there are so many ways in which every thing, as it comes up, might be told, and you can't tell which is the best. You believe there must be a *best* way; but you might spend your life in trying to satisfy yourself which was that best way, and, when you came to the close of it, find you had done nothing,—hadn't even found out the way. I have always to remind myself that something, even if it be far from the best thing, is better than nothing. Perhaps the only way to arrive at the best way is to make plenty of blunders, and find them out.

This morning I had been sitting a long time with my pen in my hand, thinking what this chapter ought to be about,—that is, what part of my own history, or of that of my neighbors interwoven therewith, I ought to take up next,—when my third child, my little Cecilia, aged five, came into the room, and said,—

"Mamma, there's a poor man at the door, and Jemima won't give him any thing."

"Quite right, my dear. We must give what we can to people we know. We are sure then that it is not wasted."

"But he's so *very* poor, mamma!"

"How do you know that?"

"Poor man! he has *only* three children. I heard him tell Jemima. He was *so* sorry! And *I*'m very sorry, too."

"But don't you know you mustn't go to the door when any one is talking to Jemima?" I said.

"Yes, mamma. I didn't go to the door: I stood in the hall and peeped."

"But you mustn't even stand in the hall," I said. "Mind that."

This was, perhaps, rather an oppressive reading of a proper enough rule; but I had a very special reason for it, involving an important event in my story, which occurred about two years after what I have last set down.

One morning Percivale took a holiday in order to give me one, and we went to spend it at Richmond. It was the anniversary of our marriage; and as we wanted to enjoy it thoroughly, and, precious as children are, *every* pleasure is not enhanced by their company, we left ours at home,—Ethel and her brother Roger (named after Percivale's father), who was now nearly a year old, and wanted a good deal of attention. It was a lovely day, with just a sufficient number of passing clouds to glorify—that is, to do justice to—the sunshine, and a gentle breeze, which itself seemed to be taking a holiday, for it blew only just when you wanted it, and then only enough to make you think of that wind which, blowing where it lists, always blows where it is wanted. We took the train to Hammersmith; for my husband, having consulted the tide-table, and found that the river would be propitious, wished to row me from there to Richmond. How gay the river-side looked, with its fine broad landing stage, and the numberless boats ready to push off on the swift water, which kept growing and growing on the shingly shore! Percivale, however, would hire his boat at a certain builder's shed, that I might see it. That shed alone would have been worth coming to see—such a picture of loveliest gloom—as if it had been the cave where the twilight abode its time! You could not tell whether to call it light or shade,—that diffused presence of a soft elusive brown; but is what we call shade any thing but subdued light? All about, above, and below, lay the graceful creatures of the water, moveless and dead here on the shore, but there—launched into their own elemental world, and blown upon by the living wind—endowed at once with life and motion and quick response.

Not having been used to boats, I felt nervous as we got into the long, sharp-nosed, hollow fish which Percivale made them shoot out on the rising tide; but the slight fear vanished almost the moment we were afloat, when, ignorant as I was of the art of rowing, I could not help seeing how perfectly Percivale was at home in it. The oars in his hands were like knitting-needles in mine, so deftly, so swimmingly, so variously, did he wield them. Only once my fear returned, when he stood up in the swaying thing—a mere length without breadth—to pull off his coat and waistcoat; but he stood steady, sat down gently, took his oars quietly, and the same instant we were shooting so fast through the rising tide that it seemed as if *we* were pulling the water up to Richmond.

"Wouldn't you like to steer?" said my husband. "It would amuse you."

"I should like to learn," I said,—"not that I want to be amused; I am too happy to care for amusement."

"Take those two cords behind you, then, one in each hand, sitting between them. That will do. Now, if you want me to go to your right, pull your right-hand cord; if you want me to go to your left, pull your left-hand one."

I made an experiment or two, and found the predicted consequences follow: I ran him aground, first on one bank, then on the other. But when I did so a third time,—

"Come! come!" he said: "this won't do, Mrs. Percivale. You're not trying your best. There is such a thing as gradation in steering as well as in painting, or music, or any thing else that is worth doing."

"I pull the right line, don't I?" I said; for I was now in a mood to tease him.

"Yes—to a wrong result," he answered. "You must feel your rudder, as you would the mouth of your horse with the bit, and not do any thing violent, except in urgent necessity."

I answered by turning the head of the boat right towards the nearer bank.

"I see!" he said, with a twinkle in his eyes. "I have put a dangerous power into your hands. But never mind. The queen may decree as she likes; but the sinews of war, you know"—

I thought he meant that if I went on with my arbitrary behavior, he would drop his oars; and for a little while I behaved better. Soon, however, the spirit of mischief prompting me, I began my tricks again: to my surprise I found that I had no more command over the boat than over the huge barge, which, with its great red-brown sail, was slowly ascending in front of us; I couldn't turn its head an inch in the direction I wanted.

"What does it mean, Percivale?" I cried, pulling with all my might, and leaning forward that I might pull the harder.

"What does what mean?" he returned coolly.

"That I can't move the boat."

"Oh! It means that I have resumed the reins of government."

"But how? I can't understand it."

"And I am wiser than to make you too wise. Education is *not* a panacea for moral evils. I quote your father, my dear."

And he pulled away as if nothing were the matter.

"Please, I like steering," I said remonstratingly. "And I like rowing."

"I don't see why the two shouldn't go together."

"Nor I. They ought. But not only does the steering depend on the rowing, but the rower can steer himself."

"I will be a good girl, and steer properly."

"Very well; steer away."

He looked shorewards as he spoke; and then first I became aware that he had been watching my hands all the time. The boat now obeyed my lightest touch.

How merrily the water rippled in the sun and the wind! while so responsive were our feelings to the play of light and shade around us, that more than once when a cloud crossed us, I saw its shadow turn almost into sadness on the countenance of my companion,—to vanish the next moment when the one sun above and the thousand mimic suns below shone out in universal laughter. When a steamer came in sight, or announced its approach by the far-heard sound of its beating paddles, it brought with it a few moments of almost awful responsibility; but I found that the presence of danger and duty together, instead of making me feel flurried, composed my nerves, and enabled me to concentrate my whole attention on getting the head of the boat as nearly as possible at right angles with the waves from the paddles; for Percivale had told me that if one of any size struck us on the side, it would most probably capsize us. But the way to give pleasure to my readers can hardly be to let myself grow garrulous in the memory of an ancient pleasure of my own. I will say nothing more of the delights of that day. They were such a contrast to its close, that twelve months at least elapsed before I was able to look back upon them without a shudder; for I could not rid myself of the foolish feeling that our enjoyment had been somehow to blame for what was happening at home while we were thus revelling in blessed carelessness.

When we reached our little nest, rather late in the evening, I found to my annoyance that the front door was open. It had been a fault of which I thought I had cured the cook,—to leave it thus when she ran out to fetch any thing. Percivale went down to the study; and I walked into the drawing-room, about to ring the bell in anger. There, to my surprise and farther annoyance, I found Sarah, seated on the sofa with her head in her hands, and little Roger wide awake on the floor.

"What *does* this mean?" I cried. "The front door open! Master Roger still up! and you seated in the drawing-room!"

"O ma'am!" she almost shrieked, starting up the moment I spoke, and, by the time I had put my angry interrogation, just able to gasp out—"Have you found her, ma'am?"

"Found whom?" I returned in alarm, both at the question and at the face of the girl; for through the dusk I now saw that it was very pale, and that her eyes were red with crying.

"Miss Ethel," she answered in a cry choked with a sob; and dropping again on the sofa, she hid her face once more between her hands.

I rushed to the study-door, and called Percivale; then returned to question the girl. I wonder now that I did nothing outrageous; but fear kept down folly, and made me unnaturally calm.

"Sarah," I said, as quietly as I could, while I trembled all over, "tell me what has happened. Where is the child?"

"Indeed it's not my fault, ma'am. I was busy with Master Roger, and Miss Ethel was down stairs with Jemima."

"Where is she?" I repeated sternly.

"I don't know no more than the man in the moon, ma'am."

"Where's Jemima?"

"Run out to look for her?"

"How long have you missed her?"

"An hour. Or perhaps two hours. I don't know, my head's in such a whirl. I can't remember when I saw her last. O ma'am! What *shall* I do?"

Percivale had come up, and was standing beside me. When I looked round, he was as pale as death; and at the sight of his face, I nearly dropped on the floor. But he caught hold of me, and said, in a voice so dreadfully still that it frightened me more than any thing,—

"Come, my love; do not give way, for we must go to the police at once." Then, turning to Sarah, "Have you searched the house and garden?" he asked.

"Yes, sir; every hole and corner. We've looked under every bed, and into every cupboard and chest,—the coal-cellar, the boxroom,—everywhere."

"The bathroom?" I cried.

"Oh, yes, ma'am! the bathroom, and everywhere."

"Have there been any tramps about the house since we left?" Percivale asked.

"Not that I know of; but the nursery window looks into the garden, you know, sir. Jemima didn't mention it."

"Come then, my dear," said my husband.

He compelled me to swallow a glass of wine, and led me away, almost unconscious of my bodily movements, to the nearest cab-stand. I wondered afterwards, when I recalled the calm gaze with which he glanced along the line, and chose the horse whose appearance promised the best speed. In a few minutes we were telling the inspector at the police-station in Albany Street what had happened. He took a sheet of paper, and asking one question after another about her age, appearance, and dress, wrote down our answers. He then called a man, to whom he gave the paper, with some words of direction.

"The men are now going on their beats for the night," he said, turning again to us. "They will all hear the description of the child, and some of them have orders to search."

"Thank you," said my husband. "Which station had we better go to next?"

"The news will be at the farthest before you can reach the nearest," he answered. "We shall telegraph to the suburbs first."

"Then what more is there we can do?" asked Percivale.

"Nothing," said the inspector,—"except you find out whether any of the neighbors saw her, and when and where. It would be something to know in what direction she was going. Have you any ground for suspicion? Have you ever discharged a servant? Were any tramps seen about the place?"

"I know, who it is!" I cried. "It's the woman that took Theodora! It's Theodora's mother! I know it is!"

Percivale explained what I meant.

"That's what people get, you see, when they take on themselves other people's business," returned the inspector. "That child ought to have been sent to the workhouse."

He laid his head on his hand for a moment.

"It seems likely enough," he added. Then after another pause—"I have your address. The child shall be brought back to you the moment she's found. We can't mistake her after your description."

"Where are you going now?" I said to my husband, as we left the station to re-enter the cab.

"I don't know," he answered, "except we go home and question all the shops in the neighborhood."

"Let us go to Miss Clare first," I said.

"By all means," he answered.

We were soon at the entrance of Lime Court.

When we turned the corner in the middle of it, we heard the sound of a piano.

"She's at home!" I cried, with a feeble throb of satisfaction. The fear that she might be out had for the last few moments been uppermost.

We entered the house, and ascended the stairs in haste. Not a creature did we meet, except a wicked-looking cat. The top of her head was black, her forehead and face white; and the black and white were shaped so as to look like hair parted over a white forehead, which gave her green eyes a frightfully human look as she crouched in the corner of a window-sill in the light of a gas-lamp outside. But before we reached the top of the first stair we heard the sounds of dancing, as well as of music. In a moment after, with our load of gnawing fear and helpless eagerness, we stood in the midst of a merry assembly of men, women, and children, who filled Miss Clare's room to overflowing. It was Saturday night, and they were gathered according to custom for their weekly music.

They made a way for us; and Miss Clare left the piano, and came to meet us with a smile on her beautiful face. But, when she saw our faces, hers fell.

"What *is* the matter, Mrs. Percivale?" she asked in alarm.

I sunk on the chair from which she had risen.

"We've lost Ethel," said my husband quietly.

"What do you mean? You don't"—

"No, no: she's gone; she's stolen. We don't know where she is," he answered with faltering voice. "We've just been to the police."

Miss Clare turned white; but, instead of making any remark, she called out to some of her friends whose good manners were making them leave the room,—

"Don't go, please; we want you." Then turning to me, she asked, "May I do as I think best?"

"Yes, certainly," answered my husband.

"My friend, Mrs. Percivale," she said, addressing the whole assembly, "has lost her little girl."

A murmur of dismay and sympathy arose.

"What can we do to find her?" she went on.

They fell to talking among themselves. The next instant, two men came up to us, making their way from the neighborhood of the door. The one was a keen-faced, elderly man, with iron-gray whiskers and clean-shaved chin; the other was my first acquaintance in the neighborhood, the young bricklayer. The elder addressed my husband, while the other listened without speaking.

"Tell us what she's like, sir, and how she was dressed—though that ain't much use. She'll be all different by this time."

The words shot a keener pang to my heart than it had yet felt. My darling stripped of her nice clothes, and covered with dirty, perhaps infected garments. But it was no time to give way to feeling.

My husband repeated to the men the description he had given the police, loud enough for the whole room to hear; and the women in particular, Miss Clare told me afterwards, caught it up with remarkable accuracy. They would not have done so, she said, but that their feelings were touched.

"Tell them also, please, Mr. Percivale, about the child Mrs. Percivale's father and mother found and brought up. That may have something to do with this."

My husband told them all the story; adding that the mother of the child might have found out who we were, and taken ours as a pledge for the recovery of her own.

Here one of the women spoke.

"That dark woman you took in one night—two years ago, miss—she say something. I was astin' of her in the mornin' what her trouble was, for that trouble *she* had on *her* mind was plain to see, and she come over something, half-way like, about losin' of a child; but whether it were dead, or strayed, or stolen, or what, I couldn't tell; and no more, I believe, she wanted me to."

Here another woman spoke.

"I'm 'most sure I saw her—the same woman—two days ago, and no furrer off than Gower Street," she said. "You're too good by half, miss," she went on, "to the likes of sich. They ain't none of them respectable."

"Perhaps you'll see some good come out of it before long," said Miss Clare in reply.

The words sounded like a rebuke, for all this time I had hardly sent a thought upwards for help. The image of my child had so filled my heart, that there was no room left for the thought of duty, or even of God.

Miss Clare went on, still addressing the company, and her words had a tone of authority.

"I will tell you what you must do," she said. "You must, every one of you, run and tell everybody you know, and tell every one to tell everybody else. You mustn't stop to talk it over with each other, or let those you tell it to stop to talk to you about it; for it is of the greatest consequence no time should be lost in making it as quickly and as widely known as possible. Go, please."

In a few moments the room was empty of all but ourselves. The rush on the stairs was tremendous for a single minute, and then all was still. Even the children had rushed out to tell what other children they could find.

"What must we do next?" said my husband.

Miss Clare thought for a moment.

"I would go and tell Mr. Blackstone," she said. "It is a long way from here, but whoever has taken the child would not be likely to linger in the neighborhood. It is best to try every thing."

"Right," said my husband. "Come, Wynnie."

"Wouldn't it be better to leave Mrs. Percivale with me?" said Miss Clare. "It is dreadfully fatiguing to go driving over the stones."

It was very kind of her; but if she had been a mother she would not have thought of parting me from my husband; neither would she have fancied that I could remain inactive so long as it was possible even to imagine I was doing something; but when I told her how I felt, she saw at once that it would be better for me to go.

We set off instantly, and drove to Mr. Blackstone's. What a long way it was! Down Oxford Street and Holborn we rattled and jolted, and then through many narrow ways in which I had never been, emerging at length in a broad road, with many poor and a few fine old houses in it; then again plunging into still more shabby regions of small houses, which, alas! were new, and yet wretched! At length, near an open space, where yet not a blade of grass could grow for the trampling of many feet, and for the smoke from tall chimneys, close by a gasometer of awful size, we found the parsonage, and Mr. Blackstone in his study. The moment he heard our story he went to the door and called his servant. "Run, Jabez," he said, "and tell the sexton to ring the church-bell. I will come to him directly I hear it."

I may just mention that Jabez and his wife, who formed the whole of Mr. Blackstone's household, did not belong to his congregation, but were members of a small community in the neighborhood, calling themselves Peculiar Baptists.

About ten minutes passed, during which little was said: Mr. Blackstone never seemed to have any mode of expressing his feelings except action, and where that was impossible they took hardly any recognizable shape. When the first boom of the big bell filled the little study in which we sat, I gave a cry, and jumped up from my chair: it sounded in my ears like the knell of my lost baby, for at the moment I was thinking of her as once when a baby she lay for dead in my arms. Mr. Blackstone got up and left the room, and my husband rose and would have followed him; but, saying he would be back in a few minutes, he shut the door and left us. It was half an hour, a dreadful half-hour, before he returned; for to sit doing nothing, not even being carried somewhere to do something, was frightful.

"I've told them all about it," he said. "I couldn't do better than follow Miss Clare's example. But my impression is, that, if the woman you suspect be the culprit, she would make her way out to the open as quickly as possible. Such people are most at home on the commons: they are of a less gregarious nature than the wild animals of the town. What shall you do next?"

"That is just what I want to know," answered my husband.

He never asked advice except when he did not know what to do; and never except from one whose advice he meant to follow.

"Well," returned Mr. Blackstone, "I should put an advertisement into every one of the morning papers."

"But the offices will all be closed," said Percivale.

"Yes, the publishing, but not the printing offices."

"How am I to find out where they are?"

"I know one or two of them, and the people there will tell us the rest."

"Then you mean to go with us?"

"Of course I do,—that is, if you will have me. You don't think I would leave you to go alone? Have you had any supper?"

"No. Would you like something, my dear?" said Percivale turning to me.

"I couldn't swallow a mouthful," I said.

"Nor I either," said Percivale.

"Then I'll just take a hunch of bread with me," said Mr. Blackstone, "for I am hungry. I've had nothing since one o'clock."

We neither asked him not to go, nor offered to wait till he had had his supper. Before we reached Printing-House Square he had eaten half a loaf.

"Are you sure," said my husband, as we were starting, "that they will take an advertisement at the printing-office?"

"I think they will. The circumstances are pressing. They will see that we are honest people, and will make a push to help us. But for any thing I know it may be quite *en règle*."

"We must pay, though," said Percivale, putting his hand in his pocket, and taking out his purse. "There! Just as I feared! No money!—Two—three shillings—and sixpence!"

Mr. Blackstone stopped the cab.

"I've not got as much," he said. "But it's of no consequence. I'll run and write a check."

"But where can you change it? The little shops about here won't be able."

"There's the Blue Posts."

"Let me take it, then. You won't be seen going into a public-house?" said Percivale.

"Pooh! pooh!" said Mr. Blackstone. "Do you think my character won't stand that much? Besides, they wouldn't change it for you. But when I think of it, I used the last check in my book in the beginning of the week. Never mind; they will lend me five pounds."

We drove to the Blue Posts. He got out, and returned in one minute with five sovereigns.

"What will people say to your borrowing five pounds at a public-house?" said Percivale.

"If they say what is right, it won't hurt me."

"But if they say what is wrong?"

"That they can do any time, and that won't hurt me, either."

"But what will the landlord himself think?"

"I have no doubt he feels grateful to me for being so friendly. You can't oblige a man more than by asking a *light* favor of him."

"Do you think it well in your position to be obliged to a man in his?" asked Percivale.

"I do. I am glad of the chance. It will bring me into friendly relations with him."

"Do you wish, then, to be in friendly relations with him?"

"Indubitably. In what other relations do you suppose a clergyman ought to be with one of his parishioners?"

"You didn't invite *him* into your parish, I presume."

"No; and he didn't invite me. The thing was settled in higher quarters. There we are, anyhow; and I have done quite a stroke of business in borrowing that money of him."

Mr. Blackstone laughed, and the laugh sounded frightfully harsh in my ears.

"A man"—my husband went on, who was surprised that a clergyman should be so liberal—"a man who sells drink!—in whose house so many of your parishioners will to-morrow night get too drunk to be in church the next morning!"

"I wish having been drunk were what *would* keep them from being in church. Drunk or sober, it would be all the same. Few of them care to go. They are turning out better, however, than when first I came. As for the publican, who knows what chance of doing him a good turn it may put in my way?"

"You don't expect to persuade him to shut up shop?"

"No: he must persuade himself to that."

"What good, then, can you expect to do him?"

"Who knows? I say. You can't tell what good may or may not come out of it, any more than you can tell which of your efforts, or which of your helpers, may this night be the means of restoring your child."

"What do you expect the man to say about it?"

"I shall provide him with something to say. I don't want him to attribute it to some foolish charity. He might. In the New Testament, publicans are acknowledged to have hearts."

"Yes; but the word has a very different meaning in the New Testament."

"The feeling religious people bear towards them, however, comes very near to that with which society regarded the publicans of old."

"They are far more hurtful to society than those tax-gatherers."

"They may be. I dare say they are. Perhaps they are worse than the sinners with whom their namesakes of the New Testament are always coupled."

I will not follow the conversation further. I will only give the close of it. Percivale told me afterwards that he had gone on talking in the hope of diverting my thoughts a little.

"What, then, do you mean to tell him?" asked Percivale.

"The truth, the whole truth, and nothing but the truth," said Mr. Blackstone. "I shall go in to-morrow morning, just at the time when there will probably be far too many people at the bar,—a little after noon. I shall return him his five sovereigns, ask for a glass of ale, and tell him the whole story,—how my friend, the celebrated painter, came with his wife,—and the rest of it, adding, I trust, that the child is all right, and at the moment probably going out for a walk with her mother, who won't let her out of her sight for a moment."

He laughed again, and again I thought him heartless; but I understand him better now. I wondered, too, that Percivale *could* go on talking, and yet I found that their talk did make the time go a little quicker. At length we reached the printing-office of "The Times,"—near Blackfriars' Bridge, I think.

After some delay, we saw an overseer, who, curt enough at first, became friendly when he heard our case. If he had not had children of his own, we might perhaps have fared worse. He took down the description and address, and promised that the advertisement should appear in the morning's paper in the best place he could now find for it.

Before we left, we received minute directions as to the whereabouts of the next nearest office. We spent the greater part of the night in driving from one printing-office to another. Mr. Blackstone declared he would not leave us until we had found her.

"You have to preach twice to-morrow," said Percivale: it was then three o'clock.

"I shall preach all the better," he returned. "Yes: I feel as if I should give them *one* good sermon to-morrow."

"The man talks as if the child were found already!" I thought, with indignation. "It's a pity he hasn't a child of his own! he would be more sympathetic." At the same time, if I had been honest, I should have confessed to myself that his confidence and hope helped to keep me up.

At last, having been to the printing-office of every daily paper in London, we were on our dreary way home.

Oh, how dreary it was!—and the more dreary that the cool, sweet light of a spring dawn was growing in every street, no smoke having yet begun to pour from the multitudinous chimneys to sully its purity! From misery and want of sleep, my soul and body both felt like a gray foggy night. Every now and then the thought of my child came with a fresh pang,—not that she was one moment absent from me, but that a new thought about her would dart a new sting into the ever-burning throb of the wound. If you had asked me the one blessed thing in the world, I should have said *sleep*—with my husband and children beside me. But I dreaded sleep now, both for its visions and for the frightful waking. Now and then I would start violently, thinking I heard my Ethel cry; but from the cab-window no child was ever to be seen, down all the lonely street. Then I would sink into a succession of efforts to picture to myself her little face,—white with terror and misery, and smeared with the dirt of the pitiful hands that rubbed the streaming eyes. They might have beaten her! she might have cried herself to sleep in some wretched hovel; or, worse, in some fever-stricken and crowded lodging-house, with horrible sights about her and horrible voices in her ears! Or she might at that moment be dragged wearily along a country-road, farther and farther from her mother!

I could have shrieked, and torn my hair. What if I should never see her again? She might be murdered, and I never know it! O my darling! my darling!

At the thought a groan escaped me. A hand was laid on my arm. That I knew was my husband's. But a voice was in my ear, and that was Mr. Blackstone's.

"Do you think God loves the child less than you do? Or do you think he is less able to take care of her than you are? When the disciples thought themselves sinking, Jesus rebuked them for being afraid. Be still, and you will see the hand of God in this. Good you cannot foresee will come out of it."

I could not answer him, but I felt both rebuked and grateful.

All at once I thought of Roger. What would he say when he found that his pet was gone, and we had never told him?

"Roger!" I said to my husband. "We've never told him!"

"Let us go now," he returned.

We were at the moment close to North Crescent. After a few thundering raps at the door, the landlady came down. Percivale rushed up, and in a few minutes returned with Roger. They got into the cab. A great talk followed; but I heard hardly any thing, or rather I heeded nothing. I only recollect that Roger was very indignant with his brother for having been out all night without him to help.

"I never thought of you, Roger," said Percivale.

"So much the worse!" said Roger.

"No," said Mr. Blackstone. "A thousand things make us forget. I dare say your brother all but forgot God in the first misery of his loss. To have thought of you, and not to have told you, would have been another thing."

A few minutes after, we stopped at our desolate house, and the cabman was dismissed with one of the sovereigns from the Blue Posts. I wondered afterwards what manner of man or woman had changed it there. A dim light was burning in the drawing-room. Percivale took his pass-key, and opened the door. I hurried in, and went straight to my own room; for I longed to be alone that I might weep—nor weep only. I fell on my knees by the bedside, buried my face, and sobbed, and tried to pray. But I could not collect my thoughts; and, overwhelmed by a fresh access of despair, I started again to my feet.

Could I believe my eyes? What was that in the bed? Trembling as with an ague,—in terror lest the vision should by vanishing prove itself a vision,—I stooped towards it. I heard a breathing! It was the fair hair and the rosy face of my darling—fast asleep—without one trace of suffering on her angelic loveliness! I remember no more for a while. They tell me I gave a great cry, and fell on the floor. When I came to myself I was lying on the bed. My husband was bending over me, and Roger and Mr. Blackstone were both in the room. I could not speak, but my husband understood my questioning gaze.

"Yes, yes, my love," he said quietly: "she's all right—safe and sound, thank God!"

And I did thank God.

Mr. Blackstone came to the bedside, with a look and a smile that seemed to my conscience to say, "I told you so." I held out my hand to him, but could only weep. Then I remembered how we had vexed Roger, and called him.

"Dear Roger," I said, "forgive me, and go and tell Miss Clare."

I had some reason to think this the best amends I could make him.

"I will go at once," he said. "She will be anxious."

"And I will go to my sermon," said Mr. Blackstone, with the same quiet smile.

They shook hands with me, and went away. And my husband and I rejoiced over our first-born.

# CHAPTER XXV.

## ITS SEQUEL.

My darling was recovered neither through Miss Clare's injunctions nor Mr. Blackstone's bell-ringing. A woman was walking steadily westward, carrying the child asleep in her arms, when a policeman stopped her at Turnham Green. She betrayed no fear, only annoyance, and offered no resistance, only begged he would not wake the child, or take her from her. He brought them in a cab to the police-station, whence the child was sent home. As soon as she arrived, Sarah gave her a warm bath, and put her to bed; but she scarcely opened her eyes.

Jemima had run about the streets till midnight, and then fallen asleep on the doorstep, where the policeman found her when he brought the child. For a week she went about like one dazed; and the blunders she made were marvellous. She ordered a brace of cod from the poulterer, and a pound of anchovies at the crockery shop. One day at dinner, we could not think how the chops were so pulpy, and we got so many bits of bone in our mouth: she had powerfully beaten them, as if they had been steaks. She sent up melted butter for bread-sauce, and stuffed a hare with sausages.

After breakfast, Percivale walked to the police-station, to thank the inspector, pay what expenses had been incurred, and see the woman. I was not well enough to go with him. My Marion is a white-faced thing, and her eyes look much too big for her small face. I suggested that he should take Miss Clare. As it was early, he was fortunate enough to find her at home, and she accompanied him willingly, and at once recognized the woman as the one she had befriended.

He told the magistrate he did not wish to punish her, but that there were certain circumstances which made him desirous of detaining her until a gentleman, who, he believed, could identify her, should arrive. The magistrate therefore remanded her.

The next day but one my father came. When he saw her, he had little doubt she was the same that had carried off Theo; but he could not be absolutely certain, because he had seen her only by moonlight. He told the magistrate the whole story, saying, that, if she should prove the mother of the child, he was most anxious to try what he could do for her. The magistrate expressed grave doubts whether he would find it possible to befriend her to any effectual degree. My father said he would try, if he could but be certain she was the mother.

"If she stole the child merely to compel the restitution of her own," he said. "I cannot regard her conduct with any abhorrence. But, if she is not the mother of the child, I must leave her to the severity of the law."

"I once discharged a woman," said the magistrate, "who had committed the same offence, for I was satisfied she had done so purely from the desire to possess the child."

"But might not a thief say he was influenced merely by the desire to add another sovereign to his hoard?"

"The greed of the one is a natural affection; that of the other a vice."

"But the injury to the loser is far greater in the one case than in the other."

"To set that off, however, the child is more easily discovered. Besides, the false appetite grows with indulgence; whereas one child would still the natural one."

"Then you would allow her to go on stealing child after child, until she succeeded in keeping one," said my father, laughing.

"I dismissed her with the warning, that, if ever she did so again, this would be brought up against her, and she would have the severest punishment the law could inflict. It may be right to pass a first offence, and wrong to pass a second. I tried to make her measure the injury done to the mother, by her own sorrow at losing the child; and I think not without effect. At all events, it was some years ago, and I have not heard of her again."

Now came in the benefit of the kindness Miss Clare had shown the woman. I doubt if any one else could have got the truth from her. Even she found it difficult; for to tell her that if she was Theo's mother she should not be punished, might be only to tempt her to lie. All Miss Clare could do was to assure her of the kindness of every one concerned, and to urge her to disclose her reasons for doing such a grievous wrong as steal another woman's child.

"They stole my child," she blurted out at last, when the cruelty of the action was pressed upon her.

"Oh, no!" said Miss Clare: "you left her to die in the cold."

"No, no!" she cried. "I wanted somebody to hear her, and take her in. I wasn't far off, and was just going to take her again, when I saw a light, and heard them searching for her. Oh, dear! Oh, dear!"

"Then how can you say they stole her? You would have had no child at all, but for them. She was nearly dead when they found her. And in return you go and steal their grandchild!"

"They took her from me afterwards. They wouldn't let me have my own flesh and blood. I wanted to let them know what it was to have *their* child taken from them."

"How could they tell she was your child, when you stole her away like a thief? It might, for any thing they knew, be some other woman stealing her, as you stole theirs the other day? What would have become of you if it had been so?"

To this reasoning she made no answer.

"I want my child; I want my child," she moaned. Then breaking out—"I shall kill myself if I don't get my child!" she cried. "Oh, lady, you don't know what it is to have a child and not have her! I shall kill myself if they don't give me her back. They can't say I did their child any harm. I was as good to her as if she had been my own."

"They know that quite well, and don't want to punish you. Would you like to see your child?"

She clasped her hands above her head, fell on her knees at Miss Clare's feet, and looked up in her face without uttering a word.

"I will speak to Mr. Walton," said Miss Clare; and left her.

The next morning she was discharged, at the request of my husband, who brought her home with him.

Sympathy with the mother-passion in her bosom had melted away all my resentment. She was a fine young woman, of about five and twenty, though her weather-browned complexion made her look at first much older. With the help of the servants, I persuaded her to have a bath, during which they removed her clothes, and substituted others. She objected to putting them on; seemed half-frightened at them, as if they might involve some shape of bondage, and begged to have her own again. At last Jemima, who, although so sparingly provided with brains, is not without genius, prevailed upon her, insisting that her little girl would turn away from her if she wasn't well dressed, for she had been used to see ladies about her. With a deep sigh, she yielded; begging, however, to have her old garments restored to her.

She had brought with her a small bundle, tied up in a cotton handkerchief; and from it she now took a scarf of red silk, and twisted it up with her black hair in a fashion I had never seen before. In this head-dress she had almost a brilliant look; while her carriage had a certain dignity hard of association with poverty—not inconsistent, however, with what I have since learned about the gypsies. My husband admired her even more than I did, and made a very good sketch of her. Her eyes were large and dark—unquestionably fine; and if there was not much of the light of thought in them, they had a certain wildness which in a measure made up for the want. She had rather a Spanish than an Eastern look, I thought, with an air of defiance that prevented me from feeling at ease with her; but in the presence of Miss Clare she seemed humbler, and answered her questions more readily than ours. If Ethel was in the room, her eyes would be constantly wandering after her, with a wistful, troubled, eager look. Surely, the mother-passion must have infinite relations and destinies.

As I was unable to leave home, my father persuaded Miss Clare to accompany him and help him to take charge of her. I confess it was a relief to me when she left the house; for though I wanted to be as kind to her as I could, I felt considerable discomfort in her presence.

When Miss Clare returned, the next day but one, I found she had got from her the main points of her history, fully justifying previous conjectures of my father's, founded on what he knew of the character and customs of the gypsies.

She belonged to one of the principal gypsy families in this country. The fact that they had no settled habitation, but lived in tents, like Abraham and Isaac, had nothing to do with poverty. The silver buttons on her father's coat, were, she said, worth nearly twenty pounds; and when a friend of any distinction came to tea with them, they spread a table-cloth of fine linen on the grass, and set out upon it the best of china, and a tea-service of hall-marked silver. She said her friends—as much as any gentleman in the land—scorned stealing; and affirmed that no real gypsy would "risk his neck for his belly," except he were driven by hunger. All her family could read, she said, and carried a big Bible about with them.

One summer they were encamped for several months in the neighborhood of Edinburgh, making horn-spoons and baskets, and some of them working in tin. There they were visited by a clergyman, who talked and read the Bible to them, and prayed with them. But all their visitors were not of the same sort with him. One of them was a young fellow of loose character, a clerk in the city, who, attracted by her appearance, prevailed upon her to meet him often. She was not then eighteen. Any aberration from the paths of modesty is exceedingly rare among the gypsies, and regarded with severity; and her father, hearing of this, gave her a terrible punishment with the whip he used in driving his horses. In terror of what would follow when the worst came to be known, she ran away; and, soon forsaken by her so-called lover, wandered about, a common vagrant, until her baby was born—under the stars, on a summer night, in a field of long grass.

For some time she wandered up and down, longing to join some tribe of her own people, but dreading unspeakably the disgrace of her motherhood. At length, having found a home for her child, she associated herself with a gang of gypsies of inferior character, amongst whom she had many hardships to endure. Things, however, bettered a little after one of their number was hanged for stabbing a cousin, and her position improved. It was not, however, any intention of carrying off her child to share her present lot, but the urgings of mere mother-hunger for a sight of her, that drove her to the Hall. When she had succeeded in enticing her out of sight of the house, however, the longing to possess her grew fierce; and braving all consequences, or rather, I presume, unable to weigh them, she did carry her away. Foiled in this attempt, and seeing that her chances of future success in any similar one were diminished by it, she sought some other plan. Learning that one of the family was married, and had removed to London, she succeeded, through gypsy acquaintances who lodged occasionally near Tottenham Court Road, in finding out where we lived, and carried off Ethel with the vague intent, as we had rightly conjectured, of using her as a means for the recovery of her own child.

Theodora was now about seven years of age—almost as wild as ever. Although tolerably obedient, she was not nearly so much so as the other children had been at her age; partly, perhaps, because my father could not bring himself to use that severity to the child of other people with which he had judged it proper to treat his own.

Miss Clare was present, with my father and the rest of the family, when the mother and daughter met. They were all more than curious to see how the child would behave, and whether there would be any signs of an instinct that drew her to her parent. In this, however, they were disappointed.

It was a fine warm forenoon when she came running on to the lawn where they were assembled,—the gypsy mother with them.

"There she is!" said my father to the woman. "Make the best of yourself you can."

Miss Clare said the poor creature turned very pale, but her eyes glowed with such a fire!

With the cunning of her race, she knew better than bound forward and catch up the child in her arms. She walked away from the rest, and stood watching the little damsel, romping merrily with Mr. Wagtail. They thought she recognized the dog, and was afraid of him. She had put on a few silver ornaments which she had either kept or managed to procure, notwithstanding her poverty; for both the men and women of her race manifest in a strong degree that love for barbaric adornment which, as well as their other peculiarities, points to an Eastern origin. The glittering of these in the sun, and the glow of her red scarf in her dark hair, along with the strangeness of her whole appearance, attracted the child, and she approached to look at her nearer. Then the mother took from her pocket a large gilded ball, which had probably been one of the ornaments on the top of a clock, and rolled it gleaming golden along the grass. Theo and Mr. Wagtail bounded after it with a shriek and a bark. Having examined it for a moment, the child threw it again along the lawn; and this time the mother, lithe as a leopard and fleet as a savage, joined in the chase, caught it first, and again sent it spinning away, farther from the assembled group. Once more all three followed in swift pursuit; but this time the mother took care to allow the child to seize the treasure. After the sport had continued a little while, what seemed a general consultation, of mother, child, and dog, took place over the bauble; and presently they saw that Theo was eating something.

"I trust," said my mother, "she won't hurt the child with any nasty stuff."

"She will not do so wittingly," said my father, "you may be sure. Anyhow, we must not interfere."

In a few minutes more the mother approached them with a subdued look of triumph, and her eyes overflowing with light, carrying the child in her arms. Theo was playing with some foreign coins which adorned her hair, and with a string of coral and silver beads round her neck.

For the rest of the day they were left to do much as they pleased; only every one kept good watch.

But in the joy of recovering her child, the mother seemed herself to have gained a new and childlike spirit. The more than willingness with which she hastened to do what, even in respect of her child, was requested of her, as if she fully acknowledged the right of authority in those who had been her best friends, was charming. Whether this would last when the novelty of the new experience had worn off, whether jealousy would not then come in for its share in the ordering of her conduct, remained to be shown; but in the mean time the good in her was uppermost.

She was allowed to spend a whole fortnight in making friends with her daughter, before a word was spoken about the future; the design of my father being through the child to win the mother. Certain people considered him not eager enough to convert the wicked: whatever apparent indifference he showed in that direction arose from his utter belief in the guiding of God, and his dread of outrunning his designs. He would *follow* the operations of the Spirit.

"Your forced hot-house fruits," he would say, "are often finer to look at than those which have waited for God's wind and weather; but what are they worth in respect of all for the sake of which fruit exists?"

Until an opportunity, then, was thrown in his way, he would hold back; but when it was clear to him that he had to minister, then was he thoughtful, watchful, instant, unswerving. You might have seen him during this time, as the letters of Connie informed me, often standing for minutes together watching the mother and daughter, and pondering in his heart concerning them.

Every advantage being thus afforded her, not without the stirring of some natural pangs in those who had hitherto mothered the child, the fortnight had not passed, before, to all appearance, the unknown mother was with the child the greatest favorite of all. And it was my father's expectation, for he was a profound believer in blood, that the natural and generic instincts of the child would be developed together; in other words, that as she grew in what was common to humanity, she would grow likewise in what belonged to her individual origin. This was not an altogether comforting expectation to those of us who neither had so much faith as he, nor saw so hopefully the good that lay in every evil.

One twilight, he overheard the following talk between them. When they came near where he sat, Theodora, carried by her mother, and pulling at her neck with her arms, was saying, "Tell me; tell me; tell me," in the tone of one who would compel an answer to a question repeatedly asked in vain.

"What do you want me to tell you?" said her mother. "You know well enough.
Tell me your name."

In reply, she uttered a few words my father did not comprehend, and took to be Zingaree. The child shook her petulantly and with violence, crying,—

"That's nonsense. I don't know what you say, and I don't know what to call you."

My father had desired the household, if possible, to give no name to the woman in the child's hearing.

"Call me mam, if you like."

"But you're not a lady, and I won't say ma'am to you," said Theo, rude as a child will sometimes be when least she intends offence.

Her mother set her down, and gave a deep sigh. Was it only that the child's restlessness and roughness tired her? My father thought otherwise.

"Tell me; tell me," the child persisted, beating her with her little clenched fist. "Take me up again, and tell me, or I will make you."

My father thought it time to interfere. He stepped forward. The mother started with a little cry, and caught up the child.

"Theo," said my father, "I cannot allow you to be rude, especially to one who loves you more than any one else loves you."

The woman set her down again, dropped on her knees, and caught and kissed his hand.

The child stared; but she stood in awe of my father,—perhaps the more that she had none for any one else,—and, when her mother lifted her once more, was carried away in silence.

The difficulty was got over by the child's being told to call her mother *Nurse.*

My father was now sufficiently satisfied with immediate results to carry out the remainder of his contingent plan, of which my mother heartily approved. The gardener and his wife being elderly people, and having no family, therefore not requiring the whole of their cottage, which was within a short distance of the house, could spare a room, which my mother got arranged for the gypsy; and there she was housed, with free access to her child, and the understanding that when Theo liked to sleep with her, she was at liberty to do so.

She was always ready to make herself useful; but it was little she could do for some time, and it was with difficulty that she settled to any occupation at all continuous.

Before long it became evident that her old habits were working in her and making her restless. She was pining after the liberty of her old wandering life, with sun and wind, space and change, all about her. It was spring; and the reviving life of nature was rousing in her the longing for motion and room and variety engendered by the roving centuries which had passed since first her ancestors were driven from their homes in far Hindostan. But my father had foreseen the probability, and had already thought over what could be done for her if the wandering passion should revive too powerfully. He reasoned that there was nothing bad in such an impulse,—one doubtless, which would have been felt in all its force by Abraham himself, had he quitted his tents and gone to dwell in a city,—however much its indulgence might place her at a disadvantage in the midst of a settled social order. He saw, too, that any attempt to coerce it would probably result in entire frustration; that the passion for old forms of freedom would gather tenfold vigor in consequence. It would be far better to favor its indulgence, in the hope that the love of her child would, like an elastic but infrangible cord, gradually tame her down to a more settled life.

He proposed, therefore, that she should, as a matter of duty, go and visit her parents, and let them know of her welfare. She looked alarmed.

"Your father will show you no unkindness, I am certain, after the lapse of so many years," he added. "Think it over, and tell me to-morrow how you feel about it. You shall go by train to Edinburgh, and once there you will soon be able to find them. Of course you couldn't take the child with you; but she will be safe with us till you come back."

The result was that she went; and having found her people, and spent a fortnight with them, returned in less than a month. The rest of the year she remained quietly at home, stilling her desires by frequent and long rambles with her child, in which Mr. Wagtail always accompanied them. My father thought it better to run the risk of her escaping, than force the thought of it upon her by appearing not to trust her. But it came out that she had a suspicion that the dog was there to prevent, or at least expose, any such imprudence. The following spring she went on a second visit to her friends, but was back within a week, and the next year did not go at all.

Meantime my father did what he could to teach her, presenting every truth as something it was necessary she should teach her child. With this duty, he said, he always baited the hook with which he fished for her; "or, to take a figure from the old hawking days, her eyas is the lure with which I would reclaim the haggard hawk."

What will be the final result, who dares prophesy? At my old home she still resides; grateful, and in some measure useful, idolizing, but not altogether spoiling her child, who understands the relation between them, and now calls her mother.

Dora teaches Theo, and the mother comes in for what share she inclines to appropriate. She does not take much to reading, but she is fond of listening; and is a regular and devout attendant at public worship. Above all, they have sufficing proof that her conscience is awake, and that she gives some heed to what it says.

Mr. Blackstone was right when he told me that good I was unable to foresee would result from the loss which then drowned me in despair.

# CHAPTER XXVI.

## TROUBLES.

In the beginning of the following year, the lady who filled Miss Clare's place was married, and Miss Clare resumed the teaching of Judy's children. She was now so handsomely paid for her lessons, that she had reduced the number of her engagements very much, and had more time to give to the plans in which she labored with Lady Bernard. The latter would willingly have settled such an annuity upon her as would have enabled her to devote all her time to this object; but Miss Clare felt that the earning of her bread was one of the natural ties that bound her in the bundle of social life; and that in what she did of a spiritual kind, she must be untrammelled by money-relations. If she could not do both,—provide for herself and assist others,—it would be a different thing, she said; for then it would be clear that Providence intended her to receive the hire of the laborer for the necessity laid upon her. But what influenced her chiefly was the dread of having anything she did for her friends attributed to professional motives, instead of the recognition of eternal relations. Besides, as she said, it would both lessen the means at Lady Bernard's disposal, and cause herself to feel bound to spend all her energies in that one direction; in which case she would be deprived of the recreative influences of change and more polished society. In her labor, she would yet feel her freedom, and would not serve even Lady Bernard for money, except she saw clearly that such was the will of the one Master. In thus refusing her offer, she but rose in her friend's estimation.

In the spring, great trouble fell upon the Morleys. One of the children was taken with scarlet-fever; and then another and another was seized in such rapid succession—until five of them were lying ill together—that there was no time to think of removing them. Cousin Judy would accept no assistance in nursing them, beyond that of her own maids, until her strength gave way, and she took the infection herself in the form of diphtheria; when she was compelled to take to her bed, in such agony at the thought of handing her children over to hired nurses, that there was great ground for fearing her strength would yield.

She lay moaning, with her eyes shut, when a hand was laid on hers, and Miss Clare's voice was in her ear. She had come to give her usual lesson to one of the girls who had as yet escaped the infection: for, while she took every precaution, she never turned aside from her work for any dread of consequences; and when she heard that Mrs. Morley had been taken ill, she walked straight to her room.

"Go away!" said Judy. "Do you want to die too?"

"Dear Mrs. Morley," said Miss Clare, "I will just run home, and make a few arrangements, and then come back and nurse you."

"Never mind me," said Judy. "The children! the children! What *shall* I do?"

"I am quite able to look after you all—if you will allow me to bring a young woman to help me."

"You are an angel!" said poor Judy. "But there is no occasion to bring any one with you. My servants are quite competent."

"I must have every thing in my own hands," said Miss Clare; "and therefore must have some one who will do exactly as I tell her. This girl has been with me now for some time, and I can depend upon her. Servants always look down upon governesses."

"Do whatever you like, you blessed creature," said Judy. "If any one of my servants behaves improperly to you, or neglects your orders, she shall go as soon as I am up again."

"I would rather give them as little opportunity as I can of running the risk. If I may bring this friend of my own, I shall soon have the house under hospital regulations. But I have been talking too much. I might almost have returned by this time. It is a bad beginning if I have hurt you already by saying more than was necessary."

She had hardly left the room before Judy had fallen asleep, so much was she relieved by the offer of her services. Ere she awoke, Marion was in a cab on her way back to Bolivar Square, with her friend and two carpet-bags. Within an hour, she had intrenched herself in a spare bedroom, had lighted a fire, got encumbering finery out of the way, arranged all the medicines on a chest of drawers, and set the clock on the mantle-piece going; made the round of the patients, who were all in adjoining rooms, and the round of the house, to see that the disinfectants were fresh and active, added to their number, and then gone to await the arrival of the medical attendant in Mrs. Morley's room.

"Dr. Brand might have been a little more gracious," said Judy; "but I thought it better not to interrupt him by explaining that you were not the professional nurse he took you for."

"Indeed, there was no occasion," answered Miss Clare. "I should have told him so myself, had it not been that I did a nurse's regular work in St. George's Hospital for two months, and have been there for a week or so, several times since, so that I believe I have earned the right to be spoken to as such. Anyhow, I understood every word he said."

Meeting Mr. Morley in the hall, the doctor advised him not to go near his wife, diphtheria being so infectious; but comforted him with the assurance that the nurse appeared an intelligent young person, who would attend to all his directions; adding,—

"I could have wished she had been older; but there is a great deal of illness about, and experienced nurses are scarce."

Miss Clare was a week in the house before Mr. Morley saw her, or knew she was there. One evening she ran down to the dining-room, where he sat over his lonely glass of Madeira, to get some brandy, and went straight to the sideboard. As she turned to leave the room, he recognized her, and said, in some astonishment,—

"You need not trouble yourself, Miss Clare. The nurse can get what she wants from Hawkins. Indeed, I don't see"—

"Excuse me, Mr. Morley. If you wish to speak to me, I will return in a few minutes; but I have a good deal to attend to just at this moment."

She left the room; and, as he had said nothing in reply, did not return.

Two days after, about the same hour, whether suspecting the fact, or for some other reason, he requested the butler to send the nurse to him.

"The nurse from the nursery, sir; or the young person as teaches the young ladies the piano?" asked Hawkins.

"I mean the sick-nurse," said his master.

In a few minutes Miss Clare entered the dining-room, and approached Mr. Morley.

"How do you do, Miss Clare?" he said stiffly; for to any one in his employment he was gracious only now and then. "Allow me to say that I doubt the propriety of your being here so much. You cannot fail to carry the infection. I think your lessons had better be postponed until *all* your pupils are able to benefit by them. I have just sent for the nurse; and,—if you please"—

"Yes. Hawkins told me you wanted me," said Miss Clare.

"I did not want you. He must have mistaken."

"I am the nurse, Mr. Morley."

"Then I *must* say it is not with my approval," he returned, rising from his chair in anger. "I was given to understand that a properly-qualified person was in charge of my wife and family. This is no ordinary case, where a little coddling is all that is wanted."

"I am perfectly qualified, Mr. Morley."

He walked up and down the room several times.

"I must speak to Mrs. Morley about this." he said.

"I entreat you will not disturb her. She is not so well this afternoon."

"How *is* this, Miss Clare? Pray explain to me how it is that you come to be taking a part in the affairs of the family so very different from that for which Mrs. Morley—which—was arranged between Mrs. Morley and yourself."

"It is but an illustration of the law of supply and demand," answered Marion. "A nurse was wanted; Mrs. Morley had strong objections to a hired nurse, and I was very glad to be able to set her mind at rest."

"It was very obliging in you, no doubt," he returned, forcing the admission; "but—but"—

"Let us leave it for the present, if you please; for while I am nurse, I must mind my business. Dr. Brand expresses himself quite satisfied with me, so far as we have gone; and it is better for the children, not to mention Mrs. Morley, to have some one about them they are used to."

She left the room without waiting further parley.

Dr. Brand, however, not only set Mr. Morley's mind at rest as to her efficiency, but when a terrible time of anxiety was at length over, during which one after another, and especially Judy herself, had been in great danger, assured him that, but for the vigilance and intelligence of Miss Clare, joined to a certain soothing influence which she exercised over every one of her patients, he did not believe he could have brought Mrs. Morley through. Then, indeed, he changed his tone to her, in a measure, still addressing her as from a height of superiority.

They had recovered so far that they were to set out the next morning for Hastings, when he thus addressed her, having sent for her once more to the dining-room:—

"I hope you will accompany them, Miss Clare," he said. "By this time you must be in no small need of a change yourself."

"The best change for me will be Lime Court," she answered, laughing.

"Now, pray don't drive your goodness to the verge of absurdity," he said pleasantly.

"Indeed, I am anxious about my friends there," she returned. "I fear they have not been getting on quite so well without me. A Bible-woman and a Roman Catholic have been quarrelling dreadfully, I hear."

Mr. Morley compressed his lips. It *was* annoying to be so much indebted to one who, from whatever motives, called such people her friends.

"Oblige me, then," he said loftily, taking an envelope from the mantle-piece, and handing it to her, "by opening that at your leisure."

"I will open it now, if you please," she returned.

It contained a bank-note for a hundred pounds. Mr. Morley, though a hard man, was not by any means stingy. She replaced it in the envelope, and laid it again on the chimney-piece.

"You owe me nothing, Mr. Morley," she said.

"Owe you nothing! I owe you more than I can ever repay."

"Then don't try it, please. You are *very* generous; but indeed I could not accept it."

"You must oblige me. You *might* take it from *me*," he added, almost pathetically, as if the bond was so close that money was nothing between them.

"You are the last—one of the last I *could* take money from, Mr. Morley."

"Why?"

"Because you think so much of it, and yet would look down on me the more if
I accepted it."

He bit his lip, rubbed his forehead with his hand, threw back his head, and turned away from her.

"I should be very sorry to offend you," she said; "and, believe me, there is hardly any thing I value less than money. I have enough, and could have plenty more if I liked. I would rather have your friendship than all the money you possess. But that cannot be, so long as"—

She stopped: she was on the point of going too far, she thought.

"So long as what?" he returned sternly.

"So long as you are a worshipper of Mammon," she answered; and left the room.

She burst out crying when she came to this point. She had narrated the whole with the air of one making a confession.

"I am afraid it was very wrong," she said; "and if so, then it was very rude as well. But something seemed to force it out of me. Just think: there was a generous heart, clogged up with self-importance and wealth! To me, as he stood there on the hearth-rug, he was a most pitiable object—with an impervious wall betwixt him and the kingdom of heaven! He seemed like a man in a terrible dream, from which I *must* awake him by calling aloud in his ear—except that, alas! the dream was not terrible to him, only to me! If he had been one of my poor friends, guilty of some plain fault, I should have told him so without compunction; and why not, being what he was? There he stood,—a man of estimable qualities, of beneficence, if not bounty; no miser, nor consciously unjust; yet a man whose heart the moth and rust were eating into a sponge!—who went to church every Sunday, and had many friends, not one of whom, not even his own wife, would tell him that he was a Mammon-worshipper, and losing his life. It may have been useless, it may have been wrong; but I felt driven to it by bare human pity for the misery I saw before me."

"It looks to me as if you had the message given you to give him," I said.

"But—though I don't know it—what if I was annoyed with him for offering me that wretched hundred pounds,—in doing which he was acting up to the light that was in him?"

I could not help thinking of the light which is darkness, but I did not say so. Strange tableau, in this our would-be grand nineteenth century,—a young and poor woman prophet-like rebuking a wealthy London merchant on his own hearth-rug, as a worshipper of Mammon! I think she was right; not because he was wrong, but because, as I firmly believe, she did it from no personal motives whatever, although in her modesty she doubted herself. I believe it was from pure regard for the man and for the truth, urging her to an irrepressible utterance. If so, should we not say that she spoke by the Spirit? Only I shudder to think what utterance might, with an equal outward show, be attributed to the same Spirit. Well, to his own master every one standeth or falleth; whether an old prophet who, with a lie in his right hand, entraps an honorable guest, or a young prophet who, with repentance in his heart, walks calmly into the jaws of the waiting lion. [Footnote: See the Sermons of the Rev. Henry Whitehead, vicar of St. John's, Limehouse; as remarkable for the profundity of their insight us for the noble severity of their literary modelling.—G.M.D.]

And no one can tell what effects the words may have had upon him. I do not believe he ever mentioned the circumstance to his wife. At all events, there was no change in her manner to Miss Clare. Indeed, I could not help fancying that a little halo of quiet reverence now encircled the love in every look she cast upon her.

She firmly believed that Marion had saved her life, and that of more than one of her children. Nothing, she said, could equal the quietness and tenderness and tirelessness of her nursing. She was never flurried, never impatient, and never frightened. Even when the tears would be flowing down her face, the light never left her eyes nor the music her voice; and when they were all getting better, and she had the nursery piano brought out on the landing in the middle of the sick-rooms, and there played and sung to them, it was, she said, like the voice of an angel, come fresh to the earth, with the same old news of peace and good-will. When the children—this I had from the friend she brought with her—were tossing in the fever, and talking of strange and frightful things they saw, one word from her would quiet them; and her gentle, firm command was always sufficient to make the most fastidious and rebellious take his medicine.

She came out of it very pale, and a good deal worn. But the day they set off for Hastings, she returned to Lime Court. The next day she resumed her lessons, and soon recovered her usual appearance. A change of work, she always said, was the best restorative. But before a month was over I succeeded in persuading her to accept my mother's invitation to spend a week at the Hall; and from this visit she returned quite invigorated. Connie, whom she went to see,—for by this time she was married to Mr. Turner,—was especially delighted with her delight in the simplicities of nature. Born and bred in the closest town-environment, she had yet a sensitiveness to all that made the country so dear to us who were born in it, which Connie said surpassed ours, and gave her special satisfaction as proving that my oft recurring dread lest such feelings might but be the result of childish associations was groundless, and that they were essential to the human nature, and so felt by God himself. Driving along in the pony-carriage,—for Connie is not able to walk much, although she is well enough to enjoy life thoroughly,—Marion would remark upon ten things in a morning, that my sister had never observed. The various effects of light and shade, and the variety of feeling they caused, especially interested her. She would spy out a lurking sunbeam, as another would find a hidden flower. It seemed as if not a glitter in its nest of gloom could escape her. She would leave the carriage, and make a long round through the fields or woods, and, when they met at the appointed spot, would have her hands full not of flowers only, but of leaves and grasses and weedy things, showing the deepest interest in such lowly forms as few would notice except from a scientific knowledge, of which she had none: it was the thing itself—its look and its home—that drew her attention. I cannot help thinking that this insight was profoundly one with her interest in the corresponding regions of human life and circumstance.

# CHAPTER XXVII.

## MISS CLARE AMONGST HER FRIENDS.

I must give an instance of the way in which Marion—I am tired of calling her *Miss Clare*, and about this time I began to drop it—exercised her influence over her friends. I trust the episode, in a story so fragmentary as mine, made up of pieces only of a quiet and ordinary life, will not seem unsuitable. How I wish I could give it you as she told it to me! so graphic was her narrative, and so true to the forms of speech amongst the London poor. I must do what I can, well assured it must come far short of the original representation.

One evening, as she was walking up to her attic, she heard a noise in one of the rooms, followed by a sound of weeping. It was occupied by a journeyman house-painter and his wife, who had been married several years, but whose only child had died about six months before, since which loss things had not been going on so well between them. Some natures cannot bear sorrow: it makes them irritable, and, instead of drawing them closer to their own, tends to isolate them. When she entered, she found the woman crying, and the man in a lurid sulk.

"What *is* the matter?" she asked, no doubt in her usual cheerful tone.

"I little thought it would come to this when I married him," sobbed the woman, while the man remained motionless and speechless on his chair, with his legs stretched out at full length before him.

"Would you mind telling me about it? There may be some mistake, you know."

"There ain't no mistake in *that*," said the woman, removing the apron she had been holding to her eyes, and turning a cheek towards Marion, upon which the marks of an open-handed blow were visible enough. "I didn't marry him to be knocked about like that."

"She calls that knocking about, do she?" growled the husband. "What did she go for to throw her cotton gownd in my teeth for, as if it was my blame she warn't in silks and satins?"

After a good deal of questioning on her part, and confused and recriminative statement on theirs, Marion made out the following as the facts of the case:—

For the first time since they were married, the wife had had an invitation to spend the evening with some female friends. The party had taken place the night before; and although she had returned in ill-humor, it had not broken out until just as Marion entered the house. The cause was this: none of the guests were in a station much superior to her own, yet she found herself the only one who had not a silk dress: hers was a print, and shabby. Now, when she was married, she had a silk dress, of which she said her husband had been proud enough when they were walking together. But when she saw the last of it, she saw the last of its sort, for never another had he given her to her back; and she didn't marry him to come down in the world—that she didn't!

"Of course not," said Marion. "You married him because you loved him, and thought him the finest fellow you knew."

"And so he was then, grannie. But just look at him now!"

The man moved uneasily, but without bending his outstretched legs. The fact was, that since the death of the child he had so far taken to drink that he was not unfrequently the worse for it; which had been a rare occurrence before.

"It ain't my fault," he said, "when work ain't a-goin,' if I don't dress her like a duchess. I'm as proud to see my wife rigged out as e'er a man on 'em; and that *she* know! and when she cast the contrairy up to me, I'm blowed if I could keep my hands off on her. She ain't the woman I took her for, miss. She *'ave* a temper!"

"I don't doubt it," said Marion. "Temper is a troublesome thing with all of us, and makes us do things we're sorry for afterwards. *You*'re sorry for striking her—ain't you, now?"

There was no response. Around the sullen heart silence closed again. Doubtless he would have given much to obliterate the fact, but he would not confess that he had been wrong. We are so stupid, that confession seems to us to fix the wrong upon us, instead of throwing it, as it does, into the depths of the eternal sea.

"I may have my temper," said the woman, a little mollified at finding, as she thought, that Miss Clare took her part; "but here am I, slaving from morning to night to make both ends meet, and goin' out every job I can get a-washin' or a-charin', and never 'avin' a bit of fun from year's end to year's end, and him off to his club, as he calls it!—an' it's a club he's like to blow out my brains with some night, when he comes home in a drunken fit; for it's worse *and* worse he'll get, miss, like the rest on 'em, till no woman could be proud, as once I was, to call him hers. And when I do go out to tea for once in a way, to be jeered at by them as is no better nor no worse 'n myself, acause I ain't got a husband as cares enough for me to dress me decent!—that do stick i' my gizzard. I do dearly love to have neighbors think my husband care a bit about me, let-a-be 'at he don't, one hair; and when he send me out like that"—

Here she broke down afresh.

"Why didn't ye stop at home then? I didn't tell ye to go," he said fiercely, calling her a coarse name.

"Richard," said Marion, "such words are not fit for *me* to hear, still less for your own wife."

"Oh! never mind me: I'm used to sich," said the woman spitefully.

"It's a lie," roared the man: "I never named sich a word to ye afore. It do make me mad to hear ye. I drink the clothes off your back, do I? If I bed the money, ye might go in velvet and lace for aught I cared!"

"*She* would care little to go in gold and diamonds, if *you* didn't care to see her in them," said Marion.

At this the woman burst into fresh tears, and the man put on a face of contempt,—the worst sign, Marion said, she had yet seen in him, not excepting the blow; for to despise is worse than to strike.

I can't help stopping my story here to put in a reflection that forces itself upon me. Many a man would regard with disgust the idea of striking his wife, who will yet cherish against her an aversion which is infinitely worse. The working-man who strikes his wife, but is sorry for it, and tries to make amends by being more tender after it, a result which many a woman will consider cheap at the price of a blow endured,—is an immeasurably superior husband to the gentleman who shows his wife the most absolute politeness, but uses that very politeness as a breastwork to fortify himself in his disregard and contempt.

Marion saw that while the tides ran thus high, nothing could be done; certainly, at least, in the way of argument. Whether the man had been drinking she could not tell, but suspected that must have a share in the evil of his mood. She went up to him, laid her hand on his shoulder, and said,—

"You're out of sorts, Richard. Come and have a cup of tea, and I will sing to you."

"I don't want no tea."

"You're fond of the piano, though. And you like to hear me sing, don't you?"

"Well, I do," he muttered, as if the admission were forced from him.

"Come with me, then."

He dragged himself up from his chair, and was about to follow her.

"You ain't going to take him from me, grannie, after he's been and struck me?" interposed his wife, in a tone half pathetic, half injured.

"Come after us in a few minutes," said Marion, in a low voice, and led the way from the room.

Quiet as a lamb Richard followed her up stairs. She made him sit in the easy-chair, and began with a low, plaintive song, which she followed with other songs and music of a similar character. He neither heard nor saw his wife enter, and both sat for about twenty minutes without a word spoken. Then Marion made a pause, and the wife rose and approached her husband. He was fast asleep.

"Don't wake him," said Marion; "let him have his sleep out. You go down and get the place tidy, and a nice bit of supper for him—if you can."

"Oh, yes! he brought me home his week's wages this very night."

"The whole?"

"Yes, grannie"

"Then weren't you too hard upon him? Just think: he had been trying to behave himself, and had got the better of the public-house for once, and come home fancying you'd be so pleased to see him; and you"—

"He'd been drinking," interrupted Eliza. "Only he said as how it was but a pot of beer he'd won in a wager from a mate of his."

"Well, if, after that beginning, he yet brought you home his money, he ought to have had another kind of reception. To think of the wife of a poor man making such a fuss about a silk dress! Why, Eliza, I never had a silk dress in my life; and I don't think I ever shall."

"Laws, grannie! who'd ha' thought that now!"

"You see I have other uses for my money than buying things for show."

"That you do, grannie! But you see," she added, somewhat inconsequently, "we ain't got no child, and Dick he take it ill of me, and don't care to save his money; so he never takes me out nowheres, and I do be so tired o' stopping indoors, every day and all day long, that it turns me sour, I do believe. I didn't use to be cross-grained, miss. But, laws! I feels now as if I'd let him knock me about ever so, if only he wouldn't say as how it was nothing to him if I was dressed ever so fine."

"You run and get his supper."

Eliza went; and Marion, sitting down again to her instrument, improvised for an hour. Next to her New Testament, this was her greatest comfort. She sung and prayed both in one then, and nobody but God heard any thing but the piano. Nor did it impede the flow of her best thoughts, that in a chair beside her slumbered a weary man, the waves of whose evil passions she had stilled, and the sting of whose disappointments she had soothed, with the sweet airs and concords of her own spirit. Who could say what tender influences might not be stealing over him, borne on the fair sounds? for even the formless and the void was roused into life and joy by the wind that roamed over the face of its deep. No humanity jarred with hers. In the presence of the most degraded, she felt God there. A face, even if besotted, *was* a face, only in virtue of being in the image of God. That a man was a man at all, must be because he was God's. And this man was far indeed from being of the worst. With him beside her, she could pray with most of the good of having the door of her closet shut, and some of the good of the gathering together as well. Thus was love, as ever, the assimilator of the foreign, the harmonizer of the unlike; the builder of the temple in the desert, and of the chamber in the market-place.

As she sat and discoursed with herself, she perceived that the woman was as certainly suffering from *ennui* as any fine lady in Mayfair.

"Have you ever been to the National Gallery, Richard?" she asked, without turning her head, the moment she heard him move.

"No, grannie," he answered with a yawn. "Don'a' most know what sort of a place it be now. Waxwork, ain't it?"

"No. It's a great place full of pictures, many of them hundreds of years old. They're taken care of by the Government, just for people to go and look at. Wouldn't you like to go and see them some day?"

"Donno as I should much."

"If I were to go with you, now, and explain some of them to you? I want you to take your wife and me out for a holiday. You can't think, you who go out to your work every day, how tiresome it is to be in the house from morning to night, especially at this time of the year, when the sun's shining, and the very sparrows trying to sing!"

"She may go out when she please, grannie. I ain't no tyrant."

"But she doesn't care to go without you. You wouldn't have her like one of those slatternly women you see standing at the corners, with their fists in their sides and their elbows sticking out, ready to talk to anybody that comes in the way."

"*My* wife was never none o' sich, grannie. I knows her as well's e'er a one, though she do 'ave a temper of her own."

At this moment Eliza appeared in the door-way, saying,—

"Will ye come to yer supper, Dick? I ha' got a slice o' ham an' a hot tater for ye. Come along."

"Well, I don't know as I mind—jest to please *you*, Liza. I believe I ha' been asleep in grannie's cheer there, her a playin' an' a singin', I make no doubt, like a werry nightingerl, bless her, an' me a snorin' all to myself, like a runaway locomotive! Won't *you* come and have a slice o' the 'am, an' a tater, grannie? The more you ate, the less we'd grudge it."

"I'm sure o' that," chimed in Eliza. "Do now, grannie; please do."

"I will, with pleasure," said Marion; and they went down together.

Eliza had got the table set out nicely, with a foaming jug of porter beside the ham and potatoes. Before they had finished, Marion had persuaded Richard to take his wife and her to the National Gallery, the next day but one, which, fortunately for her purpose, was Whit Monday, a day whereon Richard, who was from the north always took a holiday.

At the National Gallery, the house-painter, in virtue of his craft, claimed the exercise of criticism; and his remarks were amusing enough. He had more than once painted a sign-board for a country inn, which fact formed a bridge between the covering of square yards with color and the painting of pictures; and he naturally used the vantage-ground thus gained to enhance his importance with his wife and Miss Clare. He was rather a clever fellow too, though as little educated in any other direction than that of his calling as might well be.

All the woman seemed to care about in the pictures was this or that something which reminded her, often remotely enough I dare say, of her former life in the country. Towards the close of their visit, they approached a picture—one of Hobbima's, I think—which at once riveted her attention.

"Look, look, Dick!" she cried. "There's just such a cart as my father used to drive to the town in. Farmer White always sent *him* when the mistress wanted any thing and he didn't care to go hisself. And, O Dick! there's the very moral of the cottage we lived in! Ain't it a love, now?"

"Nice enough," Dick replied. "But it warn't there I seed you, Liza. It wur at the big house where you was housemaid, you know. That'll be it, I suppose,—away there like, over the trees."

They turned and looked at each other, and Marion turned away. When she looked again, they were once more gazing at the picture, but close together, and hand in hand, like two children.

As they went home in the omnibus, the two averred they had never spent a happier holiday in their lives; and from that day to this no sign of their quarrelling has come to Marion's knowledge. They are not only her regular attendants on Saturday evenings, but on Sunday evenings as well, when she holds a sort of conversation-sermon with her friends.

# CHAPTER XXVIII.

## MR. MORLEY.

As soon as my cousin Judy returned from Hastings, I called to see her, and found them all restored, except Amy, a child of between eight and nine. There was nothing very definite the matter with her, but she was white and thin, and looked wistful; the blue of her eyes had grown pale, and her fair locks had nearly lost the curl which had so well suited her rosy cheeks. She had been her father's pride for her looks, and her mother's for her sayings,—at once odd and simple. Judy that morning reminded me how, one night, when she was about three years old, some time after she had gone to bed, she had called her nurse, and insisted on her mother's coming. Judy went, prepared to find her feverish; for there had been jam-making that day, and she feared she had been having more than the portion which on such an occasion fell to her share. When she reached the nursery, Amy begged to be taken up that she might say her prayers over again. Her mother objected; but the child insisting, in that pretty, petulant way which so pleased her father, she yielded, thinking she must have omitted some clause in her prayers, and be therefore troubled in her conscience. Amy accordingly kneeled by the bedside in her night-gown, and, having gone over all her petitions from beginning to end, paused a moment before the final word, and inserted the following special and peculiar request: "And, p'ease God, give me some more jam to-morrow-day, for ever and ever. Amen."

I remember my father being quite troubled when he heard that the child had been rebuked for offering what was probably her very first genuine prayer. The rebuke, however, had little effect on the equanimity of the petitioner, for she was fast asleep a moment after it.

"There is one thing that puzzles and annoys me," said Judy. "I can't think what it means. My husband tells me that Miss Clare was so rude to him, the day before we left for Hastings, that he would rather not be aware of it any time she is in the house. Those were his very words. 'I will not interfere with your doing as you think proper,' he said, 'seeing you consider yourself under such obligation to her; and I should be sorry to deprive her of the advantage of giving lessons in a house like this; but I wish you to be careful that the girls do not copy her manners. She has not by any means escaped the influence of the company she keeps.' I was utterly astonished, you may well think; but I could get no further explanation from him. He only said that when I wished to have her society of an evening, I must let him know, because he would then dine at his club. Not knowing the grounds of his offence, there was little other argument I could use than the reiteration of my certainty that he must have misunderstood her. 'Not in the least,' he said. 'I have no doubt she is to you every thing amiable; but she has taken some unaccountable aversion to me, and loses no opportunity of showing it. And I *don't* think I deserve it.' I told him I was so sure he did not deserve it, that I must believe there was some mistake. But he only shook his head and raised his newspaper. You must help me, little coz."

"How am I to help you, Judy dear?" I returned. "I can't interfere between husband and wife, you know. If I dared such a thing, he would quarrel with me too—and rightly."

"No, no," she returned, laughing: "I don't want your intercession. I only want you to find out from Miss Clare whether she knows how she has so mortally offended my husband. I believe she knows nothing about it. She *has* a rather abrupt manner sometimes, you know; but then my husband is not so silly as to have taken such deep offence at that. Help me, now—there's a dear!"

I promised I would, and hence came the story I have already given. But Marion was so distressed at the result of her words, and so anxious that Judy should not be hurt, that she begged me, if I could manage it without a breach of verity, to avoid disclosing the matter; especially seeing Mr. Morley himself judged it too heinous to impart to his wife.

How to manage it I could not think. But at length we arranged it between us. I told Judy that Marion confessed to having said something which had offended Mr. Morley; that she was very sorry, and hoped she need not say that such had not been her intention, but that, as Mr. Morley evidently preferred what had passed between them to remain unmentioned, to disclose it would be merely to swell the mischief. It would be better for them all, she requested me to say, that she should give up her lessons for the present; and therefore she hoped Mrs. Morley would excuse her. When I gave the message, Judy cried, and said nothing. When the children heard that Marion was not coming for a while, Amy cried, the other girls looked very grave, and the boys protested.

I have already mentioned that the fault I most disliked in those children was their incapacity for being petted. Something of it still remains; but of late I have remarked a considerable improvement in this respect. They have not only grown in kindness, but in the gift of receiving kindness. I cannot but attribute this, in chief measure, to their illness and the lovely nursing of Marion. They do not yet go to their mother for petting, and from myself will only endure it; but they are eager after such crumbs as Marion, by no means lavish of it, will vouchsafe them.

Judy insisted that I should let Mr. Morley hear Marion's message.

"But the message is not to Mr. Morley," I said. "Marion would never have thought of sending one to him."

"But if I ask you to repeat it in his hearing, you will not refuse?"

To this I consented; but I fear she was disappointed in the result. Her husband only smiled sarcastically, drew in his chin, and showed himself a little more cheerful than usual.

One morning, about two months after, as I was sitting in the drawing-room, with my baby on the floor beside me, I was surprised to see Judy's brougham pull up at the little gate—for it was early. When she got out, I perceived at once that something was amiss, and ran to open the door. Her eyes were red, and her cheeks ashy. The moment we reached the drawing-room, she sunk on the couch and burst into tears.

"Judy!" I cried, "what *is* the matter? Is Amy worse?"

"No, no, cozzy dear; but we are ruined. We haven't a penny in the world. The children will be beggars."

And there were the gay little horses champing their bits at the door, and the coachman sitting in all his glory, erect and impassive!

I did my best to quiet her, urging no questions. With difficulty I got her to swallow a glass of wine, after which, with many interruptions and fresh outbursts of misery, she managed to let me understand that her husband had been speculating, and had failed. I could hardly believe myself awake. Mr. Morley was the last man I should have thought capable either of speculating, or of failing in it if he did.

Knowing nothing about business, I shall not attempt to explain the particulars. Coincident failures amongst his correspondents had contributed to his fall. Judy said he had not been like himself for months; but it was only the night before that he had told her they must give up their house in Bolivar Square, and take a small one in the suburbs. For any thing he could see, he said, he must look out for a situation.

"Still you may be happier than ever, Judy. I can tell you that happiness does not depend on riches," I said, though I could not help crying with her.

"It's a different thing though, after you've been used to them," she answered. "But the question is of bread for my children, not of putting down my carriage."

She rose hurriedly.

"Where are you going? Is there any thing I can do for you?" I asked.

"Nothing," she answered. "I left my husband at Mr. Baddeley's. He is as rich as Croesus, and could write him a check that would float him."

"He's too rich to be generous, I'm afraid," I said.

"What do you mean by that?" she asked.

"If he be so generous, how does it come that he is so rich?"

"Why, his father made the money."

"Then he most likely takes after his father. Percivale says he does not believe a huge fortune was ever made of nothing, without such pinching of one's self and such scraping of others, or else such speculation, as is essentially dishonorable."

"He stands high," murmured Judy hopelessly.

"Whether what is dishonorable be also disreputable depends on how many there are of his own sort in the society in which he moves."

"Now, coz, you know nothing to his discredit, and he's our last hope."

"I will say no more," I answered. "I hope I may be quite wrong. Only I should expect nothing of *him*."

When she reached Mr. Baddeley's her husband was gone. Having driven to his counting-house, and been shown into his private room, she found him there with his head between his hands. The great man had declined doing any thing for him, and had even rebuked him for his imprudence, without wasting a thought on the fact that every penny he himself possessed was the result of the boldest speculation on the part of his father. A very few days only would elapse before the falling due of certain bills must at once disclose the state of his affairs.

As soon as she had left me, Percivale not being at home, I put on my bonnet, and went to find Marion. I must tell *her* every thing that caused me either joy or sorrow; and besides, she had all the right that love could give to know of Judy's distress. I knew all her engagements, and therefore where to find her; and sent in my card, with the pencilled intimation that I would wait the close of her lesson. In a few minutes she came out and got into the cab. At once I told her my sad news.

"Could you take me to Cambridge Square to my next engagement?" she said.

I was considerably surprised at the cool way in which she received the communication, but of course I gave the necessary directions.

"Is there any thing to be done?" she asked, after a pause.

"I know of nothing," I answered.

Again she sat silent for a few minutes.

"One can't move without knowing all the circumstances and particulars," she said at length. "And how to get at them? He wouldn't make a confidante of *me*," she said, smiling sadly.

"Ah! you little think what vast sums are concerned in such a failure as his!" I remarked, astounded that one with her knowledge of the world should talk as she did.

"It will be best," she said, after still another pause, "to go to Mr. Blackstone. He has a wonderful acquaintance with business for a clergyman, and knows many of the city people."

"What could any clergyman do in such a case?" I returned. "For Mr. Blackstone, Mr. Morley would not accept even consolation at his hands."

"The time for that is not come yet," said Marion. "We must try to help him some other way first. We will, if we can, make friends with him by means of the very Mammon that has all but ruined him."

She spoke of the great merchant just as she might of Richard, or any of the bricklayers or mechanics, whose spiritual condition she pondered that she might aid it.

"But what could Mr. Blackstone do?" I insisted.

"All I should want of him would be to find out for me what Mr. Morley's liabilities are, and how much would serve to tide him over the bar of his present difficulties. I suspect he has few friends who would risk any thing for him. I understand he is no favorite in the city; and, if friendship do not come in, he must be stranded. You believe him an honorable man,—do you not?" she asked abruptly.

"It never entered my head to doubt it," I replied.

The moment we reached Cambridge Square she jumped out, ran up the steps, and knocked at the door. I waited, wondering if she was going to leave me thus without a farewell. When the door was opened, she merely gave a message to the man, and the same instant was again in the cab by my side.

"Now I am free!" she said, and told the man to drive to Mile End.

"I fear I can't go with you so far, Marion," I said. "I must go home—I have so much to see to, and you can do quite as well without me. I don't know what you intend, but *please* don't let any thing come out. I can trust *you*, but"—

"If you can trust me, I can trust Mr. Blackstone. He is the most cautious man in the world. Shall I get out, and take another cab?"

"No. You can drop me at Tottenham Court Road, and I will go home by omnibus. But you must let me pay the cab."

"No, no; I am richer than you: I have no children. What fun it is to spend money for Mr. Morley, and lay him under an obligation he will never know!" she said, laughing.

The result of her endeavors was, that Mr. Blackstone, by a circuitous succession of introductions, reached Mr. Morley's confidential clerk, whom he was able so far to satisfy concerning his object in desiring the information, that he made him a full disclosure of the condition of affairs, and stated what sum would be sufficient to carry them over their difficulties; though, he added, the greatest care, and every possible reduction of expenditure for some years, would be indispensable to their complete restoration.

Mr. Blackstone carried his discoveries to Miss Clare and she to Lady Bernard.

"My dear Marion," said Lady Bernard, "this is a serious matter you suggest. The man may be honest, and yet it may be of no use trying to help him. I don't want to bolster him up for a few months in order to see my money go after his. That's not what I've got to do with it. No doubt I could lose as much as you mention, without being crippled by it, for I hope it's no disgrace in me to be rich, as it's none in you to be poor; but I hate waste, and I will *not* be guilty of it. If Mr. Morley will convince me and any friend or man of business to whom I may refer the matter, that there is good probability of his recovering himself by means of it, then, and not till then, I shall feel justified in risking the amount. For, as you say, it would prevent much misery to many besides that good-hearted creature, Mrs. Morley, and her children. It is worth doing if it can be done—not worth trying if it can't."

"Shall I write for you, and ask him to come and see you?"

"No, my dear. If I do a kindness, I must do it humbly. It is a great liberty to take with a man to offer him a kindness. I must go to him. I could not use the same freedom with a man in misfortune as with one in prosperity. I would have such a one feel that his money or his poverty made no difference to me; and Mr. Morley wants that lesson, if any man does. Besides, after all, I may not be able to do it for him, and he would have good reason to be hurt if I had made him dance attendance on me."

The same evening Lady Bernard's shabby one-horse-brougham stopped at Mr. Morley's door. She asked to see Mrs. Morley, and through her had an interview with her husband. Without circumlocution, she told him that if he would lay his affairs before her and a certain accountant she named, to use their judgment regarding them in the hope of finding it possible to serve him, they would wait upon him for that purpose at any time and place he pleased. Mr. Morley expressed his obligation,—not very warmly, she said,—

repudiating, however, the slightest objection to her ladyship's knowing now what all the world must know the next day but one.

Early the following morning Lady Bernard and the accountant met Mr. Morley at his place in the city, and by three o'clock in the afternoon fifteen thousand pounds were handed in to his account at his banker's.

The carriage was put down, the butler, one of the footmen, and the lady's maid, were dismissed, and household arrangements fitted to a different scale.

One consequence of this chastisement, as of the preceding, was, that the whole family drew yet more closely and lovingly together; and I must say for Judy, that, after a few weeks of what she called poverty, her spirits seemed in no degree the worse for the trial.

At Marion's earnest entreaty no one told either Mr. or Mrs. Morley of the share she had had in saving his credit and social position. For some time she suffered from doubt as to whether she had had any right to interpose in the matter, and might not have injured Mr. Morley by depriving him of the discipline of poverty; but she reasoned with herself, that, had it been necessary for him, her efforts would have been frustrated; and reminded herself, that, although his commercial credit had escaped, it must still be a considerable trial to him to live in reduced style.

But that it was not all the trial needful for him, was soon apparent; for his favorite Amy began to pine more rapidly, and Judy saw, that, except some change speedily took place, they could not have her with them long. The father, however, refused to admit the idea that she was in danger. I suppose he felt as if, were he once to allow the possibility of losing her, from that moment there would be no stay between her and the grave: it would be a giving of her over to death. But whatever Dr. Brand suggested was eagerly followed. When the chills of autumn drew near, her mother took her to Ventnor; but little change followed, and before the new year she was gone. It was the first death, beyond that of an infant, they had had in their family, and took place at a time when the pressure of business obligations rendered it impossible for her father to be out of London: he could only go to lay her in the earth, and bring back his wife. Judy had never seen him weep before. Certainly I never saw such a change in a man. He was literally bowed with grief, as if he bore a material burden on his back. The best feelings of his nature, unimpeded by any jar to his self-importance or his prejudices, had been able to spend themselves on the lovely little creature; and I do not believe any other suffering than the loss of such a child could have brought into play that in him which was purely human.

He was at home one morning, ill for the first time in his life, when Marion called on Judy. While she waited in the drawing-room, he entered. He turned the moment he saw her, but had not taken two steps towards the door, when he turned again, and approached her. She went to meet him. He held out his hand.

"She was very fond of you, Miss Clare," he said. "She was talking about you the very last time I saw her. Let by-gones be by-gones between us."

"I was very rough and rude to you, Mr. Morley, and I am very sorry," said Marion.

"But you spoke the truth," he rejoined. "I thought I was above being spoken to like a sinner, but I don't know now why not."

He sat down on a couch, and leaned his head on his hand. Marion took a chair near him, but could not speak.

"It is very hard," he murmured at length.

"Whom the Lord loveth he chasteneth," said Marion.

"That may be true in some cases, but I have no right to believe it applies to me. He loved the child, I would fain believe; for I dare not think of her either as having ceased to be, or as alone in the world to which she has gone. You do think, Miss Clare, do you not, that we shall know our friends in another world?"

"I believe," answered Marion, "that God sent you that child for the express purpose of enticing you back to himself; and, if I believe any thing at all, I believe that the gifts of God are without repentance."

Whether or not he understood her she could not tell, for at this point Judy came in. Seeing them together she would have withdrawn again; but her husband called her, with more tenderness in his voice than Marion could have imagined belonging to it.

"Come, my dear. Miss Clare and I were talking about our little angel. I didn't think ever to speak of her again, but I fear I am growing foolish. All the strength is out of me; and I feel so tired,—so weary of every thing!"

She sat down beside him, and took his hand. Marion crept away to the children. An hour after, Judy found her in the nursery, with the youngest on her knee, and the rest all about her. She was telling them that we were sent into this world to learn to be good, and then go back to God from whom we came, like little Amy.

"When I go out to-mowwow," said one little fellow, about four years old, "I'll look up into the sky vewy hard, wight up; and then I shall see Amy, and God saying to her, 'Hushaby, poo' Amy! You bette' now, Amy?' Sha'n't

I,
Mawion?"

She had taught them to call her Marion.

"No, my pet: you might look and look, all day long, and every day, and never see God or Amy."

"Then they *ain't* there!" he exclaimed indignantly.

"God is there, anyhow," she answered; "only you can't see him that way."

"I don't care about seeing God," said the next elder: "it's Amy I want to see. Do tell me, Marion, how we are to see Amy. It's too bad if we're never to see her again; and I don't think it's fair."

"I will tell you the only way I know. When Jesus was in the world, he told us that all who had clean hearts should see God. That's how Jesus himself saw God."

"It's Amy, I tell you, Marion—it's not God I want to see," insisted the one who had last spoken.

"Well, my dear, but how can you see Amy if you can't even see God? If Amy be in God's arms, the first thing, in order to find her, is to find God. To be good is the only way to get near to anybody. When you're naughty, Willie, you can't get near your mamma, can you?"

"Yes, I can. I can get close up to her."

"Is that near enough? Would you be quite content with that? Even when she turns away her face and won't look at you?"

The little caviller was silent.

"Did you ever see God, Marion?" asked one of the girls.

She thought for a moment before giving an answer. "No," she said. "I've seen things just after he had done them; and I think I've heard him speak to me; but I've never seen him yet."

"Then you're not good, Marion," said the free-thinker of the group.

"No: that's just it. But I hope to be good some day, and then I *shall* see him."

"How do you grow good, Marion?" asked the girl.

"God is always trying to make me good," she answered; "and I try not to interfere with him."

"But sometimes you forget, don't you?"

"Yes, I do."

"And what do you do then?"

"Then I'm sorry and unhappy, and begin to try again."

"And God don't mind much, does he?"

"He minds very much until I mind; but after that he forgets it all,—takes all my naughtiness and throws it behind his back, and won't look at it."

"That's very good of God," said the reasoner, but with such a self-satisfied air in his approval, that Marion thought it time to stop.

She came straight to me, and told me, with a face perfectly radiant, of the alteration in Mr. Morley's behavior to her, and, what was of much more consequence, the evident change that had begun to be wrought in him.

I am not prepared to say that he has, as yet, shown a very shining light, but that some change has passed is evident in the whole man of him. I think the eternal wind must now be able to get in through some chink or other which the loss of his child has left behind. And, if the change were not going on, surely he would ere now have returned to his wallowing in the mire of Mammon; for his former fortune is, I understand, all but restored to him.

I fancy his growth in goodness might be known and measured by his progress in appreciating Marion. He still regards her as extreme in her notions; but it is curious to see how, as they gradually sink into his understanding, he comes to adopt them as, and even to mistake them for, his own.

# CHAPTER XXIX.

## A STRANGE TEXT.

For some time after the events last related, things went on pretty smoothly with us for several years. Indeed, although I must confess that what I said in my haste, when Mr. S. wanted me to write this book, namely, that nothing had ever happened to me worth telling, was by no means correct, and that I have found out my mistake in the process of writing it; yet, on the other hand, it must be granted that my story could never have reached the mere bulk required if I had not largely drawn upon the history of my friends to supplement my own. And it needs no prophetic gift to foresee that it will be the same to the end of the book. The lives of these friends, however, have had so much to do with all that is most precious to me in our own life, that, if I were to leave out only all that did not immediately touch upon the latter, the book, whatever it might appear to others, could not possibly then appear to myself any thing like a real representation of my actual life and experiences. The drawing might be correct,—but the color?

What with my children, and the increase of social duty resulting from the growth of acquaintance,—occasioned in part by my success in persuading Percivale to mingle a little more with his fellow-painters,—my heart and mind and hands were all pretty fully occupied; but I still managed to see Marion two or three times a week, and to spend about so many hours with her, sometimes alone, sometimes with her friends as well. Her society did much to keep my heart open, and to prevent it from becoming selfishly absorbed in its cares for husband and children. For love which is *only* concentrating its force, that is, which is not at the same time widening its circle, is itself doomed, and for its objects ruinous, be those objects ever so sacred. God himself could never be content that his children should love him only; nor has he allowed the few to succeed who have tried after it: perhaps their divinest success has been their most mortifying failure. Indeed, for exclusive love sharp suffering is often sent as the needful cure,—needful to break the stony crust, which, in the name of love for one's own, gathers about the divinely glowing core; a crust which, promising to cherish by keeping in the heat, would yet gradually thicken until all was crust; for truly, in things of the heart and spirit, as the warmth ceases to spread, the molten mass within ceases to glow, until at length, but for the divine care and discipline, there would be no love left for even spouse or child, only for self,—which is eternal death.

For some time I had seen a considerable change in Roger. It reached even to his dress. Hitherto, when got up for dinner, he was what I was astonished to hear my eldest boy, the other day, call "a howling swell;" but at other times he did not even escape remark,—not for the oddity merely, but the slovenliness of his attire. He had worn, for more years than I dare guess, a brown coat, of some rich-looking stuff, whose long pile was stuck together in many places with spots and dabs of paint, so that he looked like our long-haired Bedlington terrier Fido, towards the end of the week in muddy weather. This was now discarded; so far at least, as to be hung up in his brother's study, to be at hand when he did any thing for him there, and replaced by a more civilized garment of tweed, of which he actually showed himself a little careful: while, if his necktie *was* red, it was of a very deep and rich red, and he had seldom worn one at all before; and his brigand-looking felt hat was exchanged for one of half the altitude, which he did not crush on his head with quite as many indentations as its surface could hold. He also began to go to church with us sometimes.

But there was a greater and more significant change than any of these. We found that he was sticking more steadily to work. I can hardly say *his* work; for he was Jack-of-all-trades, as I have already indicated. He had a small income, left him by an old maiden aunt with whom he had been a favorite, which had hitherto seemed to do him nothing but harm, enabling him to alternate fits of comparative diligence with fits of positive idleness. I have said also, I believe, that, although he could do nothing thoroughly, application alone was wanted to enable him to distinguish himself in more than one thing. His forte was engraving on wood; and my husband said, that, if he could do so well with so little practice as he had had, he must be capable of becoming an admirable engraver. To our delight, then, we discovered, all at once, that he had been working steadily for three months for the Messrs. D——, whose place was not far from our house. He had said nothing about it to his brother, probably from having good reason to fear that he would regard it only as a *spurt*. Having now, however, executed a block which greatly pleased himself, he had brought a proof impression to show Percivale; who, more pleased with it than even Roger himself, gave him a hearty congratulation, and told him it would be a shame if he did not bring his execution in that art to perfection; from which, judging by the present specimen, he said it could not be far off. The words brought into Roger's face an expression of modest gratification which it rejoiced me to behold: he accepted Percivale's approbation more like a son than a brother, with a humid glow in his eyes and hardly a word on his lips. It seemed to me that the child in his heart had begun to throw off the swaddling clothes which foolish manhood had wrapped around it, and the germ of his being was about to assert itself. I have seldom indeed seen Percivale look so pleased.

"Do me a dozen as good as that," he said, "and I'll have the proofs framed in silver gilt."

It *has* been done; but the proofs had to wait longer for the frame than Percivale for the proofs.

But he need have held out no such bribe of brotherly love, for there was another love already at work in himself more than sufficing to the affair. But I check myself: who shall say what love is sufficing for this or for that? Who, with the most enduring and most passionate love his heart can hold, will venture to say that he could have done without the love of a brother? Who will say that he could have done without the love of the dog whose bones have lain mouldering in his garden for twenty years? It is enough to say that there was a more engrossing, a more marvellous love at work.

Roger always, however, took a half-holiday on Saturdays, and now generally came to us. On one of these occasions I said to him,—

"Wouldn't you like to come and hear Marion play to her friends this evening, Roger?"

"Nothing would give me greater pleasure," he answered; and we went.

It was delightful. In my opinion Marion is a real artist. I do not claim for her the higher art of origination, though I could claim for her a much higher faculty than the artistic itself. I suspect, for instance, that Moses was a greater man than the writer of the Book of Job, notwithstanding that the poet moves me so much more than the divine politician. Marion combined in a wonderful way the critical faculty with the artistic; which two, however much of the one may be found without the other, are mutually essential to the perfection of each. While she uttered from herself, she heard with her audience; while she played and sung with her own fingers and mouth, she at the same time listened with their ears, knowing what they must feel, as well as what she meant to utter. And hence it was, I think, that she came into such vital contact with them, even through her piano.

As we returned home, Roger said, after some remark of mine of a cognate sort,—

"Does she never try to teach them any thing, Ethel?"

"She is constantly teaching them, whether she tries or not," I answered. "If you can make any one believe that there is something somewhere to be trusted, is not that the best lesson you can give him? That can be taught only by being such that people cannot but trust you."

"I didn't need to be told that," he answered. "What I want to know is, whether or not she ever teaches them by word of mouth,—an ordinary and inferior mode, if you will."

"If you had ever heard her, you would not call hers an ordinary or inferior mode," I returned. "Her teaching is the outcome of her life, the blossom of her being, and therefore has the whole force of her living truth to back it."

"Have I offended you, Ethel?" he asked.

Then I saw, that, in my eagerness to glorify my friend, I had made myself unpleasant to Roger,—a fault of which I had been dimly conscious before now. Marion would never have fallen into that error. She always made her friends feel that she was *with* them, side by side with them, and turning her face in the same direction, before she attempted to lead them farther.

I assured him that he had not offended me, but that I had been foolishly backing him from the front, as I once heard an Irishman say,—some of whose bulls were very good milch cows.

"She teaches them every Sunday evening," I added.

"Have you ever heard her?"

"More than once. And I never heard any thing like it."

"Could you take me with you some time?" he asked, in an assumed tone of ordinary interest, out of which, however, he could not keep a slight tremble.

"I don't know. I don't quite see why I shouldn't. And yet"—

"Men do go," urged Roger, as if it were a mere half-indifferent suggestion.

"Oh, yes! you would have plenty to keep you in countenance!" I returned,—"men enough—and worth teaching, too—some of them at least!"

"Then, I don't see why she should object to me for another."

"I don't know that she would. You are not exactly of the sort, you know—that"—

"I don't see the difference. I see no essential difference, at least. The main thing is, that I am in want of teaching, as much as any of them. And, if she stands on circumstances, I am a working-man as much as any of them—perhaps more than most of them. Few of them work after midnight, I should think, as I do, not unfrequently."

"Still, all admitted, I should hardly like"—

"I didn't mean you were to take me without asking her," he said: "I should never have dreamed of that."

"And if I were to ask her, I am certain she would refuse. But," I added, thinking over the matter a little, "I will take you without asking her. Come with me to-morrow night. I don't think she will have the heart to send you away."

"I will," he answered, with more gladness in his voice than he intended, I think, to manifest itself.

We arranged that he should call for me at a certain hour.

I told Percivale, and he pretended to grumble that I was taking Roger instead of him.

"It was Roger, and not you, that made the request," I returned. "I can't say I see why you should go because Roger asked. A woman's logic is not equal to that."

"I didn't mean he wasn't to go. But why shouldn't I be done good to as well as he?"

"If you really want to go," I said, "I don't see why you shouldn't. It's ever so much better than going to any church I know of—except one. But we must be prudent. I can't take more than one the first time. We must get the thin edge of the wedge in first."

"And you count Roger the thin edge?"

"Yes."

"I'll tell him so."

"Do. The thin edge, mind, without which the thicker the rest is the more useless! Tell him that if you like. But, seriously, I quite expect to take you there, too, the Sunday after."

Roger and I went. Intending to be a little late, we found when we readied the house, that, as we had wished, the class was already begun. In going up the stairs, we saw very few of the grown inhabitants, but in several of the rooms, of which the doors stood open, elder girls taking care of the younger children; in one, a boy nursing the baby with as much interest as any girl could have shown. We lingered on the way, wishing to give Marion time to get so thoroughly into her work that she could take no notice of our intrusion. When we reached the last stair we could at length hear her voice, of which the first words we could distinguish, as we still ascended, were,—

"I will now read to you the chapter of which I spoke."

The door being open, we could hear well enough, although she was sitting where we could not see her. We would not show ourselves until the reading was ended: so much, at least, we might overhear without offence.

Before she had read many words, Roger and I began to cast strange looks on each other. For this was the chapter she read:—

"And Joseph, wheresoever he went in the city, took the Lord Jesus with him, where he was sent for to work, to make gates, or milk-pails, or sieves, or boxes; the Lord Jesus was with him wheresoever he went. And as often as Joseph had any thing in his work to make longer or shorter, or wider or narrower, the Lord Jesus would stretch his hand towards it. And presently it became as Joseph would have it. So that he had no need to finish any thing with his own hands, for he was not very skilful at his carpenter's trade.

"On a certain time the king of Jerusalem sent for him, and said, I would have thee make me a throne of the same dimensions with that place in which I commonly sit. Joseph obeyed, and forthwith began the work, and continued two years in the king's palace before he finished. And when he came to fix it in its place, he found it wanted two spans on each side of the appointed measure. Which, when the king saw, he was very angry with Joseph; and Joseph, afraid of the king's anger, went to bed without his supper, taking not any thing to eat. Then the Lord Jesus asked him what he was afraid of. Joseph replied, Because I have lost my labor in the work which I have been about these two years. Jesus said to him, Fear not, neither be cast down; do thou lay hold on one side of the throne, and I will the other, and we will bring it to its just dimensions. And when Joseph had done as the Lord Jesus said, and each of them had with strength drawn his side, the throne obeyed, and was brought to the proper dimensions of the place; which miracle when they who stood by saw, they were astonished, and praised God. The throne was made of the same wood which was in being in Solomon's time, namely, wood adorned with various shapes and figures."

Her voice ceased, and a pause followed.

"We must go in now," I whispered.

"She'll be going to say something now; just wait till she's started," said Roger.

"Now, what do you think of it?" asked Marion in a meditative tone.

We crept within the scope of her vision, and stood. A voice, which I knew, was at the moment replying to her question.

"*I* don't think it's much of a chapter, that, grannie."

The speaker was the keen-faced, elderly man, with iron-gray whiskers, who had come forward to talk to Percivale on that miserable evening when we were out searching for little Ethel. He sat near where we stood by the door, between two respectable looking women, who had been listening to the chapter as devoutly as if it had been of the true gospel.

"Sure, grannie, that ain't out o' the Bible?" said another voice, from somewhere farther off.

"We'll talk about that presently," answered Marion.

"I want to hear what Mr. Jarvis has to say to it: he's a carpenter himself, you see,—a joiner, that is, you know."

All the faces in the room were now turned towards Jarvis.

"Tell me why you don't think much of it, Mr. Jarvis," said Marion.

"'Tain't a bit likely," he answered.

"What isn't likely?"

"Why, not one single thing in the whole kit of it. And first and foremost, 'tain't a bit likely the old man 'ud ha' been sich a duffer."

"Why not? There must have been stupid people then as well as now."

"Not *his* father." said Jarvis decidedly.

"He wasn't but his step-father, like, you know, Mr. Jarvis," remarked the woman beside him in a low voice.

"Well, he'd never ha' been *hers*, then. *She* wouldn't ha' had a word to say to *him*."

"I have seen a good—and wise woman too—with a dull husband," said Marion.

"You know you don't believe a word of it yourself, grannie," said still another voice.

"Besides," she went on without heeding the interruption, "in those times, I suspect, such things were mostly managed by the parents, and the woman herself had little to do with them."

A murmur of subdued indignation arose,—chiefly of female voices.

"Well, *they* wouldn't then," said Jarvis.

"He might have been rich," suggested Marion.

"I'll go bail *he* never made the money then," said Jarvis. "An old idget! I don't believe sich a feller 'ud ha' been *let* marry a woman like her—I *don't*."

"You mean you don't think God would have let him?"

"Well, that's what I *do* mean, grannie. The thing couldn't ha' been, nohow."

"I agree with you quite. And now I want to hear more of what in the story you don't consider likely."

"Well, it ain't likely sich a workman 'ud ha' stood so high i' the trade that the king of Jerusalem would ha' sent for *him* of all the tradesmen in the town to make his new throne for him. No more it ain't likely—and let him be as big a duffer as ever was, to be a jiner at all—that he'd ha' been two year at work on that there throne—an' a carvin' of it in figures too!—and never found out it was four spans too narrer for the place it had to stand in. Do ye 'appen to know now, grannie, how much is a span?"

"I don't know. Do you know, Mrs. Percivale?"

The sudden reference took me very much by surprise; but I had not forgotten, happily, the answer I received to the same question, when anxious to realize the monstrous height of Goliath.

"I remember my father telling me," I replied, "that it was as much as you could stretch between your thumb and little finger."

"There!" cried Jarvis triumphantly, parting the extreme members of his right hand against the back of the woman in front of him—"that would be seven or eight inches! Four times that? Two foot and a half at least! Think of that!"

"I admit the force of both your objections," said Marion. "And now, to turn to a more important part of the story, what do you think of the way in which according to it he got his father out of his evil plight?"

I saw plainly enough that she was quietly advancing towards some point in her view,—guiding the talk thitherward, steadily, without haste or effort.

Before Jarvis had time to make any reply, the blind man, mentioned in a former chapter, struck in, with the tone of one who had been watching his opportunity.

"*I* make more o' that pint than the t'other," he said. "A man as is a duffer may well make a mull of a thing; but a man as knows what he's up to can't. I don't make much o' them miracles, you know, grannie—that is, I don't know, and what I don't know, I won't say as I knows; but what I'm sure of is this here one thing,—that man or boy as *could* work a miracle, you know, grannie, wouldn't work no miracle as there wasn't no good working of."

"It was to help his father," suggested Marion.

Here Jarvis broke in almost with scorn.

"To help him to pass for a clever fellow, when he was as great a duffer as ever broke bread!"

"I'm quite o' your opinion, Mr. Jarvis," said the blind man. "It 'ud ha' been more like him to tell his father what a duffer he was, and send him home to learn his trade."

"He couldn't do that, you know," said Marion gently. "He *couldn't* use such words to his father, if he were ever so stupid."

"His step-father, grannie," suggested the woman who had corrected Jarvis on the same point. She spoke very modestly, but was clearly bent on holding forth what light she had.

"Certainly, Mrs. Renton; but you know he couldn't be rude to any one,—leaving his own mother's husband out of the question."

"True for you, grannie," returned the woman.

"I think, though," said Jarvis, "for as hard as he'd ha' found it, it would ha' been more like him to set to work and teach his father, than to scamp up his mulls."

"Certainly," acquiesced Marion. "To hide any man's faults, and leave him not only stupid, but, in all probability, obstinate and self-satisfied, would not be like *him*. Suppose our Lord had had such a father: what do you think he would have done?"

"He'd ha' done all he could to make a man of him," answered Jarvis.

"Wouldn't he have set about making him comfortable then, in spite of his blunders?" said Marion.

A significant silence followed this question.

"Well, *no*; not first thing, I don't think," returned Jarvis at length. "He'd ha' got him o' some good first, and gone in to make him comfortable arter."

"Then I suppose you would rather be of some good and uncomfortable, than of no good and comfortable?" said Marion.

"I hope so, grannie," answered Jarvis; and "*I* would;" "Yes;" "That I would," came from several voices in the little crowd, showing what an influence Marion must have already had upon them.

"Then," she said,—and I saw by the light which rose in her eyes that she was now coming to the point,—"Then, surely it must be worth our while to bear discomfort in order to grow of some good! Mr. Jarvis has truly said, that, if Jesus had had such a father, he would have made him of some good before he made him comfortable: that is just the way your Father in heaven is acting with you. Not many of you would say you are of much good yet; but you would like to be better. And yet,—put it to yourselves,—do you not grumble at every thing that comes to you that you don't like, and call it bad luck, and worse—yes, even when you know it comes of your own fault, and nobody else's? You think if you had only this or that to make you comfortable, you would be content; and you call it very hard that So-and-so should be getting on well, and saving money, and you down on your luck, as you say. Some of you even grumble that your neighbors' children should be healthy when yours are pining. You would allow that you are not of much good yet; but you forget that to make you comfortable as you are would be the same as to pull out Joseph's misfitted thrones and doors, and make his misshapen buckets over again for him. That you think so absurd that you can't believe the story a bit; but you would be helped out of all *your* troubles, even those you bring on yourselves, not thinking what the certain consequence would be, namely, that you would grow of less and less value, until you were of no good, either to God or man. If you think about it, you will see that I am right. When, for instance, are you most willing to do right? When are you most ready to hear about good things? When are you most inclined to pray to God? When you have plenty of money in your pockets, or when you are in want? when you have had a good dinner, or when you have not enough to get one? when you are in jolly health, or when the life seems ebbing out of you in misery and pain? No matter that you may have brought it on yourselves; it is no less God's way of bringing you back to him, for he decrees that suffering shall follow sin: it is just then you most need it; and, if it drives you to God, that is its end, and there will be an end of it. The prodigal was himself to blame for the want that made him a beggar at the swine's trough; yet that want was the greatest blessing God could give to him, for it drove him home to his father.

"But some of you will say you are no prodigals; nor is it your fault that you find yourselves in such difficulties that life seems hard to you. It would be very wrong in me to set myself up as your judge, and to tell you that it *was* your fault. If it is, God will let you know it. But if it be not your fault, it does not follow that you need the less to be driven back to God. It is not only in punishment of our sins that we are made to suffer: God's runaway children must be brought back to their home and their blessedness,—back to their Father in heaven. It is not always a sign that God is displeased with us when he makes us suffer. 'Whom the Lord loveth he chasteneth, and scourgeth every son whom he receiveth. If ye endure chastening, God dealeth with you as with sons.' But instead of talking more about it, I must take it to myself; and learn not to grumble when *my* plans fail."

"That's what *you* never goes and does, grannie," growled a voice from somewhere.

I learned afterwards it was that of a young tailor, who was constantly quarrelling with his mother.

"I think I have given up grumbling at my circumstances," she rejoined; "but then I have nothing to grumble at in them. I haven't known hunger or cold for a great many years now. But I do feel discontented at times when I see some of you not getting better so fast as I should like. I ought to have patience, remembering how patient God is with my conceit and stupidity, and not expect too much of you. Still, it can't be wrong to wish that you tried a good deal more to do what he wants of you. Why should his children not be his friends? If you would but give yourselves up to him, you would find his yoke so easy, his burden so light! But you do it half only, and some of you not at all.

"Now, however, that we have got a lesson from a false gospel, we may as well get one from the true."

As she spoke, she turned to her New Testament which lay beside her. But Jarvis interrupted her.

"Where did you get that stuff you was a readin' of to us, grannie?" he asked.

"The chapter I read to you," she answered, "is part of a pretended gospel, called, 'The First Gospel of the Infancy of Jesus Christ.' I can't tell you who wrote it, or how it came to be written. All I can say is, that, very early in the history of the church, there were people who indulged themselves in inventing things about Jesus, and seemed to have had no idea of the importance of keeping to facts, or, in other words, of speaking and writing only the truth. All they seemed to have cared about was the gratifying of their own feelings of love and veneration; and so they made up tales about him, in his honor as they supposed, no doubt, just as if he had been a false god of the Greeks or Romans. It is long before some people learn to speak the truth, even after they know it is wicked to lie. Perhaps, however, they did not expect their stories to be received as facts, intending them only as a sort of recognized fiction about him,—amazing presumption at the best."

"Did anybody, then, ever believe the likes of that, grannie?" asked Jarvis.

"Yes: what I read to you seems to have been believed within a hundred years after the death of the apostles. There are several such writings, with a great deal of nonsense in them, which were generally accepted by Christian people for many hundreds of years."

"I can't imagine how anybody could go inwentuating such things!" said the blind man.

"It is hard for us to imagine. They could not have seen how their inventions would, in later times, be judged any thing but honoring to him in whose honor they wrote them. Nothing, be it ever so well invented, can be so good as the bare truth. Perhaps, however, no one in particular invented some of them, but the stories grew, just as a report often does amongst yourselves. Although everybody fancies he or she is only telling just what was told to him or her, yet, by degrees, the pin's-point of a fact is covered over with lies upon lies, almost everybody adding something, until the report has grown to be a mighty falsehood. Why, you had such a story yourselves, not so very long ago, about one of your best friends! One comfort is, such a story is sure not to be consistent with itself; it is sure to show its own falsehood to any one who is good enough to doubt it, and who will look into it, and examine it well. You don't, for instance, want any other proof than the things themselves to show you that what I have just read to you can't be true."

"But then it puzzles me to think how anybody could believe them," said the blind man.

"Many of the early Christians were so childishly simple that they would believe almost any thing that was told them. In a time when such nonsense could be written, it is no great wonder there should be many who could believe it."

"Then, what was their faith worth," said the blind man, "if they believed false and true all the same?"

"Worth no end to them," answered Marion with eagerness; "for all the false things they might believe about him could not destroy the true ones, or prevent them from believing in Jesus himself, and bettering their ways for his sake. And as they grew better and better, by doing what he told them, they would gradually come to disbelieve this and that foolish or bad thing."

"But wouldn't that make them stop believing in him altogether?"

"On the contrary, it would make them hold the firmer to all that they saw to be true about him. There are many people, I presume, in other countries, who believe those stories still; but all the Christians I know have cast aside every one of those writings, and keep only to those we call the Gospels. To throw away what is not true, because it is not true, will always help the heart to be truer; will make it the more anxious to cleave to what it sees must be true. Jesus remonstrated with the Jews that they would not of themselves judge what was right; and the man who lets God teach him is made abler to judge what is right a thousand-fold."

"Then don't you think it likely this much is true, grannie,"—said Jarvis, probably interested in the question, in part at least, from the fact that he was himself a carpenter,—"that he worked with his father, and helped him in his trade?"

"I do, indeed," answered Marion. "I believe that is the one germ of truth in the whole story. It is possible even that some incidents of that part of his life may have been handed down a little way, at length losing all their shape, however, and turning into the kind of thing I read to you. Not to mention that they called him the carpenter, is it likely he who came down for the express purpose of being a true man would see his father toiling to feed him and his mother and his brothers and sisters, and go idling about, instead of putting to his hand to help him? Would that have been like him?"

"Certainly not," said Mr. Jarvis.

But a doubtful murmur came from the blind man, which speedily took shape in the following remark:—

"I can't help thinkin', grannie, of one time—you read it to us not long ago—when he laid down in the boat and went fast asleep, takin' no more heed o' them a slavin' o' theirselves to death at their oars, than if they'd been all comfortable like hisself; that wasn't much like takin' of his share—was it now?"

"John Evans," returned Marion with severity, "it is quite right to put any number of questions, and express any number of doubts you honestly feel; but you have no right to make remarks you would not make if you were anxious to be as fair to another as you would have another be to you. Have you considered that he had been working hard all day long, and was, in fact, worn out? You don't think what hard work it is, and how exhausting, to speak for hours to great multitudes, and in the open air too, where your voice has no help to make it heard. And that's not all; for he had most likely been healing many as well; and I believe every time the power went out of him to cure, he suffered in the relief he gave; it left him weakened,—with so much the less of strength to support his labors,—so that, even in his very body, he took our iniquities and bare our infirmities. Would you, then, blame a weary man, whose perfect faith in God rendered it impossible for him to fear any thing, that he lay down to rest in God's name, and left his friends to do their part for the redemption of the world in rowing him to the other side of the lake,—a thing they were doing every other day of their lives? You ought to consider before you make such remarks, Mr. Evans. And you forget also that the moment they called him, he rose to help them."

"And find fault with them," interposed Evans, rather viciously I thought.

"Yes; for they were to blame for their own trouble, and ought to send it away."

"What! To blame for the storm? How could they send that away?"

"Was it the storm that troubled them then? It was their own fear of it. The storm could not have troubled them if they had had faith in their Father in heaven."

"They had good cause to be afraid of it, anyhow."

"He judged they had not, for he was not afraid himself. You judge they had, because you would have been afraid."

"He could help himself, you see."

"And they couldn't trust either him or his Father, notwithstanding all he had done to manifest himself and his Father to them. Therefore he saw that the storm about them was not the thing that most required rebuke."

"I never pretended to much o' the sort," growled Evans. "Quite the contrairy."

"And why? Because, like an honest man, you wouldn't pretend to what you hadn't got. But, if you carried your honesty far enough, you would have taken pains to understand our Lord first. Like his other judges, you condemn him beforehand. You will not call that honesty?"

"I don't see what right you've got to badger me like this before a congregation o' people," said the blind man, rising in indignation. "If I ain't got my heyesight, I ha' got my feelin's."

"And do you think *he* has no feelings, Mr. Evans? You have spoken evil of *him*: I have spoken but the truth of *you*!"

"Come, come, grannie," said the blind man, quailing a little; "don't talk squash. I'm a livin' man afore the heyes o' this here company, an' he ain't nowheres. Bless you, *he* don't mind!"

"He minds so much," returned Marion, in a subdued voice, which seemed to tremble with coming tears, "that he will never rest until you think fairly of him. And he is here now; for he said, 'I am with you alway, to the end of the world;' and he has heard every word you have been saying against him. He isn't angry like me; but your words may well make him feel sad—for your sake, John Evans—that you should be so unfair."

She leaned her forehead on her hand, and was silent. A subdued murmur arose. The blind man, having stood irresolute for a moment, began to make for the door, saying,—

"I think I'd better go. I ain't wanted here."

"If you *are* an honest man, Mr. Evans," returned Marion, rising, "you will sit down and hear the case out."

With a waving, fin-like motion of both his hands, Evans sank into his seat, and spoke no word.

After but a moment's silence, she resumed as if there had been no interruption.

"That he should sleep, then, during the storm was a very different thing from declining to assist his father in his workshop; just as the rebuking of the sea was a very different thing from hiding up his father's bad work in miracles. Had that father been in danger, he might perhaps have aided him as he did the disciples. But"—

"Why do you say *perhaps*, grannie?" interrupted a bright-eyed boy who sat on the hob of the empty grate. "Wouldn't he help his father as soon as his disciples?"

"Certainly, if it was good for his father; certainly not, if it was not good for him: therefore I say *perhaps*. But now," she went on, turning to the joiner, "Mr. Jarvis, will you tell me whether you think the work of the carpenter's son would have been in any way distinguishable from that of another man?"

"Well, I don't know, grannie. He wouldn't want to be putting of a private mark upon it. He wouldn't want to be showing of it off—would he? He'd use his tools like another man, anyhow."

"All that we may be certain of. He came to us a man, to live a man's life, and do a man's work. But just think a moment. I will put the question again: Do you suppose you would have been able to distinguish his work from that of any other man?"

A silence followed. Jarvis was thinking. He and the blind man were of the few that can think. At last his face brightened.

"Well, grannie," he said, "I think it would be very difficult in any thing easy, but very easy in any thing difficult."

He laughed,—for he had not perceived the paradox before uttering it.

"Explain yourself, if you please, Mr. Jarvis. I am not sure that I understand you," said Marion.

"I mean, that, in an easy job, which any fair workman could do well enough, it would not be easy to tell his work. But, where the job was difficult, it would be so much better done, that it would not be difficult to see the better hand in it."

"I understand you, then, to indicate, that the chief distinction would lie in the quality of the work; that whatever he did, he would do in such a thorough manner, that over the whole of what he turned out, as you would say, the perfection of the work would be a striking characteristic. Is that it?"

"That is what I do mean, grannie."

"And that is just the conclusion I had come to myself."

"*I* should like to say just one word to it, grannie, so be you won't cut up crusty," said the blind man.

"If you are fair, I sha'n't be crusty, Mr. Evans. At least, I hope not," said Marion.

"Well, it's this: Mr. Jarvis he say as how the jiner-work done by Jesus Christ would be better done than e'er another man's,—tip-top fashion,—and there would lie the differ. Now, it do seem to me as I've got no call to come to that 'ere conclusion. You been tellin' on us, grannie, I donno how long now, as how Jesus Christ was the Son of God, and that he come to do the works of God,—down here like, afore our faces, that we might see God at work, by way of. Now, I ha' nothin' to say agin that: it may be, or it mayn't be—I can't tell. But if that be the way on it, then I don't see how Mr. Jarvis can be right; the two don't curryspond,—not by no means. For the works o' God—there ain't one on'em as I can see downright well managed—tip-top jiner's work, as I may say; leastways,—Now stop a bit, grannie; don't trip a man up, and then say as he fell over his own dog,—leastways, I don't say about the moon an' the stars an' that; I dessay the sun he do get up the werry moment he's called of a mornin', an' the moon when she ought to for her night-work,—I ain't no 'stronomer strawnry, and I ain't heerd no complaints about *them*; but I do say as how, down here, we ha' got most uncommon bad weather more'n at times; and the walnuts they turns out, every now an' then, full o' mere dirt; an' the oranges awful. There 'ain't been a good crop o' hay, they tells me, for many's the year. An' i' furren parts, what wi' earthquakes an' wolcanies an' lions an' tigers, an' savages as eats their wisiters, an' chimley-pots blowin' about, an' ships goin' down, an' fathers o' families choked an' drownded an' burnt i' coal-pits by the hundred,—it do seem to me that if his jinerin' hadn't been tip-top, it would ha' been but like the rest on it. There, grannie! Mind, I mean no offence; an' I don't doubt you ha' got somethink i' your weskit pocket as 'll turn it all topsy-turvy in a moment. Anyhow, I won't purtend to nothink, and that's how it look to me."

"I admit," said Marion, "that the objection is a reasonable one. But why do you put it, Mr. Evans, in such a triumphant way, as if you were rejoiced to think it admitted of no answer, and believed the world would be ever so much better off if the storms and the tigers had it all their own way, and there were no God to look after things."

"Now, you ain't fair to *me*, grannie. Not avin' of my heyesight like the rest on ye, I may be a bit fond of a harguyment; but I tries to hit fair, and when I hears what ain't logic, I can no more help comin' down upon it than I can help breathin' the air o' heaven. And why shouldn't I? There ain't no law agin a harguyment. An' more an' over, it do seem to me as how you and Mr. Jarvis is wrong i' *it is* harguyment."

"If I was too sharp upon you, Mr. Evans, and I may have been," said Marion, "I beg your pardon."

"It's granted, grannie."

"I don't mean, you know, that I give in to what you say,—not one bit."

"I didn't expect it of you. I'm a-waitin' here for you to knock me down."

"I don't think a mere victory is worth the breath spent upon it," said Marion. "But we should all be glad to get or give more light upon any subject, if it be by losing ever so many arguments. Allow me just to put a question or two to Mr. Jarvis, because he's a joiner himself—and that's a great comfort to me to-night: What would you say, Mr. Jarvis, of a master who planed the timber he used for scaffolding, and tied the crosspieces with ropes of silk?"

"I should say he was a fool, grannie,—not only for losin' of his money and his labor, but for weakenin' of his scaffoldin',—summat like the old throne-maker i' that chapter, I should say."

"What's the object of a scaffold, Mr. Jarvis?"

"To get at something else by means of,—say build a house."

"Then, so long as the house was going up all right, the probability is there wouldn't be much amiss with the scaffold?"

"Certainly, provided it stood till it was taken down."

"And now, Mr. Evans," she said next, turning to the blind man, "I am going to take the liberty of putting a question or two to you."

"All right, grannie. Fire away."

"Will you tell me, then, what the object of this world is?"

"Well, most people makes it their object to get money, and make theirselves comfortable."

"But you don't think that is what the world was made for?"

"Oh! as to that, how should I know, grannie? And not knowin', I won't say."

"If you saw a scaffold," said Marion, turning again to Jarvis, "would you be in danger of mistaking it for a permanent erection?"

"Nobody wouldn't be such a fool," he answered. "The look of it would tell you that."

"You wouldn't complain, then, if it should be a little out of the square, and if there should be no windows in it?"

Jarvis only laughed.

"Mr. Evans," Marion went on, turning again to the blind man, "do you think the design of this world was to make men comfortable?"

"If it was, it don't seem to ha' succeeded," answered Evans.

"And you complain of that—don't you?"

"Well, yes, rather,"—said the blind man, adding, no doubt, as he recalled the former part of the evening's talk,—"for harguyment, ye know, grannie."

"You think, perhaps, that God, having gone so far to make this world a pleasant and comfortable place to live in, might have gone farther and made it quite pleasant and comfortable for everybody?"

"Whoever could make it at all could ha' done that, grannie."

"Then, as he hasn't done it, the probability is he didn't mean to do it?"

"Of course. That's what I complain of."

"Then he meant to do something else?"

"It looks like it."

"The whole affair has an unfinished look, you think?"

"I just do."

"What if it were not meant to stand, then? What if it were meant only for a temporary assistance in carrying out something finished and lasting, and of unspeakably more importance? Suppose God were building a palace for you, and had set up a scaffold, upon which he wanted you to help him; would it be reasonable in you to complain that you didn't find the scaffold at all a comfortable place to live in?—that it was draughty and cold? This World is that scaffold; and if you were busy carrying stones and mortar for the palace, you would be glad of all the cold to cool the glow of your labor."

"I'm sure I work hard enough when I get a job as my heyesight will enable me to do," said Evans, missing the spirit of her figure.

"Yes: I believe you do. But what will all the labor of a workman who does not fall in with the design of the builder come to? You may say you don't understand the design: will you say also that you are under no obligation to put so much faith in the builder, who is said to be your God and Father, as to do the thing he tells you? Instead of working away at the palace, like men, will you go on tacking bits of matting and old carpet about the corners of the scaffold to keep the wind off, while that same wind keeps tearing them away and scattering them? You keep trying to live in a scaffold, which not all you could do to all eternity would make a house of. You see what I mean, Mr. Evans?"

"Well, not ezackly," replied the blind man.

"I mean that God wants to build you a house whereof the walls shall be *goodness*: you want a house whereof the walls shall be *comfort*. But God knows that such walls cannot be built,—that that kind of stone crumbles away in the foolish workman's hands. He would make you comfortable; but neither is that his first object, nor can it be gained without the first, which is to make you good. He loves you so much that he would infinitely rather have you good and uncomfortable, for then he could take you to his heart as his own children, than comfortable and not good, for then he could not come near you, or give you any thing he counted worth having for himself or worth giving to you."

"So," said Jarvis, "you've just brought us round, grannie, to the same thing as before."

"I believe so," returned Marion. "It comes to this, that when God would build a palace for himself to dwell in with his children, he does not want his scaffold so constructed that they shall be able to make a house of it for themselves, and live like apes instead of angels."

"But if God can do any thing he please," said Evans, "he might as well *make* us good, and there would be an end of it."

"That is just what he is doing," returned Marion. "Perhaps, by giving them perfect health, and every thing they wanted, with absolute good temper, and making them very fond of each other besides, God might have provided himself a people he would have had no difficulty in governing, and amongst whom, in consequence, there would have been no crime and no struggle or suffering. But I have known a dog with more goodness than that would come to. We cannot be good without having consented to be made good. God shows us the good and the bad; urges us to be good; wakes good thoughts and desires in us; helps our spirit with his Spirit, our thought with his thought: but we must yield; we must turn to him; we must consent, yes, try to be made good. If we could grow good without trying, it would be a poor goodness: *we* should not be good, after all; at best, we should only be not bad. God wants us to choose to be good, and so be partakers of his holiness; he would have us lay hold of him. He who has given his Son to suffer for us will make us suffer too, bitterly if needful, that we may bethink ourselves, and turn to him. He would make us as good as good can be, that is, perfectly good; and therefore will rouse us to take the needful hand in the work ourselves,—rouse us by discomforts innumerable.

"You see, then, it is not inconsistent with the apparent imperfections of the creation around us, that Jesus should have done the best possible carpenter's work; for those very imperfections are actually through their imperfection the means of carrying out the higher creation God has in view, and at which he is working all the time.

"Now let me read you what King David thought upon this question."

She read the hundred and seventh Psalm. Then they had some singing, in which the children took a delightful part. I have seldom heard children sing pleasantly. In Sunday schools I have always found their voices painfully harsh. But Marion made her children restrain their voices, and sing softly; which had, she said, an excellent moral effect on themselves, all squalling and screeching, whether in art or morals, being ruinous to either.

Toward the close of the singing, Roger and I slipped out. We had all but tacitly agreed it would be best to make no apology, but just vanish, and come again with Percivale the following Sunday.

The greater part of the way home we walked in silence.

"What did you think of that, Roger?" I asked at length.

"Quite Socratic as to method," he answered, and said no more.

I sent a full report of the evening to my father, who was delighted with it, although, of course, much was lost in the reporting of the mere words, not to mention the absence of her sweet face and shining eyes, of her quiet, earnest, musical voice. My father kept the letter, and that is how I am able to give the present report.

# CHAPTER XXX.

## ABOUT SERVANTS.

I went to call on Lady Bernard the next day: for there was one subject on which I could better talk with her than with Marion; and that subject was Marion herself. In the course of our conversation, I said that I had had more than usual need of such a lesson as she gave us the night before,—I had been, and indeed still was, so vexed with my nurse.

"What is the matter?" asked Lady Bernard.

"She has given me warning," I answered.

"She has been with you some time—has she not?"

"Ever since we were married."

"What reason does she give?"

"Oh! she wants *to better herself*, of course," I replied,—in such a tone, that Lady Bernard rejoined,—

"And why should she not better herself?"

"But she has such a false notion of bettering herself. I am confident what she wants will do any thing but better her, if she gets it."

"What is her notion, then? Are you sure you have got at the real one?"

"I believe I have *now*. When I asked her first, she said she was very comfortable, and condescended to inform me that she had nothing against either me or her master, but thought it was time she was having more wages; for a friend of hers, who had left home a year after herself, was having two more pounds than she had."

"It is very natural, and certainly not wrong, that she should wish for more wages."

"I told her she need not have taken such a round-about way of asking for an advance, and said I would raise her wages with pleasure. But, instead of receiving the announcement with any sign of satisfaction, she seemed put out by it; and, after some considerable amount of incoherence, blurted out that the place was dull, and she wanted a change. At length, however, I got at her real reason, which was simply ambition: she wanted to rise in the world,—to get a place where men-servants were kept,—a more fashionable place, in fact."

"A very mistaken ambition certainly," said Lady Bernard, "but one which would be counted natural enough in any other line of life. Had she given you ground for imagining higher aims in her?"

"She had been so long with us, that I thought she must have some regard for us."

"She has probably a good deal more than she is aware of. But change is as needful to some minds, for their education, as an even tenor of life is to others. Probably she has got all the good she is capable of receiving from you, and there may be some one ready to take her place for whom you will be able to do more. However inconvenient it may be for you to change, the more young people pass through your house the better."

"If it were really for her good, I hope I shouldn't mind."

"You cannot tell what may be needful to cause the seed you have sown to germinate. It may be necessary for her to pass to another class in the school of life, before she can realize what she learned in yours."

I was silent, for I was beginning to feel ashamed; and Lady Bernard went on,—

"When I hear mistresses lamenting, over some favorite servant, as marrying certain misery in exchange for a comfortable home, with plenty to eat and drink and wear, I always think of the other side to it, namely, how, through the instincts of his own implanting, God is urging her to a path in which, by passing through the fires and waters of suffering, she may be stung to the life of a true humanity. And such suffering is far more ready to work its perfect work on a girl who has passed through a family like yours."

"I wouldn't say a word to keep her if she were going to be married," I said; "but you will allow there is good reason to fear she will be no better for such a change as she desires."

"You have good reason to fear, my child," said Lady Bernard, smiling so as to take all sting out of the reproof, "that you have too little faith in the God who cares for your maid as for you. It is not indeed likely that she will have such help as yours where she goes next; but the loss of it may throw her back on herself, and bring out her individuality, which is her conscience. Still, I am far from wondering at your fear for her,—knowing well what dangers she may fall into. Shall I tell you what first began to open my eyes to the evils of a large establishment? Wishing to get rid of part of the weight of my affairs, and at the same time to assist a relative who was in want of employment, I committed to him, along with larger matters, the oversight of my household expenses, and found that he saved me the whole of his salary. This will be easily understood from a single fact. Soon after his appointment, he called on a tradesman to pay him his bill. The man, taking him for a new butler, offered him the same discount he had been in the habit of giving his supposed predecessor, namely, twenty-five per cent,—a discount, I need not say, never intended to reach my knowledge, any more than my purse. The fact was patent: I had been living in a hotel, of which I not only paid the rent, but paid the landlord for cheating me. With such a head to an establishment, you may judge what the members may become."

"I remember an amusing experience my brother-in-law, Roger Percivale, once had of your household," I said.

"I also remember it perfectly," she returned. "That was how I came to know him. But I knew something of his family long before. I remember his grandfather, a great buyer of pictures and marbles."

Lady Bernard here gave me the story from her point of view; but Roger's narrative being of necessity the more complete, I tell the tale as he told it me.

At the time of the occurrence, he was assisting Mr. F., the well-known sculptor, and had taken a share in both the modelling and the carving of a bust of Lady Bernard's father. When it was finished, and Mr. F. was about to take it home, he asked Roger to accompany him, and help him to get it safe into the house and properly placed.

Roger and the butler between them carried it to the drawing-room, where were Lady Bernard and a company of her friends, whom she had invited to meet Mr. F, at lunch, and see the bust. There being no pedestal yet ready, Mr. F. made choice of a certain small table for it to stand upon, and then accompanied her ladyship and her other guests to the dining-room, leaving Roger to uncover the bust, place it in the proper light, and do whatever more might be necessary to its proper effect on the company when they should return. As she left the room, Lady Bernard told Roger to ring for a servant to clear the table for him, and render what other assistance he might want. He did so. A lackey answered the bell, and Roger requested him to remove the things from the table. The man left the room, and did not return. Roger therefore cleared and moved the table himself, and with difficulty got the bust upon it. Finding then several stains upon the pure half transparency of the marble, he rang the bell for a basin of water and a sponge. Another man appeared, looked into the room, and went away. He rang once more, and yet another servant came. This last condescended to hear him; and, informing him that he could get what he wanted in the scullery, vanished in his turn. By this time Roger confesses to have been rather in a rage; but what could he do? Least of all allow Mr. F.'s work, and the likeness of her ladyship's father, to make its debut with a spot on its nose; therefore, seeing he could not otherwise procure what was necessary, he set out in quest of the unknown appurtenances of the kitchen.

It is unpleasant to find one's self astray, even in a moderately sized house; and Roger did not at all relish wandering about the huge place, with no finger-posts to keep him in its business-thoroughfares, not to speak of directing him to the remotest recesses of a house "full," as Chaucer says, "of crenkles." At last, however, he found himself at the door of the servants' hall. Two men were lying on their backs on benches, with their knees above their heads in the air; a third was engaged in emptying a pewter pot, between his draughts tossing *facetiæ* across its mouth to a damsel who was removing the remains of some private luncheon; and a fourth sat in one of the windows reading "Bell's Life." Roger took it all in at a glance, while to one of the giants supine, or rather to a perpendicular pair of white stockings, he preferred his request for a basin and a sponge. Once more he was informed that he would find what he wanted in the scullery. There was no time to waste on unavailing demands, therefore he only begged further to be directed how to find it. The fellow, without raising his head or lowering his knees, jabbered out such instructions as, from the rapidity with which he delivered them, were, if not unintelligible, at all events incomprehensible; and Roger had to set out again on the quest, only not quite so bewildered as before. He found a certain long passage mentioned, however, and happily, before he arrived at the end of it, met a maid, who with the utmost civility gave him full instructions to find the place. The scullery-maid was equally civil; and Roger returned with basin and sponge to the drawing-room, where he speedily removed the too troublesome stains from the face of the marble.

When the company re-entered, Mr. F. saw at once, from the expression and bearing of Roger, that something had happened to discompose him, and asked him what was amiss. Roger having briefly informed him, Mr. F. at once recounted the facts to Lady Bernard, who immediately requested a full statement from Roger himself, and heard the whole story.

She walked straight to the bell, and ordered up every one of her domestics, from the butler to the scullery-maid.

Without one hasty word, or one bodily sign of the anger she was in, except the flashing of her eyes, she told them she could not have had a suspicion that such insolence was possible in her house; that they had disgraced her in her own eyes, as having gathered such people about her; that she would not add to Mr. Percivale's annoyance by asking him to point out the guilty persons, but that they might assure themselves she would henceforth keep both eyes and ears open, and if the slightest thing of the sort happened again, she would most assuredly dismiss every one of them at a moment's warning. She then turned to Roger and said,—

"Mr. Percivale, I beg your pardon for the insults you have received from my servants."

"I did think," she said, as she finished telling me the story, "to dismiss them all on the spot, but was deterred by the fear of injustice. The next morning, however, four or five of them gave my housekeeper warning: I gave orders that they should leave the house at once, and from that day I set about reducing my establishment. My principal objects were two: first, that my servants might have more work; and second, that I might be able to know something of every one of them; for one thing I saw, that, until I ruled my own house well, I had no right to go trying to do good out of doors. I think I do know a little of the nature and character of every soul under my roof now; and I am more and more confident that nothing of real and lasting benefit can be done for a class except through personal influence upon the individual persons who compose it—such influence, I mean, as at the very least sets for Christianity."

# CHAPTER XXXI.

## ABOUT PERCIVALE.

I should like much, before in my narrative approaching a certain hard season we had to encounter, to say a few words concerning my husband, if I only knew how. I find women differ much, both in the degree and manner in which their feelings will permit them to talk about their husbands. I have known women set a whole community against their husbands by the way in which they trumpeted their praises; and I have known one woman set everybody against herself by the way in which she published her husband's faults. I find it difficult to believe either sort. To praise one's husband is so like praising one's self, that to me it seems immodest, and subject to the same suspicion as self-laudation; while to blame one's husband, even justly and openly, seems to me to border upon treachery itself. How, then, am I to discharge a sort of half duty my father has laid upon me by what he has said in "The Seaboard Parish," concerning my husband's opinions? My father is one of the few really large-minded men I have yet known; but I am not certain that he has done Percivale justice. At the same time, if he has not, Percivale himself is partly to blame, inasmuch as he never took pains to show my father what he was; for, had he done so, my father of all men would have understood him. On the other hand, this fault, if such it was, could have sprung only from my husband's modesty, and his horror of possibly producing an impression on my father's mind more favorable than correct. It is all right now, however.

Still, my difficulty remains as to how I am to write about him. I must encourage myself with the consideration that none but our own friends, with whom, whether they understood us or not, we are safe, will know to whom the veiled narrative points.

But some acute reader may say,—

"You describe your husband's picture: he will be known by that."

In this matter I have been cunning—I hope not deceitful, inasmuch as I now reveal my cunning. Instead of describing any real picture of his, I have always substituted one he has only talked about. The picture actually associated with the facts related is not the picture I have described.

Although my husband left the impression on my father's mind, lasting for a long time, that he had some definite repugnance to Christianity itself, I had been soon satisfied, perhaps from his being more open with me, that certain unworthy representations of Christianity, coming to him with authority, had cast discredit upon the whole idea of it. In the first year or two of our married life, we had many talks on the subject; and I was astonished to find what things he imagined to be acknowledged essentials of Christianity, which have no place whatever in the New Testament; and I think it was in proportion as he came to see his own misconceptions, that, although there was little or no outward difference to be perceived in him, I could more and more clearly distinguish an under-current of thought and feeling setting towards the faith which Christianity preaches. He said little or nothing, even when I attempted to draw him out on the matter; for he was almost morbidly careful not to seem to know any thing he did not know, or to appear what he was not. The most I could get out of him was—but I had better give a little talk I had with him on one occasion. It was some time before we began to go to Marion's on a Sunday evening, and I had asked him to go with me to a certain, little chapel in the neighborhood.

"What!" he said merrily, "the daughter of a clergyman be seen going to a conventicle?"

"If I did it, I would be seen doing it," I answered.

"Don't you know that the man is no conciliatory, or even mild dissenter, but a decided enemy to Church and State and all that?" pursued Percivale.

"I don't care," I returned. "I know nothing about it. What I know is, that he's a poet and a prophet both in one. He stirs up my heart within me, and makes me long to be good. He is no orator, and yet breaks into bursts of eloquence such as none of the studied orators, to whom you profess so great an aversion, could ever reach."

"You may well be right there. It is against nature for a speaker to be eloquent throughout his discourse, and the false will of course quench the true. I don't mind going if you wish it. I suppose he believes what he says, at least."

"Not a doubt of it. He could not speak as he does from less than a thorough belief."

"Do you mean to say, Wynnie, that he is *sure* of every thing,—I don't want to urge an unreasonable question,—but is he *sure* that the story of the New Testament is, in the main, actual fact? I should be very sorry to trouble your faith, but"—

"My father says," I interrupted, "that a true faith is like the Pool of Bethesda: it is when troubled that it shows its healing power."

"That depends on where the trouble comes from, perhaps," said Percivale.

"Anyhow," I answered, "it is only that which cannot be shaken that shall remain."

"Well, I will tell you what seems to me a very common-sense difficulty. How is any one to be *sure* of the things recorded? I cannot imagine a man of our time absolutely certain of them. If you tell me I have testimony, I answer, that the testimony itself requires testimony. I never even saw the people who bear it; have just as good reason to doubt their existence, as that of him concerning whom they bear it; have positively no means of verifying it, and indeed, have so little confidence in all that is called evidence, knowing how it can be twisted, that I should distrust any conclusion I might seem about to come to on the one side or the other. It does appear to me, that, if the thing were of God, he would have taken care that it should be possible for an honest man to place a hearty confidence in its record."

He had never talked to me so openly, and I took it as a sign that he had been thinking more of these things than hitherto. I felt it a serious matter to have to answer such words, for how could I have any better assurance of that external kind than Percivale himself? That I was in the same intellectual position, however, enabled me the better to understand him. For a short time I was silent, while he regarded me with a look of concern,—fearful, I fancied, lest he should have involved me in his own perplexity.

"Isn't it possible, Percivale," I said, "that God may not care so much for beginning at that end?"

"I don't quite understand you, Wynnie," he returned.

"A man might believe every fact recorded concerning our Lord, and yet not have the faith in him that God wishes him to have."

"Yes, certainly. But will you say the converse of that is true?"

"Explain, please."

"Will you say a man may have the faith God cares for without the faith you say he does not care for?"

"I didn't say that God does not care about our having assurance of the facts; for surely, if every thing depends on those facts, much will depend on the degree of our assurance concerning them. I only expressed a doubt whether, in the present age, he cares that we should have that assurance first. Perhaps he means it to be the result of the higher kind of faith which rests in the will."

"I don't, at the moment, see how the higher faith, as you call it, can precede the lower."

"It seems to me possible enough. For what is the test of discipleship the Lord lays down? Is it not obedience? 'If ye love me, keep my commandments.' 'If a man love me, he will keep my commandments.' 'I never knew you: depart from me, ye workers of iniquity.' Suppose a man feels in himself that he must have some saviour or perish; suppose he feels drawn, by conscience, by admiration, by early memories, to the form of Jesus, dimly seen through the mists of ages; suppose he cannot be sure there ever was such a man, but reads about him, and ponders over the words attributed to him, until he feels they are the right thing, whether *he* said them or not, and that if he could but be sure there were such a being, he would believe in him with heart and soul; suppose also that he comes upon the words, 'If any man is willing to do the will of the Father, he shall know whether I speak of myself or he sent me;' suppose all these things, might not the man then say to himself, 'I cannot tell whether all this is true, but I know nothing that seems half so good, and I will try to do the will of the Father in the hope of the promised knowledge'? Do you think God would, or would not, count that to the man for faith?"

I had no more to say, and a silence followed. After a pause of some duration, Percivale said,—

"I will go with you, my dear;" and that was all his answer.

When we came out of the little chapel,—the same into which Marion had stepped on that evening so memorable to her,—we walked homeward in silence, and reached our own door ere a word was spoken. But, when I went to take off my things, Percivale followed me into the room and said,—

"Whether that man is *certain* of the facts or not, I cannot tell yet; but I am perfectly satisfied he believes in the manner of which you were speaking,—that of obedience, Wynnie. He must believe with his heart and will and life."

"If so, he can well afford to wait for what light God will give him on things that belong to the intellect and judgment."

"I would rather think," he returned, "that purity of life must re-act on the judgment, so as to make it likewise clear, and enable it to recognize the true force of the evidence at command."

"That is how my father came to believe," I said.

"He seems to me to rest his conviction more upon external proof."

"That is only because it is easier to talk about. He told me once that he was never able to estimate the force and weight of the external arguments until after he had believed for the very love of the eternal truth he saw in the story. His heart, he said, had been the guide of his intellect."

"That is just what I would fain believe. But, O Wynnie! the pity of it if that story should not be true, after all!"

"Ah, my love!" I cried, "that very word makes me surer than ever that it cannot but be true. Let us go on putting it to the hardest test; let us try it until it crumbles in our hands,—try it by the touchstone of action founded on its requirements."

"There may be no other way," said Percivale, after a thoughtful pause, "of becoming capable of recognizing the truth. It may be beyond the grasp of all but the mind that has thus yielded to it. There may be no contact for it with any but such a mind. Such a conviction, then, could neither be forestalled nor communicated. Its very existence must remain doubtful until it asserts itself. I see that."

# CHAPTER XXXII.

## MY SECOND TERROR.

"Please, ma'am, is Master Fido to carry Master Zohrab about by the back o' the neck?" said Jemima, in indignant appeal, one afternoon late in November, bursting into the study where I sat with my husband.

Fido was our Bedlington terrier, which, having been reared by Newcastle colliers, and taught to draw a badger,—whatever that may mean,—I am hazy about it,—had a passion for burrowing after any thing buried. Swept away by the current of the said passion, he had with his strong forepaws unearthed poor Zohrab, which, being a tortoise, had ensconced himself, as he thought, for the winter, in the earth at the foot of a lilac-tree; but now, much to his jeopardy, from the cold and the shock of the surprise more than from the teeth of his friend, was being borne about the garden in triumph, though whether exactly as Jemima described may be questionable. Her indignation at the inroad of the dog upon the personal rights of the tortoise had possibly not lessened her general indifference to accuracy.

Alarmed at the danger to the poor animal, of a kind from which his natural defences were powerless to protect him, Percivale threw down his palette and brushes, and ran to the door.

"Do put on your coat and hat, Percivale!" I cried; but he was gone.

Cold as it was, he had been sitting in the light blouse he had worn at his work all the summer. The stove had got red-hot, and the room was like an oven, while outside a dank fog filled the air. I hurried after him with his coat, and found him pursuing Fido about the garden, the brute declining to obey his call, or to drop the tortoise. Percivale was equally deaf to my call, and not until he had beaten the dog did he return with the rescued tortoise in his hands. The consequences were serious,—first the death of Zohrab, and next a terrible illness to my husband. He had caught cold: it settled on his lungs, and passed into bronchitis.

It was a terrible time to me; for I had no doubt, for some days, that he was dying. The measures taken seemed thoroughly futile.

It is an awful moment when first Death looks in at the door. The positive recognition of his presence is so different from any vividest imagination of it! For the moment I believed nothing,—felt only the coming blackness of absolute loss. I cared neither for my children, nor for my father or mother. Nothing appeared of any worth more. I had conscience enough left to try to pray, but no prayer would rise from the frozen depths of my spirit. I could only move about in mechanical and hopeless ministration to one whom it seemed of no use to go on loving any more; for what was nature but a soulless machine, the constant clank of whose motion sounded only, "Dust to dust; dust to dust," forevermore? But I was roused from this horror-stricken mood by a look from my husband, who, catching a glimpse of my despair, motioned me to him with a smile as of sunshine upon snow, and whispered in my ear,—

"I'm afraid you haven't much more faith than myself, after all, Wynnie."

It stung me into life,—not for the sake of my professions, not even for the honor of our heavenly Father, but by waking in me the awful thought of my beloved passing through the shadow of death with no one beside him to help or comfort him, in absolute loneliness and uncertainty. The thought was unendurable. For a moment I wished he might die suddenly, and so escape the vacuous despair of a conscious lingering betwixt life and the something or the nothing beyond it.

"But I cannot go with you!" I cried; and, forgetting all my duty as a nurse, I wept in agony.

"Perhaps another will, my Wynnie,—one who knows the way," he whispered; for he could not speak aloud, and closed his eyes.

It was as if an arrow of light had slain the Python coiled about my heart. If *he* believed, *I* could believe also; if *he* could encounter the vague dark, *I* could endure the cheerless light. I was myself again, and, with one word of endearment, left the bedside to do what had to be done.

At length a faint hope began to glimmer in the depths of my cavernous fear. It was long ere it swelled into confidence; but, although I was then in somewhat feeble health, my strength never gave way. For a whole week I did not once undress, and for weeks I was half-awake all the time I slept. The softest whisper would rouse me thoroughly; and it was only when Marion took my place that I could sleep at all.

I am afraid I neglected my poor children dreadfully. I seemed for the time to have no responsibility, and even, I am ashamed to say, little care for them. But then I knew that they were well attended to: friends were very kind—especially Judy—in taking them out; and Marion's daily visits were like those of a mother. Indeed, she was able to mother any thing human except a baby, to whom she felt no attraction,—any more than to the inferior animals, for which she had little regard beyond a negative one: she would hurt no creature that was not hurtful; but she had scarcely an atom of kindness for dog or cat, or any thing that is petted of woman. It is the only defect I am aware of in her character.

My husband slowly recovered, but it was months before he was able to do any thing he would call work. But, even in labor, success is not only to the strong. Working a little at the short best time of the day with him, he managed, long before his full recovery, to paint a small picture which better critics than I have thought worthy of Angelico, I will attempt to describe it.

Through the lighted windows of a great hall, the spectator catches broken glimpses of a festive company. At the head of the table, pouring out the red wine, he sees one like unto the Son of man, upon whom the eyes of all are turned. At the other end of the hall, seated high in a gallery, with rapt looks and quaint yet homely angelican instruments, he sees the orchestra pouring out their souls through their strings and trumpets. The hall is filled with a jewelly glow, as of light suppressed by color, the radiating centre of which is the red wine on the table; while mingled wings, of all gorgeous splendors, hovering in the dim height, are suffused and harmonized by the molten ruby tint that pervades the whole.

Outside, in the drizzly darkness, stands a lonely man. He stoops listening, with one ear laid almost against the door. His half-upturned face catches a ray of the light reflected from a muddy pool in the road. It discloses features wan and wasted with sorrow and sickness, but glorified with the joy of the music. He is like one who has been four days dead, to whose body the music has recalled the soul. Down by his knee he holds a violin, fashioned like those of the orchestra within; which, as he listens, he is tuning to their pitch.

To readers acquainted with a poem of Dr. Donne's,—"Hymn to God, my God, in my sickness,"—this description of mine will at once suggest the origin of the picture. I had read some verses of it to him in his convalescence; and, having heard them once, he requested them often again. The first stanza runs thus:—

"Since I am coming to that holy room
Where with the choir of saints forevermore
I shall be made thy musique, as I come,
I tune the instrument here at the door;
And what I must do then, think here before."

The painting is almost the only one he has yet refused to let me see before it was finished; but, when it was, he hung it up in my own little room off the study, and I became thoroughly acquainted with it. I think I love it more than any thing else he has done. I got him, without telling him why, to put a touch or two to the listening figure, which made it really like himself.

During this period of recovery, I often came upon him reading his Greek New Testament, which he would shove aside when I entered. At length, one morning, I said to him,—

"Are you ashamed of the New Testament, Percivale? One would think it was a bad book from the way you try to hide it."

"No, my love," he said: "it is only that I am jealous of appearing to do that from suffering and weakness only, which I did not do when I was strong and well. But sickness has opened my eyes a good deal I think; and I am sure of this much, that, whatever truth there is here, I want it all the same whether I am feeling the want or not. I had no idea what there was in this book."

"Would you mind telling me," I said, "what made you take to reading it?"

"I will try. When I thought I was dying, a black cloud seemed to fall over every thing. It was not so much that I was afraid to die,—although I did dread the final conflict,—as that I felt so forsaken and lonely. It was of little use saying to myself that I mustn't be a coward, and that it was the part of a man to meet his fate, whatever it might be, with composure; for I saw nothing worth being brave about: the heart had melted out of me; there was nothing to give me joy, nothing for my life to rest up on, no sense of love at the heart of things. Didn't you feel something the same that terrible day?"

"I did," I answered. "I hope I never believed in Death all the time; and yet for one fearful moment the skeleton seemed to swell and grow till he blotted out the sun and the stars, and was himself all in all, while the life beyond was too shadowy to show behind him. And so Death was victorious, until the thought of your loneliness in the dark valley broke the spell; and for your sake I hoped in God again."

"And I thought with myself,—Would God set his children down in the dark, and leave them to cry aloud in anguish at the terrors of the night? Would he not make the very darkness light about them? Or, if they must pass through such tortures, would he not at least let them know that he was with them? How, then, can there be a God? Then arose in my mind all at once the old story, how, in the person of his Son, God himself had passed through the darkness now gathering about me; had gone down to the grave, and had conquered death by dying. If this was true, this was to be a God indeed. Well might he call on us to endure, who had himself borne the far heavier share. If there were an Eternal Life who would perfect my life, I could be brave; I could endure what he chose to lay upon me; I could go whither he led."

"And were you able to think all that when you were so ill, my love?" I said.

"Something like it,—practically very like it," he answered. "It kept growing in my mind,—coming and going, and gathering clearer shape. I thought with myself, that, if there was a God, he certainly knew that I would give myself to him if I could; that, if I knew Jesus to be verily and really his Son, however it might seem strange to believe in him and hard to obey him, I would try to do so; and then a verse about the smoking flax and the bruised reed came into my head, and a great hope arose in me. I do not know if it was what the good people would call faith; but I had no time and no heart to think about words: I wanted God and his Christ. A fresh spring of life seemed to burst up in my heart; all the world grew bright again: I seemed to love you and the children twice as much as before; a calmness came down upon my spirit which seemed to me like nothing but the presence of God; and, although I dare say you did not then perceive a change, I am certain that the same moment I began to recover."

# CHAPTER XXXIII.

## THE CLOUDS AFTER THE RAIN.

But the clouds returned after the rain. It will be easily understood how the little money we had in hand should have rapidly vanished during Percivale's illness. While he was making nothing, the expenses of the family went on as usual; and not that only, but many little delicacies had to be got for him, and the doctor was yet to pay. Even up to the time when he had been taken ill, we had been doing little better than living from hand to mouth; for as often as we thought income was about to get a few yards ahead in the race with expense, something invariably happened to disappoint us.

I am not sorry that I have no *special* faculty for saving; for I have never known any, in whom such was well developed, who would not do things they ought to be ashamed of. The savings of such people seem to me to come quite as much off other people as off themselves; and, especially in regard of small sums, they are in danger of being first mean, and then dishonest. Certainly, whoever makes saving *the* end of her life, must soon grow mean, and will probably grow dishonest. But I have never succeeded in drawing the line betwixt meanness and dishonesty: what is mean, so far as I can see, slides by indistinguishable gradations into what is plainly dishonest. And what is more, the savings are commonly made at the cost of the defenceless. It is better far to live in constant difficulties than to keep out of them by such vile means as must, besides, poison the whole nature, and make one's judgments, both of God and her neighbors, mean as her own conduct. It is nothing to say that you must be just before you are generous, for that is the very point I am insisting on; namely, that one must be just to others before she is generous to herself. It will never do to make your two ends meet by pulling the other ends from the hands of those who are likewise puzzled to make them meet.

But I must now put myself at the bar, and cry *Peccavi*; for I was often wrong on the other side, sometimes getting things for the house before it was quite clear I could afford them, and sometimes buying the best when an inferior thing would have been more suitable, if not to my ideas, yet to my purse. It is, however, far more difficult for one with an uncertain income to learn to save, or even to be prudent, than for one who knows how much exactly every quarter will bring.

My husband, while he left the whole management of money matters to me, would yet spend occasionally without consulting me. In fact, he had no notion of money, and what it would or would not do. I never knew a man spend less upon himself; but he would be extravagant for me, and I dared hardly utter a foolish liking lest he should straightway turn it into a cause of shame by attempting to gratify it. He had, besides, a weakness for over-paying people, of which neither Marion nor I could honestly approve, however much we might admire the disposition whence it proceeded.

Now that I have confessed, I shall be more easy in my mind; for, in regard of the troubles that followed, I cannot be sure that I was free of blame. One word more in self-excuse, and I have done: however imperative, it is none the less hard to cultivate two opposing virtues at one and the same time.

While my husband was ill, not a picture had been disposed of; and even after he was able to work a little, I could not encourage visitors: he was not able for the fatigue, and in fact shrunk, with an irritability I had never perceived a sign of before, from seeing any one. To my growing dismay, I saw my little stock—which was bodily in my hand, for we had no banking account—rapidly approaching its final evanishment.

Some may think, that, with parents in the position of mine, a temporary difficulty need have caused me no anxiety: I must, therefore, mention one or two facts with regard to both my husband and my parents.

In the first place, although he had as complete a confidence in him as I had, both in regard to what he said and what he seemed, my husband could not feel towards my father as I felt. He had married me as a poor man, who yet could keep a wife; and I knew it would be a bitter humiliation to him to ask my father for money, on the ground that he had given his daughter. I should have felt nothing of the kind; for I should have known that my father would do him as well as me perfect justice in the matter, and would consider any money spent upon us as used to a divine purpose. For he regarded the necessaries of life as noble, its comforts as honorable, its luxuries as permissible,—thus reversing altogether the usual judgment of rich men, who in general like nothing worse than to leave their hoards to those of their relatives who will degrade them to the purchase of mere bread and cheese, blankets and clothes and coals. But I had no right to go against my husband's feeling. So long as the children had their bread and milk, I would endure with him. I am confident I could have starved as well as he, and should have enjoyed letting him see it.

But there were reasons because of which even I, in my fullest freedom, could not have asked help from my father just at this time. I am ashamed to tell the fact, but I must: before the end of his second year at Oxford, just over, the elder of my two brothers had, without any vice I firmly believe, beyond that of thoughtlessness and folly, got himself so deeply mired in debt, both to tradespeople and money-lenders, that my father had to pay two thousand pounds for him. Indeed, as I was well assured, although he never told me so, he had to borrow part of the money on a fresh mortgage in order to clear him. Some lawyer, I believe, told him that he was not bound to pay: but my father said, that, although such creditors deserved no protection of the law, he was not bound to give them a lesson in honesty at the expense of weakening the bond between himself and his son, for whose misdeeds he acknowledged a large share of responsibility; while, on the other hand, he was bound to give his son the lesson of the suffering brought on his family by his selfishness; and therefore would pay the money—if not gladly, yet willingly. How the poor boy got through the shame and misery of it, I can hardly imagine; but this I can say for him, that it was purely of himself that he accepted a situation in Ceylon, instead of returning to Oxford. Thither he was now on his way, with the intention of saving all he could in order to repay his father; and if at length he succeeds in doing so, he will doubtless make a fairer start the second time, because of the discipline, than if he had gone out with the money in his pocket.

It was natural, then, that in such circumstances a daughter should shrink from adding her troubles to those caused by a son. I ought to add, that my father had of late been laying out a good deal in building cottages for the laborers on his farms, and that the land was not yet entirely freed from the mortgages my mother had inherited with it.

Percivale continued so weak, that for some time I could not bring myself to say a word to him about money. But to keep them as low as possible did not prevent the household debts from accumulating, and the servants' wages were on the point of coming due. I had been careful to keep the milkman paid; and for the rest of the tradesmen, I consoled myself with the certainty, that, if the worst came to the worst, there was plenty of furniture in the house to pay every one of them. Still, of all burdens, next to sin, that of debt, I think, must be heaviest.

I tried to keep cheerful; but at length, one night, during our supper of bread and cheese, which I could not bear to see my poor, pale-faced husband eating, I broke down.

"What *is* the matter, my darling?" asked Percivale.

I took a half-crown from my pocket, and held it out on the palm of my hand.

"That's all I've got, Percivale," I said.

"Oh! that all—is it?" he returned lightly.

"Yes,—isn't that enough?" I said with some indignation.

"Certainly—for to-night," he answered, "seeing the shops are shut. But is that all that's troubling you?" he went on.

"It seems to me quite enough," I said again; "and if you had the housekeeping to do, and the bills to pay, you would think a solitary half-crown quite enough to make you miserable."

"Never mind—so long as it's a good one," he said. "I'll get you more to-morrow."

"How can you do that?" I asked.

"Easily," he answered. "You'll see. Don't you trouble your dear heart about it for a moment."

I felt relieved, and asked him no more questions.

The next morning, when I went into the study to speak to him, he was not there; and I guessed that he had gone to town to get the money, for he had not been out before since his illness, at least without me. But I hoped of all things he was not going to borrow it of a money-lender, of which I had a great and justifiable horror, having heard from himself how a friend of his had in such a case fared. I would have sold three-fourths of the things in the house rather. But as I turned to leave the study, anxious both about himself and his proceedings, I thought something was different, and soon discovered that a certain favorite picture was missing from the wall: it was clear he had gone either to sell it or raise money upon it.

By our usual early dinner-hour, he returned, and put into my hands, with a look of forced cheerfulness, two five-pound notes.

"Is that all you got for that picture?" I said.

"That is all Mr. —— would advance me upon it," he answered. "I thought he had made enough by me to have risked a little more than that; but picture-dealers—Well, never mind. That is enough to give time for twenty things to happen."

And no doubt twenty things did happen, but none of them of the sort he meant. The ten pounds sank through my purse like water through gravel. I paid a number of small bills at once, for they pressed the more heavily upon me that I knew the money was wanted; and by the end of another fortnight we were as badly off as before, with an additional trouble, which in the circumstances was any thing but slight.

In conjunction with more than ordinary endowments of stupidity and self-conceit, Jemima was possessed of a furious temper, which showed itself occasionally in outbursts of unendurable rudeness. She had been again and again on the point of leaving me, now she, now I, giving warning; but, ere the day arrived, her better nature had always got the upper hand,—she had broken down and given in. These outbursts had generally followed a season of better behavior than usual, and were all but certain if I ventured the least commendation; for she could stand any thing better than praise. At the least subsequent rebuke, self would break out in rage, vulgarity, and rudeness. On this occasion, however, I cannot tell whence it was that one of these cyclones arose in our small atmosphere; but it was Jemima, you may well believe, who gave warning, for it was out of my power to pay her wages; and there was no sign of her yielding.

My reader may be inclined to ask in what stead the religion I had learned of my father now stood me. I will endeavor to be honest in my answer.

Every now and then I tried to pray to God to deliver us; but I was far indeed from praying always, and still farther from not fainting. A whole day would sometimes pass under a weight of care that amounted often to misery; and not until its close would I bethink me that I had been all the weary hours without God. Even when more hopeful, I would keep looking and looking for the impossibility of something to happen of itself, instead of looking for some good and perfect gift to come down from the Father of lights; and, when I awoke to the fact, the fog would yet lie so deep on my soul, that I could not be sorry for my idolatry and want of faith. It was, indeed, a miserable time. There was, besides, one definite thought that always choked my prayers: I could not say in my conscience that I had been sufficiently careful either in my management or my expenditure. "If," I thought, "I could be certain that I had done my best, I should be able to trust in God for all that lies beyond my power; but now he may mean to punish me for my carelessness." Then why should I not endure it calmly and without complaint? Alas! it was not I alone that thus would be punished, but my children and my husband as well. Nor could I avoid coming on my poor father at last, who, of course, would interfere to prevent a sale; and the thought was, from the circumstances I have mentioned, very bitter to me. Sometimes, however, in more faithful moods, I would reason with myself that God would not be hard upon me, even if I had not been so saving as I ought. My father had taken his son's debts on himself, and would not allow him to be disgraced more than could be helped; and, if an earthly parent would act thus for his child, would our Father in heaven be less tender with us? Still, for very love's sake, it might be necessary to lay some disgrace upon me, for of late I had been thinking far too little of the best things. The cares more than the duties of life had been filling my mind. If it brought me nearer to God, I must then say it had been good for me to be afflicted; but while my soul was thus oppressed, how could my feelings have any scope? Let come what would, however, I must try and bear it,—even disgrace, if it was *his* will. Better people than I had been thus disgraced, and it might be my turn next. Meantime, it had not come to that, and I must not let the cares of to-morrow burden to-day.

Every day, almost, as it seems in looking back, a train of thought something like this would pass through my mind. But things went on, and grew no better. With gathering rapidity, we went sliding, to all appearance, down the inclined plane of disgrace.

Percivale at length asked Roger if he had any money by him to lend him a little; and he gave him at once all he had, amounting to six pounds,—a wonderful amount for Roger to have accumulated; with the help of which we got on to the end of Jemima's month. The next step I had in view was to take my little valuables to the pawnbroker's,—amongst them a watch, whose face was encircled with a row of good-sized diamonds. It had belonged to my great-grandmother, and my mother had given it me when I was married.

We had had a piece of boiled neck of mutton for dinner, of which we, that is my husband and I, had partaken sparingly, in order that there might be enough for the servants. Percivale had gone out; and I was sitting in the drawing-room, lost in any thing but a blessed reverie, with all the children chattering amongst themselves beside me, when Jemima entered, looking subdued.

"If you please, ma'am, this is my day," she said.

"Have you got a place, then, Jemima?" I asked; for I had been so much occupied with my own affairs that I had thought little of the future of the poor girl to whom I could have given but a lukewarm recommendation for any thing prized amongst housekeepers.

"No, ma'am. Please, ma'am, mayn't I stop?"

"No, Jemima. I am very sorry, but I can't afford to keep you. I shall have to do all the work myself when you are gone."

I thought to pay her wages out of the proceeds of my jewels, but was willing to delay the step as long as possible; rather, I believe, from repugnance to enter the pawn-shop, than from disinclination to part with the trinkets. But, as soon as I had spoken, Jemima burst into an Irish wail, mingled with sobs and tears, crying between the convulsions of all three,—

I thought there was something wrong, mis'ess. You and master looked so scared-like. Please, mis'ess, don't send me away."

"I never wanted to send you away, Jemima. You wanted to go yourself."

"No, ma'am; *that* I didn't. I only wanted you to ask me to stop. Wirra! wirra! It's myself is sorry I was so rude. It's not me; it's my temper, mis'ess. I do believe I was born with a devil inside me."

I could not help laughing, partly from amusement, partly from relief.

"But you see I can't ask you to stop," I said. "I've got no money,—not even enough to pay you to-day; so I can't keep you."

"I don't want no money, ma'am. Let me stop, and I'll cook for yez, and wash and scrub for yez, to the end o' my days. An' I'll eat no more than'll keep the life in me. I *must* eat something, or the smell o' the meat would turn me sick, ye see, ma'am; and then I shouldn't be no good to yez. Please 'm, I ha' got fifteen pounds in the savings bank: I'll give ye all that, if ye'll let me stop wid ye."

When I confess that I burst out crying, my reader will be kind enough to take into consideration that I hadn't had much to eat for some time; that I was therefore weak in body as well as in mind; and that this was the first gleam of sunshine I had had for many weeks.

"Thank you very much, Jemima," I said, as soon as I could speak. "I won't take your money, for then you would be as poor as I am. But, if you would like to stop with us, you shall; and I won't pay you till I'm able."

The poor girl was profuse in her thanks, and left the room sobbing in her apron.

It was a gloomy, drizzly, dreary afternoon. The children were hard to amuse, and I was glad when their bedtime arrived. It was getting late before Percivale returned. He looked pale, and I found afterwards that he had walked home. He had got wet, and had to change some of his clothes. When we went in to supper, there was the neck of mutton on the table, almost as we had left it. This led me, before asking him any questions, to relate what had passed with Jemima; at which news he laughed merrily, and was evidently a good deal relieved. Then I asked him where he had been.

"To the city," he answered.

"Have you sold another picture?" I asked, with an inward tribulation, half hope, half fear; for, much as we wanted the money, I could ill bear the thought of his pictures going for the price of mere pot-boilers.

"No," he replied: "the last is stopping the way. Mr. —— has been advertising it as a bargain for a hundred and fifty. But he hasn't sold it yet, and can't, he says, risk ten pounds on another. What's to come of it, I don't know," he added. "But meantime it's a comfort that Jemima can wait a bit for *her* money."

As we sat at supper, I thought I saw a look on Percivale's face which I had never seen there before. All at once, while I was wondering what it might mean, after a long pause, during which we had been both looking into the fire, he said,—

"Wynnie, I'm going to paint a better picture than I've ever painted yet. I can, and I will."

"But how are we to live in the mean time?" I said.

His face fell, and I saw with shame what a Job's comforter I was. Instead of sympathizing with his ardor, I had quenched it. What if my foolish remark had ruined a great picture! Anyhow, it had wounded a great heart, which had turned to labor as its plainest duty, and would thereby have been strengthened to endure and to hope. It was too cruel of me. I knelt by his knee, and told him I was both ashamed and sorry I had been so faithless and unkind. He made little of it, said I might well ask the question, and even tried to be merry over it; but I could see well enough that I had let a gust of the foggy night into his soul, and was thoroughly vexed with myself. We went to bed gloomy, but slept well, and awoke more cheerful.

# CHAPTER XXXIV.

## THE SUNSHINE.

As we were dressing, it came into my mind that I had forgotten to give him a black-bordered letter which had arrived the night before. I commonly opened his letters; but I had not opened this one, for it looked like a business letter, and I feared it might be a demand for the rent of the house, which was over due. Indeed, at this time I dreaded opening any letter the writing on which I did not recognize.

"Here is a letter, Percivale," I said. "I'm sorry I forgot to give it you last night."

"Who is it from?" he asked, talking through his towel from his dressing-room.

"I don't know. I didn't open it. It looks like something disagreeable."

"Open it now, then, and see."

"I can't just at this moment," I answered; for I had my back hair half twisted in my hands. "There it is on the chimney-piece."

He came in, took it, and opened it, while I went on with my toilet. Suddenly his arms were round me, and I felt his cheek on mine.

"Read that," he said, putting the letter into my hand.

It was from a lawyer in Shrewsbury, informing him that his god-mother, with whom he had been a great favorite when a boy, was dead, and had left him three hundred pounds.

It was like a reprieve to one about to be executed. I could only weep and thank God, once more believing in my Father in heaven. But it was a humbling thought, that, if he had not thus helped me, I might have ceased to believe in him. I saw plainly, that, let me talk to Percivale as I might, my own faith was but a wretched thing. It is all very well to have noble theories about God; but where is the good of them except we actually trust in him as a real, present, living, loving being, who counts us of more value than many sparrows, and will not let one of them fall to the ground without him?

"I thought, Wynnie, if there was such a God as you believed in, and with you to pray to him, we shouldn't be long without a hearing," said my husband.

There was more faith in his heart all the time, though he could not profess the belief I thought I had, than there ever was in mine.

But our troubles weren't nearly over yet. Percivale wrote, acknowledging the letter, and requesting to know when it would be convenient to let him have the money, as he was in immediate want of it. The reply was, that the trustees were not bound to pay the legacies for a year, but that possibly they might stretch a point in his favor if he applied to them. Percivale did so, but received a very curt answer, with little encouragement to expect any thing but the extreme of legal delay. He received the money, however, about four months after; lightened, to the great disappointment of my ignorance, of thirty pounds legacy-duty.

In the mean time, although our minds were much relieved, and Percivale was working away at his new picture with great energy and courage, the immediate pressure of circumstances was nearly as painful as ever. It was a comfort, however, to know that we might borrow on the security of the legacy; but, greatly grudging the loss of the interest which that would involve, I would have persuaded Percivale to ask a loan of Lady Bernard. He objected: on what ground do you think? That it would be disagreeable to Lady Bernard to be repaid the sum she had lent us! He would have finally consented, however, I have little doubt, had the absolute necessity for borrowing arrived.

About a week or ten days after the blessed news, he had a note from Mr. ——, whom he had authorized to part with the picture for thirty guineas. How much this was under its value, it is not easy to say, seeing the money-value of pictures is dependent on so many things: but, if the fairy godmother's executors had paid her legacy at once, that picture would not have been sold for less than five times the amount; and I may mention that the last time it changed hands it fetched five hundred and seventy pounds.

Mr. —— wrote that he had an offer of five and twenty for it, desiring to know whether he might sell it for that sum. Percivale at once gave his consent, and the next day received a check for eleven pounds, odd shillings; the difference being the borrowed amount upon it, its interest, the commission charged on the sale, and the price of a small picture-frame.

The next day, Percivale had a visitor at the studio,—no less a person than Mr. Baddeley, with his shirt-front in full blossom, and his diamond wallowing in light on his fifth finger,—I cannot call it his little finger, for his hands were as huge as they were soft and white,—hands descended of generations of laborious ones, but which had never themselves done any work beyond paddling in money.

He greeted Percivale with a jolly condescension, and told him, that, having seen and rather liked a picture of his the other day, he had come to inquire whether he had one that would do for a pendant to it; as he should like to have it, provided he did not want a fancy price for it.

Percivale felt as if he were setting out his children for sale, as he invited him to look about the room, and turned round a few from against the wall. The great man flitted hither and thither, spying at one after another through the cylinder of his curved hand, Percivale going on with his painting as if no one were there.

"How much do you want for this sketch?" asked Mr. Baddeley, at length, pointing to one of the most highly finished paintings in the room.

"I put three hundred on it at the Academy Exhibition," answered Percivale. "My friends thought it too little; but as it has been on my hands a long time now, and pictures don't rise in price in the keeping of the painter, I shouldn't mind taking two for it."

"Two tens, I suppose you mean," said Mr. Baddeley.

"I gave him a look," said Percivale, as he described the interview to me; and I knew as well as if I had seen it what kind of a phenomenon that look must have been.

"Come, now," Mr. Baddeley went on, perhaps misinterpreting the look, for it was such as a man of his property was not in the habit of receiving, "you mustn't think I'm made of money, or that I'm a green hand in the market. I know what your pictures fetch; and I'm a pretty sharp man of business, I believe. What do you really mean to say and stick to? Ready money, you know."

"Three hundred," said Percivale coolly.

"Why, Mr. Percivale!" cried Mr. Baddeley, drawing himself up, as my husband said, with the air of one who knew a trick worth two of that, "I paid Mr. —— fifty pounds, neither more nor less, for a picture of yours yesterday—a picture, allow me to say, worth"—

He turned again to the one in question with a critical air, as if about to estimate to a fraction its value as compared with the other.

"Worth three of that, some people think," said Percivale.

"The price of this, then, joking aside, is—?"

"Three hundred pounds," answered Percivale,—I know well how quietly.

"I understood you wished to sell it," said Mr. Baddeley, beginning, for all his good nature, to look offended, as well he might.

"I do wish to sell it. I happen to be in want of money."

"Then I'll be liberal, and offer you the same I paid for the other. I'll send you a check this afternoon for fifty—with pleasure."

"You cannot have that picture under three hundred."

"Why!" said the rich man, puzzled, "you offered it for two hundred, not five minutes ago."

"Yes; and you pretended to think I meant two tens."

"Offended you, I fear."

"At all events, betrayed so much ignorance of painting, that I would rather not have a picture of mine in your house."

"You're the first man ever presumed to tell me I was ignorant of painting," said Mr. Baddeley, now thoroughly indignant.

"You have heard the truth, then, for the first time," said Percivale, and resumed his work.

Mr. Baddeley walked out of the study.

I am not sure that he was so very ignorant. He had been in the way of buying popular pictures for some time, paying thousands for certain of them. I suspect he had eye enough to see that my husband's would probably rise in value, and, with the true huckster spirit, was ambitious of boasting how little he had given compared with what they were really worth.

Percivale in this case was doubtless rude. He had an insuperable aversion to men of Mr. Baddeley's class,—men who could have no position but for their money, and who yet presumed upon it, as if it were gifts and graces, genius and learning, judgment and art, all in one. He was in the habit of saying that the plutocracy, as he called it, ought to be put down,—that is, negatively and honestly,—by showing them no more respect than you really entertained for them. Besides, although he had no great favors for Cousin Judy's husband, he yet bore Mr. Baddeley a grudge for the way in which he had treated one with whom, while things went well with him, he had been ready enough to exchange hospitalities.

Before long, through Lady Bernard, he sold a picture at a fair price; and soon after, seeing in a shop-window the one Mr. —— had sold to Mr. Baddeley, marked ten pounds, went in and bought it. Within the year he sold it for a hundred and fifty.

By working day and night almost, he finished his new picture in time for the Academy; and, as he had himself predicted, it proved, at least in the opinion of all his artist friends, the best that he had ever painted. It was bought at once for three hundred pounds; and never since then have we been in want of money.

# CHAPTER XXXV.

## WHAT LADY BERNARD THOUGHT OF IT.

My reader may wonder, that, in my record of these troubles, I have never mentioned Marion. The fact is, I could not bring myself to tell her of them; partly because she was in some trouble herself, from strangers who had taken rooms in the house, and made mischief between her and her grandchildren; and partly because I knew she would insist on going to Lady Bernard; and, although I should not have minded it myself, I knew that nothing but seeing the children hungry would have driven my husband to consent to it.

One evening, after it was all over, I told Lady Bernard the story. She allowed me to finish it without saying a word. When I had ended, she still sat silent for a few moments; then, laying her hand on my arm, said,—

My dear child, you were very wrong, as well as very unkind. Why did you not let me know?"

"Because my husband would never have allowed me," I answered.

"Then I must have a talk with your husband," she said.

"I wish you would," I replied; "for I can't help thinking Percivale too severe about such things."

The very next day she called, and did have a talk with him in the study to the following effect:—

"I have come to quarrel with you, Mr. Percivale," said Lady Bernard.

"I'm sorry to hear it," he returned. "You're the last person I should like to quarrel with, for it would imply some unpardonable fault in me."

"It does imply a fault—and a great one," she rejoined; "though I trust not an unpardonable one. That depends on whether you can repent of it."

She spoke with such a serious air, that Percivale grew uneasy, and began to wonder what he could possibly have done to offend her. I had told him nothing of our conversation, wishing her to have her own way with him.

When she saw him troubled, she smiled.

"Is it not a fault, Mr. Percivale, to prevent one from obeying the divine law of bearing another's burden?"

"But," said Percivale, "I read as well, that every man shall bear his own burden."

"Ah!" returned Lady Bernard; "but I learn from Mr. Conybeare that two different Greek words are there used, which we translate only by the English *burden*. I cannot tell you what they are: I can only tell you the practical result. We are to bear one another's burdens of pain or grief or misfortune or doubt,—whatever weighs one down is to be borne by another; but the man who is tempted to exalt himself over his neighbor is taught to remember that he has his own load of disgrace to bear and answer for. It is just a weaker form of the lesson of the mote and the beam. You cannot get out at that door, Mr. Percivale. I beg you will read the passage in your Greek Testament, and see if you have not misapplied it. You *ought* to have let me bear your burden."

"Well, you see, my dear Lady Bernard," returned Percivale, at a loss to reply to such a vigorous assault, "I knew how it would be. You would have come here and bought pictures you didn't want; and I, knowing all the time you did it only to give me the money, should have had to talk to you as if I were taken in by it; and I really could *not* stand it."

"There you are altogether wrong. Besides depriving me of the opportunity of fulfilling a duty, and of the pleasure and the honor of helping you to bear your burden, you have deprived me of the opportunity of indulging a positive passion for pictures. I am constantly compelled to restrain it lest I should spend too much of the money given me for the common good on my own private tastes; but here was a chance for me! I might have had some of your lovely pictures in my drawing-room now—with a good conscience and a happy heart—if you had only been friendly. It was too bad of you, Mr. Percivale! I am not pretending in the least when I assert that I am really and thoroughly disappointed."

"I haven't a word to say for myself," returned Percivale.

"You couldn't have said a better," rejoined Lady Bernard; "but I hope you will never have to say it again."

"That I shall not. If ever I find myself in any difficulty worth speaking of, I will let you know at once."

"Thank you. Then we are friends again. And now I do think I am entitled to a picture,—at least, I think it will be pardonable if I yield to the *very* strong temptation I am under at this moment to buy one. Let me see: what have you in the slave-market, as your wife calls it?"

She bought "The Street Musician," as Percivale had named the picture taken from Dr. Donne. I was more miserable than I ought to have been when I found he had parted with it, but it was a great consolation to think it was to Lady Bernard's it had gone. She was the only one, except my mother or Miss Clare, I could have borne to think of as having become its possessor.

He had asked her what I thought a very low price for it; and I judge that Lady Bernard thought the same, but, after what had passed between them, would not venture to expostulate. With such a man as my husband, I fancy, she thought it best to let well alone. Anyhow, one day soon after this, her servant brought him a little box, containing a fine brilliant.

"The good lady's kindness is long-sighted," said my husband, as he placed it on his finger. "I shall be hard up, though, before I part with this. Wynnie, I've actually got a finer diamond than Mr. Baddeley! It *is* a beauty, if ever there was one!"

My husband, with all his carelessness of dress and adornment, has almost a passion for stones. It is delightful to hear him talk about them. But he had never possessed a single gem before Lady Bernard made him this present. I believe he is child enough to be happier for it all his life.

# CHAPTER XXXVI.

## RETROSPECTIVE.

Suddenly I become aware that I am drawing nigh the close of my monthly labors for a long year. Yet the year seems to have passed more rapidly because of this addition to my anxieties. Not that I haven't enjoyed the labor while I have been actually engaged in it, but the prospect of the next month's work would often come in to damp the pleasure of the present; making me fancy, as the close of each chapter drew near, that I should not have material for another left in my head. I heard a friend once remark that it is not the cares of to-day, but the cares of to-morrow, that weigh a man down. For the day we have the corresponding strength given, for the morrow we are told to trust; it is not ours yet.

When I get my money for my work, I mean to give my husband a long holiday. I half think of taking him to Italy,—for of course I can do what I like with my own, whether husband or money,—and so have a hand in making him a still better painter. Incapable of imitation, the sight of any real work is always of great service to him, widening his sense of art, enlarging his idea of what can be done, rousing what part of his being is most in sympathy with it,—a part possibly as yet only half awake; in a word, leading him another step towards that simplicity which is at the root of all diversity, being so simple that it needs all diversity to set it forth.

How impossible it seemed to me that I should ever write a book! Well or ill done, it is almost finished, for the next month is the twelfth. I must look back upon what I have written, to see what loose ends I may have left, and whether any allusion has not been followed up with a needful explanation; for this way of writing by portions—the only way in which I could have been persuaded to attempt the work, however—is unfavorable to artistic unity; an unnecessary remark, seeing that to such unity my work makes no pretensions. It is but a collection of portions detached from an uneventful, ordinary, and perhaps in part *therefore* very blessed life. Hence, perhaps, it was specially fitted for this mode of publication. At all events, I can cast upon it none of the blame of what failure I may have to confess.

A biography cannot be constructed with the art of a novel, for this reason: that a novel is constructed on the artist's scale, with swift-returning curves; a biography on the divine scale, whose circles are so large that they shoot beyond this world, sometimes even before we are able to detect in them the curve by which they will at length round themselves back towards completion. Hence, every life must look more or less fragmentary, and more or less out of drawing perhaps; not to mention the questionable effects in color and tone where the model himself will insist on taking palette and brushes, and laying childish, if not passionate, conceited, ambitious, or even spiteful hands to the work.

I do not find that I have greatly blundered, or omitted much that I ought to have mentioned. One odd thing is, that, in the opening conversation in which they urge me to the attempt, I have not mentioned Marion. I do not mean that she was present, but that surely some one must have suggested her and her history as affording endless material for my record. A thing apparently but not really strange is, that I have never said a word about the Mrs. Cromwell mentioned in the same conversation. The fact is, that I have but just arrived at the part of my story where she first comes in. She died about three months ago; and I can therefore with the more freedom narrate in the next chapter what I have known of her.

I find also that I have, in the fourth chapter, by some odd cerebro-mechanical freak, substituted the name of my Aunt *Martha* for that of my Aunt Millicent, another sister of my father, whom he has not, I believe, had occasion to mention in either of his preceding books. My Aunt Martha is Mrs. Weir, and has no children; my Aunt Millicent is Mrs. Parsons, married to a hard-working attorney, and has twelve children, now mostly grown up.

I find also, in the thirteenth chapter, an unexplained allusion. There my husband says, "Just ask my brother his experience in regard of the word to which you object." The word was *stomach*, at the use of which I had in my ill-temper taken umbrage: however disagreeable a word in itself, surely a husband might, if need be, use it without offence. It will be proof enough that my objection arose from pure ill-temper when I state that I have since asked Roger to what Percivale referred. His reply was, that, having been requested by a certain person who had a school for young ladies—probably she called it a college—to give her pupils a few lectures on physiology, he could not go far in the course without finding it necessary to make a not unfrequent use of the word, explaining the functions of the organ to which the name belonged, as resembling those of a mill. After the lecture was over, the school-mistress took him aside, and said she really could not allow her young ladies to be made familiar with such words. Roger averred that the word was absolutely necessary to the subject upon which she had desired his lectures; and that he did not know how any instruction in physiology could be given without the free use of it. "No doubt," she returned, "you must recognize the existence of the organ in question; but, as the name of it is offensive to ears polite, could you not substitute another? You have just said that its operations resemble those of a mill: could you not, as often as you require to speak of it, refer to it in the future as *the mill*?" Roger, with great difficulty repressing his laughter, consented; but in his next lecture made far more frequent reference to *the mill* than was necessary, using the word every time—I know exactly how—with a certain absurd solemnity that must have been irresistible. The girls went into fits of laughter at the first utterance of it, and seemed, he said, during the whole lecture, intent only on the new term, at every recurrence of which their laughter burst out afresh. Doubtless their school-mistress had herself prepared them to fall into Roger's trap. The same night he received a note from her, enclosing his fee for the lectures given, and informing him that the rest of the course would not be required. Roger sent back the money, saying that to accept part payment would be to renounce his claim for the whole; and that, besides, he had already received an amount of amusement quite sufficient to reward him for his labor. I told him I thought he had been rather cruel; but he said such a woman wanted a lesson. He said also, that to see the sort of women who sometimes had the responsibility of training girls must make the angels weep; none but a heartless mortal like himself could laugh where conventionality and insincerity were taught in every hint as to posture and speech. It was bad enough, he said, to shape yourself into your own ideal; but to have to fashion yourself after the ideal of one whose sole object in teaching was to make money, was something wretched indeed.

I find, besides, that several intentions I had when I started have fallen out of the scheme. Somehow, the subjects would not well come in, or I felt that I was in danger of injuring the persons in the attempt to set forth their opinions.

# CHAPTER XXXVII.

## MRS. CROMWELL COMES.

The moment the legacy was paid, our liabilities being already nearly discharged, my husband took us all to Hastings. I had never before been to any other seacoast town where the land was worthy of the sea, except Kilkhaven. Assuredly, there is no place within easy reach of London to be once mentioned with Hastings. Of course we kept clear of the more fashionable and commonplace St. Leonard's End, where yet the sea is the same,—a sea such that, not even off Cornwall, have I seen so many varieties of ocean-aspect. The immediate shore, with its earthy cliffs, is vastly inferior to the magnificent rock about Tintagel; but there is no outlook on the sea that I know more satisfying than that from the heights of Hastings, especially the East Hill; from the west side of which also you may, when weary of the ocean, look straight down on the ancient port, with its old houses, and fine, multiform red roofs, through the gauze of blue smoke which at eve of a summer day fills the narrow valley, softening the rough goings-on of life into harmony with the gentleness of sea and shore, field and sky. No doubt the suburbs are as unsightly as mere boxes of brick and lime can be, with an ugliness mean because pretentious, an altogether modern ugliness; but even this cannot touch the essential beauty of the place.

On the brow of this East Hill, just where it begins to sink towards Ecclesbourne Glen, stands a small, old, rickety house in the midst of the sweet grass of the downs. This house my husband was fortunate in finding to let, and took for three months. I am not, however, going to give any history of how we spent them; my sole reason for mentioning Hastings at all being that there I made the acquaintance of Mrs. Cromwell. It was on this wise.

One bright day, about noon,—almost all the days of those months were gorgeous with sunlight,—a rather fashionable maid ran up our little garden, begging for some water for her mistress. Sending her on with the water, I followed myself with a glass of sherry.

The door in our garden-hedge opened immediately on a green hollow in the hill, sloping towards the glen. As I stepped from the little gate on to the grass, I saw, to my surprise, that a white fog was blowing in from the sea. The heights on the opposite side of the glen, partially obscured thereby, looked more majestic than was their wont, and were mottled with patches of duller and brighter color as the drifts of the fog were heaped or parted here and there. Far down, at the foot of the cliffs, the waves of the rising tide, driven shore-wards with the added force of a south-west breeze, caught and threw back what sunlight reached them, and thinned with their shine the fog between. It was all so strange and fine, and had come on so suddenly,—for when I had looked out a few minutes before, sea and sky were purely resplendent,—that I stood a moment or two and gazed, almost forgetting why I was there.

When I bethought myself and looked about me, I saw, in the sheltered hollow before me, a lady seated in a curiously-shaped chair; so constructed, in fact, as to form upon occasion a kind of litter. It was plain she was an invalid, from her paleness, and the tension of the skin on her face, revealing the outline of the bones beneath. Her features were finely formed, but rather small, and her forehead low; a Greek-like face, with large, pale-blue eyes, that reminded me of little Amy Morley's. She smiled very sweetly when she saw me, and shook her head at the wine.

"I only wanted a little water," she said. "This fog seems to stifle me."

"It has come on very suddenly," I said. "Perhaps it is the cold of it that affects your breathing. You don't seem very strong, and any sudden change of temperature"—

"I am not one of the most vigorous of mortals," she answered, with a sad smile; "but the day seemed of such indubitable character, that, after my husband had brought me here in the carriage, he sent it home, and left me with my maid, while he went for a long walk across the downs. When he sees the change in the weather, though, he will turn directly."

"It won't do to wait him here," I said. "We must get you in at once. Would it be wrong to press you to take a little of this wine, just to counteract a chill?"

"I daren't touch any thing but water," she replied, "It would make me feverish at once."

"Run and tell the cook," I said to the maid, "that I want her here. You and she could carry your mistress in, could you not? I will help you."

"There's no occasion for that, ma'am: she's as light as a feather," was the whispered answer.

"I am quite ashamed of giving you so much trouble," said the lady, either hearing or guessing at our words. "My husband will be very grateful to you."

"It is only an act of common humanity," I said.

But, as I spoke, I fancied her fair brow clouded a little, as if she was not accustomed to common humanity, and the word sounded harsh in her ear. The cloud, however, passed so quickly that I doubted, until I knew her better, whether it had really been there.

The two maids were now ready; and, Jemima instructed by the other, they lifted her with the utmost ease, and bore her gently towards the house. The garden-gate was just wide enough to let the chair through, and in a minute more she was upon the sofa. Then a fit of coughing came on which shook her dreadfully. When it had passed she lay quiet, with closed eyes, and a smile hovering about her sweet, thin-lipped mouth. By and by she opened them, and looked at me with a pitiful expression.

"I fear you are far from well," I said.

"I'm dying," she returned quietly.

"I hope not," was all I could answer.

"Why should you hope not?" she returned. "I am in no strait betwixt two. I desire to depart. For me to die will be all gain."

"But your friends?" I ventured to suggest, feeling my way, and not quite relishing either the form or tone of her utterance.

"I have none but my husband."

"Then your husband?" I persisted.

"Ah!" she said mournfully, "he will miss me, no doubt, for a while. But it *must* be a weight off him, for I have been a sufferer so long!"

At this moment I heard a heavy, hasty step in the passage; the next, the room door opened, and in came, in hot haste, wiping his red face, a burly man, clumsy and active, with an umbrella in his hand, followed by a great, lumbering Newfoundland dog.

"Down, Polyphemus!" he said to the dog, which crept under a chair; while he, taking no notice of my presence, hurried up to his wife.

"My love! my little dove!" he said eagerly: "did you think I had forsaken you to the cruel elements?"

"No, Alcibiades," she answered, with a sweet little drawl; "but you do not observe that I am not the only lady in the room." Then, turning to me, "This is my husband, Mr. Cromwell," she said. "I cannot tell him *your* name."

"I am Mrs. Percivale," I returned, almost mechanically, for the gentleman's two names had run together and were sounding in my head: *Alcibiades Cromwell*! How could such a conjunction have taken place without the intervention of Charles Dickens?

"I beg your pardon, ma'am," said Mr. Cromwell, bowing. "Permit my anxiety about my poor wife to cover my rudeness. I had climbed the other side of the glen before I saw the fog; and it is no such easy matter to get up and down these hills of yours. I am greatly obliged to you for your hospitality.

You have doubtless saved her life; for she is a frail flower, shrinking from the least breath of cold."

The lady closed her eyes again, and the gentleman took her hand, and felt her pulse. He seemed about twice her age,—she not thirty; he well past fifty, the top of his head bald, and his gray hair sticking out fiercely over his good-natured red cheeks. He laid her hand gently down, put his hat on the table and his umbrella in a corner, wiped his face again, drew a chair near the sofa, and took his place by her side. I thought it better to leave them.

When I re-entered after a while, I saw from the windows, which looked sea-ward, that the wind had risen, and was driving thin drifts no longer, but great, thick, white masses of sea-fog landwards. It was the storm-wind of that coast, the south-west, which dashes the pebbles over the Parade, and the heavy spray against the houses. Mr. Alcibiades Cromwell was sitting as I had left him, silent, by the side of his wife, whose blue-veined eyelids had apparently never been lifted from her large eyes.

"Is there any thing I could offer Mrs. Cromwell?" I said. "Could she not eat something?"

"It is very little she can take," he answered; "but you are very kind. If you could let her have a little beef-tea? She generally has a spoonful or two about this time of the day."

"I am sorry we have none," I said; "and it would be far too long for her to wait. I have a nice chicken, though, ready for cooking: if she could take a little chicken-broth, that would be ready in a very little while."

"Thank you a thousand times, ma'am," he said heartily; "nothing could be better. She might even be induced to eat a mouthful of the chicken. But I am afraid your extreme kindness prevents me from being so thoroughly ashamed as I ought to be at putting you to so much trouble for perfect strangers."

"It is but a pleasure to be of service to any one in want of it," I said.

Mrs. Cromwell opened her eyes and smiled gratefully. I left the room to give orders about the chicken, indeed, to superintend the preparation of it myself; for Jemima could not be altogether trusted in such a delicate affair as cooking for an invalid.

When I returned, having set the simple operation going, Mr. Cromwell had a little hymn-book of mine he had found on the table open in his hand, and his wife was saying to him,—

"That is lovely! Thank you, husband. How can it be I never saw it before? I am quite astonished."

"She little knows what multitudes of hymns there are!" I thought with myself,—my father having made a collection, whence I had some idea of the extent of that department of religious literature.

"This is a hymn-book we are not acquainted with," said Mr. Cromwell, addressing me.

"It is not much known," I answered. "It was compiled by a friend of my father's for his own schools."

"And this," he went on, "is a very beautiful hymn. You may trust my wife's judgment, Mrs. Percivale. She lives upon hymns."

He read the first line to show which he meant. I had long thought, and still think, it the most beautiful hymn I know. It was taken from the German, only much improved in the taking, and given to my father to do what he pleased with; and my father had given it to another friend for his collection. Before that, however, while still in manuscript, it had fallen into the hands of a certain clergyman, by whom it had been published without leave asked, or apology made: a rudeness of which neither my father nor the author would have complained, for it was a pleasure to think it might thus reach many to whom it would be helpful; but they both felt aggrieved and indignant that he had taken the dishonest liberty of altering certain lines of it to suit his own opinions. As I am anxious to give it all the publicity I can, from pure delight in it, and love to all who are capable of the same delight, I shall here communicate it, in the full confidence of thus establishing a claim on the gratitude of my readers.

O Lord, how happy is the time  
  When in thy love I rest!  
When from my weariness I climb  
  Even to thy tender breast!  
The night of sorrow endeth there:  
  Thou art brighter than the sun;  
And in thy pardon and thy care  
  The heaven of heaven is won.

Let the world call herself my foe,  
  Or let the world allure.  
I care not for the world: I go  
  To this dear Friend and sure.  
And when life's fiercest storms are sent  
  Upon life's wildest sea,  
My little bark is confident,  
  Because it holds by thee.

When the law threatens endless death
  Upon the awful hill,
Straightway from her consuming breath
  My soul goes higher still,—
Goeth to Jesus, wounded, slain,
  And maketh him her home,
Whence she will not go out again,
  And where death cannot come.

I do not fear the wilderness
  Where thou hast been before;
Nay, rather will I daily press
  After thee, near thee, more.
Thou art my food; on thee I lean;
  Thou makest my heart sing;
And to thy heavenly pastures green
  All thy dear flock dost bring.

And if the gate that opens there
  Be dark to other men,
It is not dark to those who share
  The heart of Jesus then.
That is not losing much of life
  Which is not losing thee,
Who art as present in the strife
  As in the victory.

Therefore how happy is the time
  When in thy love I rest!
When from my weariness I climb
  Even to thy tender breast!
The night of sorrow endeth there:
  Thou are brighter than the sun;
And in thy pardon and thy care
  The heaven of heaven is won.

In telling them a few of the facts connected with the hymn, I presume I had manifested my admiration of it with some degree of fervor.

"Ah!" said Mrs. Cromwell, opening her eyes very wide, and letting the rising tears fill them: "Ah, Mrs. Percivale! you are—you must be one of us!"

"You must tell me first who you are," I said.

She held out her hand; I gave her mine: she drew me towards her, and whispered almost in my ear—though why or whence the affectation of secrecy I can only imagine—the name of a certain small and exclusive sect. I will not indicate it, lest I should be supposed to attribute to it either the peculiar faults or virtues of my new acquaintance.

"No," I answered, speaking with the calmness of self-compulsion, for I confess I felt repelled: "I am not one of you, except in as far as we all belong to the church of Christ."

I have thought since how much better it would have been to say, "Yes: for we all belong to the church of Christ."

She gave a little sigh of disappointment, closed her eyes for a moment, opened them again with a smile, and said with a pleading tone,—

"But you do believe in personal religion?"

"I don't see," I returned, "how religion can be any thing but personal."

Again she closed her eyes, in a way that made me think how convenient bad health must be, conferring not only the privilege of passing into retirement at any desirable moment, but of doing so in such a ready and easy manner as the mere dropping of the eyelids.

I rose to leave the room once more. Mr. Cromwell, who had made way for me to sit beside his wife, stood looking out of the window, against which came sweeping the great volumes of mist. I glanced out also. Not only was the sea invisible, but even the brow of the cliffs. When he turned towards me, as I passed him, I saw that his face had lost much of its rubicund hue, and looked troubled and anxious.

"There is nothing for it," I said to myself, "but keep them all night," and so gave directions to have a bedroom prepared for them. I did not much like it, I confess; for I was not much interested in either of them, while of the sect to which she belonged I knew enough already to be aware that it was of the narrowest and most sectarian in Christendom. It was a pity she had sought to claim me by a would-be closer bond than that of the body of Christ. Still I knew I should be myself a sectary if I therefore excluded her from my best sympathies. At the same time I did feel some curiosity concerning the oddly-yoked couple, and wondered whether the lady was really so ill as she would appear. I doubted whether she might not be using her illness both as an excuse for self-indulgence, and as a means of keeping her husband's interest in her on the stretch. I did not like the wearing of her religion on her sleeve, nor the mellifluous drawl in which she spoke.

When the chicken-broth was ready, she partook daintily; but before she ended had made a very good meal, including a wing and a bit of the breast; after which she fell asleep.

"There seems little chance of the weather clearing," said Mr. Cromwell in a whisper, as I approached the window where he once more stood.

"You must make up your mind to remain here for the night," I said.

"My dear madam, I couldn't think of it," he returned,—I thought from unwillingness to incommode a strange household. "An invalid like her, sweet lamb!" he went on, "requires so many little comforts and peculiar contrivances to entice the repose she so greatly needs, that—that—in short, I must get her home."

"Where do you live?" I asked, not sorry to find his intention of going so fixed.

"We have a house in Warrior Square," he answered. "We live in London, but have been here all the past winter. I doubt if she improves, though. I doubt—I doubt."

He said the last words in a yet lower and more mournful whisper; then, with a shake of his head, turned and gazed again through the window.

A peculiar little cough from the sofa made us both look round. Mrs. Cromwell was awake, and searching for her handkerchief. Her husband understood her movements, and hurried to her assistance. When she took the handkerchief from her mouth, there was a red spot upon it. Mr. Cromwell's face turned the color of lead; but his wife looked up at him, and smiled; a sweet, consciously pathetic smile.

"He has sent for me," she said. "The messenger has come."

Her husband made no answer. His eyes seemed starting from his head.

"Who is your medical man?" I asked him.

He told me, and I sent off my housemaid to fetch him. It was a long hour before he arrived; during which, as often as I peeped in, I saw him sitting silent, and holding her hand, until the last time, when I found him reading a hymn to her. She was apparently once more asleep. Nothing could be more favorable to her recovery than such quietness of both body and mind.

When the doctor came, and had listened to Mr. Cromwell's statement, he proceeded to examine her chest with much care. That over, he averred in her hearing that he found nothing serious; but told her husband apart that there was considerable mischief, and assured me afterwards that her lungs were all but gone, and that she could not live beyond a month or two. She had better be removed to her own house, he said, as speedily as possible.

"But it would be cruelty to send her out a day like this," I returned.

"Yes, yes: I did not mean that," he said. "But to-morrow, perhaps. You'll see what the weather is like. Is Mrs. Cromwell an old friend?"

"I never saw her until to-day," I replied.

"Ah!" he remarked, and said no more.

We got her to bed as soon as possible. I may just mention that I never saw any thing to equal the *point-devise* of her underclothing. There was not a stitch of cotton about her, using the word *stitch* in its metaphorical sense. But, indeed, I doubt whether her garments were not all made with linen thread. Even her horse-hair petticoat was quilted with rose-colored silk inside.

"Surely she has no children!" I said to myself; and was right, as my mother-readers will not be surprised to learn.

It was a week before she got up again, and a month before she was carried down the hill; during which time her husband sat up with her, or slept on a sofa in the room beside her, every night. During the day I took a share in the nursing, which was by no means oppressive, for she did not suffer much, and required little. Her chief demand was for hymns, the only annoyance connected with which worth mentioning was, that she often wished me to admire with her such as I could only half like, and occasionally such as were thoroughly distasteful to me. Her husband had brought her own collection from Warrior Square, volumes of hymns in manuscript, copied by her own hand, many of them strange to me, none of those I read altogether devoid of literary merit, and some of them lovely both in feeling and form. But all, even the best, which to me were unobjectionable, belonged to one class,—a class breathing a certain tone difficult to describe; one, however, which I find characteristic of all the Roman Catholic hymns I have read. I will not indicate any of her selection; neither, lest I should be supposed to object to this or that one answering to the general description, and yet worthy of all respect, or even sympathy, will I go further with a specification of their sort than to say that what pleased me in them was their full utterance of personal devotion to the Saviour, and that what displeased me was a sort of sentimental regard of self in the matter,—an implied special, and thus partially exclusive predilection or preference of the Saviour for the individual supposed to be making use of them; a certain fundamental want of humility therefore, although the forms of speech in which they were cast might be laboriously humble. They also not unfrequently manifested a great leaning to the forms of earthly show as representative of the glories of that kingdom which the Lord says is *within us*.

Likewise the manner in which Mrs. Cromwell talked reminded me much of the way in which a nun would represent her individual relation to Christ. I can best show what I mean by giving a conversation I had with her one day when she was recovering, which she did with wonderful rapidity up to a certain point. I confess I shrink a little from reproducing it, because of the sacred name which, as it seemed to me, was far too often upon her lips, and too easily uttered. But then, she was made so different from me!

The fine weather had returned in all its summer glory, and she was lying on a couch in her own room near the window, whence she could gaze on the expanse of sea below, this morning streaked with the most delicate gradations of distance, sweep beyond sweep, line and band and ribbon of softly, often but slightly varied hue, leading the eyes on and on into the infinite. There may have been some atmospheric illusion ending off the show, for the last reaches mingled so with the air that you saw no horizon line, only a great breadth of border; no spot which could you appropriate with certainty either to sea or sky; while here and there was a vessel, to all appearance, pursuing its path in the sky, and not upon the sea. It was, as some of my readers will not require to be told, a still, gray forenoon, with a film of cloud over all the heavens, and many horizontal strata of deeper but varying density near the horizon.

Mrs. Cromwell had lain for some time with her large eyes fixed on the farthest confusion of sea and sky.

"I have been sending out my soul," she said at length, "to travel all across those distances, step by step, on to the gates of pearl. Who knows but that may be the path I must travel to meet the Bridegroom?"

"The way is wide," I said: "what if you should miss him?"

I spoke almost involuntarily. The style of her talk was very distasteful to me; and I had just been thinking of what I had once heard my father say, that at no time were people in more danger of being theatrical than when upon their death-beds.

"No," she returned, with a smile of gentle superiority; "no: that cannot be. Is he not waiting for me? Has he not chosen me, and called me for his own? Is not my Jesus mine? I shall *not* miss him. He waits to give me my new name, and clothe me in the garments of righteousness."

As she spoke, she clasped her thin hands, and looked upwards with a radiant expression. Far as it was from me to hint, even in my own soul, that the Saviour was not hers, tenfold more hers than she was able to think, I could not at the same time but doubt whether her heart and soul and mind were as close to him as her words would indicate she thought they were. She could not be wrong in trusting him; but could she be right in her notion of the measure to which her union with him had been perfected? I could not help thinking that a little fear, soon to pass into reverence, might be to her a salutary thing. The fear, I thought, would heighten and deepen the love, and purify it from that self which haunted her whole consciousness, and of which she had not yet sickened, as one day she certainly must.

"My lamp is burning," she said; "I feel it burning. I love my Lord. It would be false to say otherwise."

"Are you sure you have oil enough in your vessel as well as in your lamp?" I said.

"Ah, you are one of the doubting!" she returned kindly. "Don't you know that sweet hymn about feeding our lamps from the olive-trees of Gethsemane? The idea is taken from the lamp the prophet Zechariah saw in his vision, into which two olive-branches, through two golden pipes, emptied the golden oil out of themselves. If we are thus one with the olive-tree, the oil cannot fail us. It is not as if we had to fill our lamps from a cruse of our own. This is the cruse that cannot fail."

"True, true," I said; "but ought we not to examine our own selves whether we are in the faith?"

"Let those examine that doubt," she replied; and I could not but yield in my heart that she had had the best of the argument.

For I knew that the confidence in Christ which prevents us from thinking of ourselves, and makes us eager to obey his word, leaving all the care of our feelings to him, is a true and healthy faith. Hence I could not answer her, although I doubted whether her peace came from such confidence,—doubted for several reasons: one, that, so far from not thinking of herself, she seemed full of herself; another, that she seemed to find no difficulty with herself in any way; and, surely, she was too young for all struggle to be over! I perceived no reference to the will of God in regard of any thing she had to do, only in regard of what she had to suffer, and especially in regard of that smallest of matters, when she was to go. Here I checked myself, for what could she *do* in such a state of health? But then she never spoke as if she had any anxiety about the welfare of other people. That, however, might be from her absolute contentment in the will of God. But why did she always look to the Saviour through a mist of hymns, and never go straight back to the genuine old good news, or to the mighty thoughts and exhortations with which the first preachers of that news followed them up and unfolded the grandeur of their goodness? After all, was I not judging her? On the other hand, ought I not to care for her state? Should I not be inhuman, that is, unchristian, if I did not?

In the end I saw clearly enough, that, except it was revealed to me what I ought to say, I had no right to say any thing; and that to be uneasy about her was to distrust Him whose it was to teach her, and who would perfect that which he had certainly begun in her. For her heart, however poor and faulty and flimsy its faith might be, was yet certainly drawn towards the object of faith. I, therefore, said nothing more in the direction of opening her eyes to what I considered her condition: that view of it might, after all, be but a phantasm of my own projection. What was plainly my duty was to serve her as one of those the least of whom the Saviour sets forth as representing himself. I would do it to her as unto him.

My children were out the greater part of every day, and Dora was with me, so that I had more leisure than I had had for a long time. I therefore set myself to wait upon her as a kind of lady's maid in things spiritual. Her own maid, understanding her ways, was sufficient for things temporal. I resolved to try to help her after her own fashion, and not after mine; for, however strange the nourishment she preferred might seem, it must at least be of the *kind* she could best assimilate. My care should be to give her her gruel as good as I might, and her beef-tea strong, with chicken-broth instead of barley-water and delusive jelly. But much opportunity of ministration was not afforded me; for her husband, whose business in life she seemed to regard as the care of her,—for which, in truth, she was gently and lovingly grateful,—and who not merely accepted her view of the matter, but, I was pretty sure, had had a large share in originating it, was even more constant in his attentions than she found altogether agreeable, to judge by the way in which she would insist on his going out for a second walk, when it was clear, that, besides his desire to be with her, he was not inclined to walk any more.

I could set myself, however, as I have indicated, to find fitting pabulum for her, and that of her chosen sort. This was possible for me in virtue of my father's collection of hymns, and the aid he could give me. I therefore sent him a detailed description of what seemed to me her condition, and what I thought I might do for her. It was a week before he gave me an answer; but it arrived a thorough one, in the shape of a box of books, each bristling with paper marks, many of them inscribed with some fact concerning, or criticism upon, the hymn indicated. He wrote that he quite agreed with my notion of the right mode of serving her; for any other would be as if a besieging party were to batter a postern by means of boats instead of walking over a lowered drawbridge, and under a raised portcullis.

Having taken a survey of the hymns my father thus pointed out to me, and arranged them according to their degrees of approximation to the weakest of those in Mrs. Cromwell's collection, I judged that in all of them there was something she must appreciate, although the main drift of several would be entirely beyond her apprehension. Even these, however, it would be well to try upon her.

Accordingly, the next time she asked me to read from her collection, I made the request that she would listen to some which I believed she did not know, but would, I thought, like. She consented with eagerness, was astonished to find she knew none of them, expressed much approbation of some, and showed herself delighted with others.

That she must have had some literary faculty seems evident from the genuine pleasure she took in simple, quaint, sometimes even odd hymns of her own peculiar kind. But the very best of another sort she could not appreciate. For instance, the following, by John Mason, in my father's opinion one of the best hymn-writers, had no attraction for her:—

"Thou wast, O God, and thou was blest
  Before the world begun;
Of thine eternity possest
  Before time's glass did run.
Thou needest none thy praise to sing,
  As if thy joy could fade:
Couldst thou have needed any thing,
  Thou couldst have nothing made.

"Great and good God, it pleaseth thee
  Thy Godhead to declare;
And what thy goodness did decree,
  Thy greatness did prepare:
Thou spak'st, and heaven and earth appeared,
  And answered to thy call;
As if their Maker's voice they Heard,
  Which is the creature's All.

"Thou spak'st the word, most mighty Lord;
  Thy word went forth with speed:
Thy will, O Lord, it was thy word;
  Thy word it was thy deed.
Thou brought'st forth Adam from the ground,
  And Eve out of his side:
Thy blessing made the earth abound
  With these two multiplied.

"Those three great leaves, heaven, sea, and land,
  Thy name in figures show;
Brutes feel the bounty of thy hand,
  But I my Maker know.
Should not I here thy servant be,
  Whose creatures serve me here?
My Lord, whom should I fear but thee,
  Who am thy creatures' fear?

"To whom, Lord, should I sing but thee,
  The Maker of my tongue?
Lo! other lords would seize on me,
  But I to thee belong.
As waters haste unto their sea,
  And earth unto its earth,
So let my soul return to thee,
  From whom it had its birth.

"But, ah! I'm fallen in the night,
  And cannot come to thee:
Yet speak the word, '*Let there be light*;'
  It shall enlighten me.
And let thy word, most mighty Lord,
  Thy fallen creature raise:
Oh! make me o'er again, and I
  Shall sing my Maker's praise."

This and others, I say, she could not relish; but my endeavors were crowned with success in so far that she accepted better specimens of the sort she liked than any she had; and I think they must have had a good influence upon her.

She seemed to have no fear of death, contemplating the change she believed at hand, not with equanimity merely, but with expectation. She even wrote hymns about it,—sweet, pretty, and weak, always with herself and the love of her Saviour for *her*, in the foreground. She had not learned that the love which lays hold of that which is human in the individual, that is, which is common to the whole race, must be an infinitely deeper, tenderer, and more precious thing to the individual than any affection manifesting itself in the preference of one over another.

For the sake of revealing her modes of thought, I will give one more specimen of my conversations with her, ere I pass on. It took place the evening before her departure for her own house. Her husband had gone to make some final preparations, of which there had been many. For one who expected to be unclothed that she might be clothed upon, she certainly made a tolerable to-do about the garment she was so soon to lay aside; especially seeing she often spoke of it as an ill-fitting garment—never with peevishness or complaint, only, as it seemed to me, with far more interest than it was worth. She had even, as afterwards appeared, given her husband—good, honest, dog-like man—full instructions as to the ceremonial of its interment. Perhaps I should have been considerably less bewildered with her conduct had I suspected that she was not half so near death as she chose to think, and that she had as yet suffered little.

That evening, the stars just beginning to glimmer through the warm flush that lingered from the sunset, we sat together in the drawing-room looking out on the sea. My patient appearing, from the light in her eyes, about to go off into one of her ecstatic moods, I hastened to forestall it, if I might, with whatever came uppermost; for I felt my inability to sympathize with her in these more of a pain than my reader will, perhaps, readily imagine.

"It seems like turning you out to let you go to-morrow, Mrs. Cromwell," I said; "but, you see, our three months are up two days after, and I cannot help it."

"You have been very kind," she said, half abstractedly. "And you are really much better. Who would have thought three weeks ago to see you so well to-day?"

"Ah! you congratulate me, do you?" she rejoined, turning her big eyes full upon me; "congratulate me that I am doomed to be still a captive in the prison of this vile body? Is it kind? Is it well?"

"At least, you must remember, if you are *doomed*, who dooms you."

"'Oh that I had the wings of a dove!'" she cried, avoiding my remark, of which I doubt if she saw the drift. "Think, dear Mrs. Percivale: the society of saints and angels!—all brightness and harmony and peace! Is it not worth forsaking this world to inherit a kingdom like that? Wouldn't *you* like to go? Don't *you* wish to fly away and be at rest?"

She spoke as if expostulating and reasoning with one she would persuade to some kind of holy emigration.

"Not until I am sent for," I answered.

"I *am* sent for," she returned.

"'The wave may be cold, and the tide may be strong;
But, hark! on the shore the angels' glad song!'

"Do you know that sweet hymn, Mrs. Percivale? There I shall be able to love him aright, to serve him aright!

"'Here all my labor is so poor!
Here all my love so faint!
But when I reach the heavenly door,
I cease the weary plaint.'"

I couldn't help wishing she would cease it a little sooner.

"But suppose," I ventured to say, "it were the will of God that you should live many years yet."

"That cannot be. And why should you wish it for me? Is it not better to depart and be with him? What pleasure could it be to a weak, worn creature like me to go on living in this isle of banishment?"

"But suppose you were to recover your health: would it not be delightful to *do* something for his sake? If you would think of how much there is to be done in the world, perhaps you would wish less to die and leave it."

"Do not tempt me," she returned reproachfully.

And then she quoted a passage the application of which to her own case appeared to me so irreverent, that I confess I felt like Abraham with the idolater; so far at least as to wish her out of the house, for I could bear with her, I thought, no longer.

She did leave it the next day, and I breathed more freely than since she had entered it.

My husband came down to fetch me the following day; and a walk with him along the cliffs in the gathering twilight, during which I recounted the affectations of my late visitor, completely wiped the cobwebs from my mental windows, and enabled me to come to the conclusion that Mrs. Cromwell was but a spoiled child, who would, somehow or other, be brought to her senses before all was over. I was ashamed of my impatience with her, and believed if I could have learned her history, of which she had told me nothing, it would have explained the rare phenomenon of one apparently able to look death in the face with so little of the really spiritual to support her, for she seemed to me to know Christ only after the flesh. But had she indeed ever looked death in the face?

# CHAPTER XXXVIII.

## MRS. CROMWELL GOES.

I heard nothing more of her for about a year. A note or two passed between us, and then all communication ceased. This, I am happy to think, was not immediately my fault: not that it mattered much, for we were not then fitted for much communion; we had too little in common to commune.

"Did you not both believe in one Lord?" I fancy a reader objecting. "How, then, can you say you had too little in common to be able to commune?"

I said the same to myself, and tried the question in many ways. The fact remained, that we could not commune, that is, with any heartiness; and, although I may have done her wrong, it was, I thought, to be accounted for something in this way. The Saviour of whom she spoke so often, and evidently thought so much, was in a great measure a being of her own fancy; so much so, that she manifested no desire to find out what the Christ was who had spent three and thirty years in making a revelation of himself to the world. The knowledge she had about him was not even at second-hand, but at many removes. She did not study his words or his actions to learn his thoughts or his meanings; but lived in a kind of dreamland of her own, which could be interesting only to the dreamer. Now, if we are to come to God through Christ, it must surely be by knowing Christ; it must be through the knowledge of Christ that the Spirit of the Father mainly works in the members of his body; and it seemed to me she did not take the trouble to "know him and the power of his resurrection." Therefore we had scarcely enough of common ground, as I say, to meet upon. I could not help contrasting her religion with that of Marion Clare.

At length I had a note from her, begging me to go and see her at her house at Richmond, and apologizing for her not coming to me, on the score of her health. I felt it my duty to go, but sadly grudged the loss of time it seemed, for I expected neither pleasure nor profit from the visit. Percivale went with me, and left me at the door to have a row on the river, and call for me at a certain hour.

The house and grounds were luxurious and lovely both, two often dissociated qualities. She could have nothing to desire of this world's gifts, I thought. But the moment she entered the room into which I had been shown, I was shocked at the change I saw in her. Almost to my horror, she was in a widow's cap; and disease and coming death were plain on every feature. Such was the contrast, that the face in my memory appeared that of health.

"My dear Mrs. Cromwell!" I gasped out.

"You see," she said, and sitting down, on a straight-backed chair, looked at me with lustreless eyes.

Death had been hovering about her windows before, but had entered at last; not to take the sickly young woman longing to die, but the hale man, who would have clung to the last edge of life.

"He is taken, and I am left," she said abruptly, after a long pause.

Her drawl had vanished: pain and grief had made her simple. "Then," I thought with myself, "she did love him!" But I could say nothing. She took my silence for the sympathy it was, and smiled a heart-rending smile, so different from that little sad smile she used to have; really pathetic now, and with hardly a glimmer in it of the old self-pity. I rose, put my arms about her, and kissed her on the forehead; she laid her head on my shoulder, and wept.

"Whom the Lord loveth he chasteneth," I faltered out, for her sorrow filled me with a respect that was new.

"Yes," she returned, as gently as hopelessly; "and whom he does not love as well."

"You have no ground for saying so," I answered. "The apostle does not."

"My lamp is gone out," she said; "gone out in darkness, utter darkness. You warned me, and I did not heed the warning. I thought I knew better, but I was full of self-conceit. And now I am wandering where there is no way and no light. My iniquities have found me out."

I did not say what I thought I saw plain enough,—that her lamp was just beginning to burn. Neither did I try to persuade her that her iniquities were small.

"But the Bridegroom," I said, "is not yet come. There is time to go and get some oil."

"Where am I to get it?" she returned, in a tone of despair.

"From the Bridegroom himself," I said.

"No," she answered. "I have talked and talked and talked, and you know he says he abhors talkers. I am one of those to whom he will say 'I know you not.'"

"And you will answer him that you have eaten and drunk in his presence, and cast out devils, and—?"

"No, no: I will say he is right; that it is all my own fault; that I thought I was something when I was nothing, but that I know better now."

A dreadful fit of coughing interrupted her. As soon as it was over, I said,—

"And what will the Lord say to you, do you think, when you have said so to him?"

"Depart from me," she answered in a hollow, forced voice.

"No," I returned. "He will say, 'I know you well. You have told me the truth. Come in.'"

"*Do* you think so?" she cried. "You never used to think well of me."

"Those who were turned away," I said, avoiding her last words, "were trying to make themselves out better than they were: they trusted, not in the love of Christ, but in what they thought their worth and social standing. Perhaps, if their deeds had been as good as they thought them, they would have known better than to trust in them. If they had told him the truth; if they had said, 'Lord, we are workers of iniquity; Lord, we used to be hypocrites, but we speak the truth now: forgive us,'—do you think he would then have turned them away? No, surely. If your lamp has gone out, make haste and tell him how careless you have been; tell him all, and pray him for oil and light; and see whether your lamp will not straightway glimmer,—glimmer first and then glow."

"Ah, Mrs. Percivale!" she cried: "I would *do* something for His sake now if I might, but I cannot. If I had but resisted the disease in me for the sake of serving him, I might have been able now: but my chance is over; I cannot now; I have too much pain. And death looks such a different thing now! I used to think of it only as a kind of going to sleep, easy though sad—sad, I mean, in the eyes of mourning friends. But, alas! I have no friends, now that my husband is gone. I never dreamed of him going first. He loved me: indeed he did, though you will hardly believe it; but I always took it as a matter of course. I never saw how beautiful and unselfish he was till he was gone. I have been selfish and stupid and dull, and my sins have found me out. A great darkness has fallen upon me; and although weary of life, instead of longing for death, I shrink from it with horror. My cough will not let me sleep: there is nothing but weariness in my body, and despair in my heart. Oh how black and dreary the nights are! I think of the time in your house as of an earthly paradise. But where is the heavenly paradise I used to dream of then?" "Would it content you," I asked, "to be able to dream of it again?"

"No, no. I want something very different now. Those fancies look so uninteresting and stupid now! All I want now is to hear God say, 'I forgive you.' And my husband—I must have troubled him sorely. You don't know how good he was, Mrs. Percivale. *He* made no pretences like silly me. Do you know," she went on, lowering her voice, and speaking with something like horror in its tone, "Do you know, I cannot *bear* hymns!"

As she said it, she looked up in my face half-terrified with the anticipation of the horror she expected to see manifested there. I could not help smiling. The case was not one for argument of any kind: I thought for a moment, then merely repeated the verse,—

"When the law threatens endless death,
Upon the awful hill,
Straightway, from her consuming breath,
My soul goes higher still,—
Goeth to Jesus, wounded, slain,
And maketh him her home,
Whence she will not go out again,
And where Death cannot come."

"Ah! that is good," she said: "if only I could get to him! But I cannot get to him. He is so far off! He seems to be—nowhere."

I think she was going to say *nobody*, but changed the word.

"If you felt for a moment how helpless and wretched I feel, especially in the early morning," she went on; "how there seems nothing to look for, and no help to be had,—you would pity rather than blame me, though I know I deserve blame. I feel as if all the heart and soul and strength and mind, with which we are told to love God, had gone out of me; or, rather, as if I had never had any. I doubt if I ever had. I tried very hard for a long time to get a sight of Jesus, to feel myself in his presence; but it was of no use, and I have quite given it up now."

I made her lie on the sofa, and sat down beside her.

"Do you think," I said, "that any one, before he came, could have imagined such a visitor to the world as Jesus Christ?"

"I suppose not," she answered listlessly.

"Then, no more can you come near him now by trying to imagine him. You cannot represent to yourself the reality, the Being who can comfort you. In other words, you cannot take him into your heart. He only knows himself, and he only can reveal himself to you. And not until he does so, can you find any certainty or any peace."

"But he doesn't—he won't reveal himself to me."

"Suppose you had forgotten what some friend of your childhood was like—say, if it were possible, your own mother; suppose you could not recall a feature of her face, or the color of her eyes; and suppose, that, while you were very miserable about it, you remembered all at once that you had a portrait of her in an old desk you had not opened for years: what would you do?"

"Go and get it," she answered like a child at the Sunday school.

"Then why shouldn't you do so now? You have such a portrait of Jesus, far truer and more complete than any other kind of portrait can be,—the portrait his own deeds and words give us of him."

"I see what you mean; but that is all about long ago, and I want him now. That is in a book, and I want him in my heart."

"How are you to get him into your heart? How could you have him there, except by knowing him? But perhaps you think you do know him?"

"I am certain I do not know him; at least, as I want to know him," she said.

"No doubt," I went on, "he can speak to your heart without the record, and, I think, is speaking to you now in this very want of him you feel. But how could he show himself to you otherwise than by helping you to understand the revelation of himself which it cost him such labor to afford? If the story were millions of years old, so long as it was true, it would be all the same as if it had been ended only yesterday; for, being what he represented himself, he never can change. To know what he was then, is to know what he is now."

"But, if I knew him so, that wouldn't be to have him with me."

"No; but in that knowledge he might come to you. It is by the door of that knowledge that his Spirit, which is himself, comes into the soul. You would at least be more able to pray to him: you would know what kind of a being you had to cry to. *You* would thus come nearer to him; and no one ever drew nigh to him to whom he did not also draw nigh. If you would but read the story as if you had never read it before, as if you were reading the history of a man you heard of for the first time"—

"Surely you're not a Unitarian, Mrs. Percivale!" she said, half lifting her head, and looking at me with a dim terror in her pale eyes.

"God forbid!" I answered. "But I would that many who think they know better believed in him half as much as many Unitarians do. It is only by understanding and believing in that humanity of his, which in such pain and labor manifested his Godhead, that we can come to know it,—know that Godhead, I mean, in virtue of which alone he was a true and perfect man; that Godhead which alone can satisfy with peace and hope the poorest human soul, for it also is the offspring of God."

I ceased, and for some moments she sat silent. Then she said feebly,—

"There's a Bible somewhere in the room."

I found it, and read the story of the woman who came behind him in terror, and touched the hem of his garment. I could hardly read it for the emotion it caused in myself; and when I ceased I saw her weeping silently.

A servant entered with the message that Mr. Percivale had called for me.

"I cannot see him to-day," she sobbed.

"Of course not," I replied. "I must leave you now; but I will come again,—come often if you like."

"You are as kind as ever!" she returned, with a fresh burst of tears. "Will you come and be with me when—when—?"

She could not finish for sobs.

"I will," I said, knowing well what she meant.

This is how I imagined the change to have come about: what had seemed her faith had been, in a great measure, but her hope and imagination, occupying themselves with the forms of the religion towards which all that was highest in her nature dimly urged. The two characteristics of amicability and selfishness, not unfrequently combined, rendered it easy for her to deceive herself, or rather conspired to prevent her from undeceiving herself, as to the quality and worth of her religion. For, if she had been other than amiable, the misery following the outbreaks of temper which would have been of certain occurrence in the state of her health, would have made her aware in some degree of her moral condition; and, if her thoughts had not been centred upon herself, she would, in her care for others, have learned her own helplessness; and the devotion of her good husband, not then accepted merely as a natural homage to her worth, would have shown itself as a love beyond her deserts, and would have roused the longing to be worthy of it. She saw now that he must have imagined her far better than she was: but she had not meant to deceive him; she had but followed the impulses of a bright, shallow nature.

But that last epithet bids me pause, and remember that my father has taught me, and that I have found the lesson true, that there is no such thing as a shallow nature: every nature is infinitely deep, for the works of God are everlasting. Also, there is no nature that is not shallow to what it must become. I suspect every nature must have the subsoil ploughing of sorrow, before it can recognize either its present poverty or its possible wealth.

When her husband died, suddenly, of apoplexy, she was stunned for a time, gradually awaking to a miserable sense of unprotected loneliness, so much the more painful for her weakly condition, and the overcare to which she had been accustomed. She was an only child, and had become an orphan within a year or two after her early marriage. Left thus without shelter, like a delicate plant whose house of glass has been shattered, she speedily recognized her true condition. With no one to heed her whims, and no one capable of sympathizing with the genuine misery which supervened, her disease gathered strength rapidly, her lamp went out, and she saw no light beyond; for the smoke of that lamp had dimmed the windows at which the stars would have looked in. When life became dreary, her fancies, despoiled of the halo they had cast on the fogs of selfish comfort, ceased to interest her; and the future grew a vague darkness, an uncertainty teeming with questions to which she had no answer. Henceforth she was conscious of life only as a weakness, as the want of a deeper life to hold it up. Existence had become a during faint, and self hateful. She saw that she was poor and miserable and blind and naked,—that she had never had faith fit to support her.

But out of this darkness dawned at least a twilight, so gradual, so slow, that I cannot tell when or how the darkness began to melt. She became aware of a deeper and simpler need than hitherto she had known,—the need of life in herself, the life of the Son of God. I went to see her often. At the time when I began this history, I was going every other day,—sometimes oftener, for her end seemed to be drawing nigh. Her weakness had greatly increased: she could but just walk across the room, and was constantly restless. She had no great continuous pain, but oft-returning sharp fits of it. She looked genuinely sad, and her spirits never recovered themselves. She seldom looked out of the window; the daylight seemed to distress her: flowers were the only links between her and the outer world,—wild ones, for the scent of greenhouse-flowers, and even that of most garden ones, she could not bear. She had been very fond of music, but could no longer endure her piano: every note seemed struck on a nerve. But she was generally quiet in her mind, and often peaceful. The more her body decayed about her, the more her spirit seemed to come alive. It was the calm of a gray evening, not so lovely as a golden sunset or a silvery moonlight, but more sweet than either. She talked little of her feelings, but evidently longed after the words of our Lord. As she listened to some of them, I could see the eyes which had now grown dim with suffering, gleam with the light of holy longing and humble adoration.

For some time she often referred to her coming departure, and confessed that she "feared death; not so much what might be on the other side, as the dark way itself,—the struggle, the torture, the fainting; but by degrees her allusions to it became rarer, and at length ceased almost entirely. Once I said to her,—

"Are you afraid of death still, Eleanor?"

"No—not much," she replied, after a brief pause. "He may do with me whatever He likes."

Knowing so well what Marion could do to comfort and support, and therefore desirous of bringing them together, I took her one day with me. But certain that the thought of seeing a stranger would render my poor Eleanor uneasy, and that what discomposure a sudden introduction might cause would speedily vanish in Marion's presence, I did not tell her what I was going to do. Nor in this did I mistake. Before we left, it was plain that Marion had a far more soothing influence upon her than I had myself. She looked eagerly for her next visit, and my mind was now more at peace concerning her.

One evening, after listening to some stories from Marion about her friends, Mrs. Cromwell said,—

"Ah, Miss Clare! to think I might have done something for *Him* by doing it for *them!* Alas! I have led a useless life, and am dying out of this world without having borne any fruit! Ah, me, me!"

"You are doing a good deal for him now," said Marion, "and hard work too!" she added; "harder far than mine."

"I am only dying," she returned—so sadly!

"You are enduring chastisement," said Marion. "The Lord gives one one thing to do, and another another. We have no right to wish for other work than he gives us. It is rebellious and unchildlike, whatever it may seem. Neither have we any right to wish to be better in *our* way: we must wish to be better in *his*."

"But I *should* like to do something for *him*; bearing is only for myself. Surely I may wish that?"

"No: you may not. Bearing is not only for yourself. You are quite wrong in thinking you do nothing for him in enduring," returned Marion, with that abrupt decision of hers which seemed to some like rudeness. "What is the will of God? Is it not your sanctification? And why did he make the Captain of our salvation perfect through suffering? Was it not that he might in like manner bring many sons into glory? Then, if you are enduring, you are working with God,—for the perfection through suffering of one more: you are working for God in yourself, that the will of God may be done in you; that he may have his very own way with you. It is the only work he requires of you now: do it not only willingly, then, but contentedly. To make people good is all his labor: be good, and you are a fellow-worker with God in the highest region of labor. He does not want you for other people—*yet*."

At the emphasis Marion laid on the last word, Mrs. Cromwell glanced sharply up. A light broke over her face: she had understood, and with a smile was silent.

One evening, when we were both with her, it had grown very sultry and breathless.

"Isn't it very close, dear Mrs. Percivale?" she said.

I rose to get a fan; and Marion, leaving the window as if moved by a sudden resolve, went and opened the piano. Mrs. Cromwell made a hasty motion, as if she must prevent her. But, such was my faith in my friend's soul as well as heart, in her divine taste as well as her human faculty, that I ventured to lay my hand on Mrs. Cromwell's. It was enough for sweetness like hers: she yielded instantly, and lay still, evidently nerving herself to suffer. But the first movement stole so "soft and soullike" on her ear, trembling as it were on the border-land between sound and silence, that she missed the pain she expected, and found only the pleasure she looked not for. Marion's hands made the instrument sigh and sing, not merely as with a human voice, but as with a human soul. Her own voice next evolved itself from the dim uncertainty, in sweet proportions and delicate modulations, stealing its way into the heart, to set first one chord, then another, vibrating, until the whole soul was filled with responses. If I add that her articulation was as nearly perfect as the act of singing will permit, my reader may well believe that a song of hers would do what a song might.

Where she got the song she then sung, she always avoids telling me. I had told her all I knew and understood concerning Mrs. Cromwell, and have my suspicions. This is the song:—

"I fancy I hear a whisper
As of leaves in a gentle air:
Is it wrong, I wonder, to fancy
It may be the tree up there?—
The tree that heals the nations,
Growing amidst the street,
And dropping, for who will gather,
Its apples at their feet?

"I fancy I hear a rushing
As of waters down a slope:
Is it wrong, I wonder, to fancy
It may be the river of hope?
The river of crystal waters
That flows from the very throne,
And runs through the street of the city
With a softly jubilant tone?

"I fancy a twilight round me,
And a wandering of the breeze,

With a hush in that high city,
And a going in the trees.
But I know there will be no night there,—
No coming and going day;
For the holy face of the Father
Will be perfect light alway.

"I could do without the darkness,
And better without the sun;
But, oh, I should like a twilight
After the day was done!
Would he lay his hand on his forehead,
On his hair as white as wool,
And shine one hour through his fingers,
Till the shadow had made me cool?

"But the thought is very foolish:
If that face I did but see,
All else would be all forgotten,—
River and twilight and tree;
I should seek, I should care, for nothing,
Beholding his countenance;
And fear only to lose one glimmer
By one single sideway glance.

"'Tis but again a foolish fancy
To picture the countenance so.
Which is shining in all our spirits,
Making them white as snow.
Come to me, shine in me, Master,
And I care not for river or tree,—
Care for no sorrow or crying,
If only thou shine in me.

"I would lie on my bed for ages,
Looking out on the dusty street,
Where whisper nor leaves nor waters,
Nor any thing cool and sweet;
At my heart this ghastly fainting,
And this burning in my blood,—
If only I knew thou wast with me,—
Wast with me and making me good."

When she rose from the piano, Mrs. Cromwell stretched out her hand for hers, and held it some time, unable to speak. Then she said,—

"That has done me good, I hope. I will try to be more patient, for I think He *is* teaching me."

She died, at length, in my arms. I cannot linger over that last time. She suffered a good deal, but dying people are generally patient. She went without a struggle. The last words I heard her utter were, "Yes, Lord;" after which she breathed but once. A half-smile came over her face, which froze upon it, and remained, until the coffin-lid covered it. But I shall see it, I trust, a whole smile some day.

# CHAPTER XXXIX.

## ANCESTRAL WISDOM.

I did think of having a chapter about children before finishing my book; but this is not going to be the kind of chapter I thought of. Like most mothers, I suppose, I think myself an authority on the subject; and, which is to me more assuring than any judgment of my own, my father says that I have been in a measure successful in bringing mine up,—only they're not brought up very far yet. Hence arose the temptation to lay down a few practical rules I had proved and found answer. But, as soon as I began to contemplate the writing of them down, I began to imagine So-and-so and So-and-so attempting to carry them out, and saw what a dreadful muddle they would make of it, and what mischief would thence lie at my door. Only one thing can be worse than the attempt to carry out rules whose principles are not understood; and that is the neglect of those which are understood, and seen to be right. Suppose, for instance, I were to say that corporal punishment was wholesome, involving less suffering than most other punishments, more effectual in the result, and leaving no sting or sense of unkindness; whereas mental punishment, considered by many to be more refined, and therefore less degrading, was often cruel to a sensitive child, and deadening to a stubborn one: suppose I said this, and a woman like my Aunt Millicent were to take it up: *her* whippings would have no more effect than if her rod were made of butterflies' feathers; they would be a mockery to her children, and bring law into contempt; while if a certain father I know were to be convinced by my arguments, he would fill his children with terror of him now, and with hatred afterwards. Of the last-mentioned result of severity, I know at least one instance. At present, the father to whom I refer disapproves of whipping even a man who has been dancing on his wife with hob-nailed shoes, because it would tend to brutalize him. But he taunts and stings, and confines in solitude for lengthened periods, high-spirited boys, and that for faults which I should consider very venial.

Then, again, if I were to lay down the rule that we must be as tender of the feelings of our children as if they were angel-babies who had to learn, alas! to understand our rough ways, how would that be taken by a certain French couple I know, who, not appearing until after the dinner to which they had accepted an invitation was over, gave as the reason, that it had been quite out of their power; for darling Désirée, their only child, had declared they shouldn't go, and that she would cry if they did; nay, went so far as to insist on their going to bed, which they were, however reluctant, compelled to do. They had actually undressed, and pretended to retire for the night; but, as soon as she was safely asleep, rose and joined their friends, calm in the consciousness of abundant excuse.

The marvel to me is that so many children turn out so well.

After all, I think there can be no harm in mentioning a few general principles laid down by my father. They are such as to commend themselves most to the most practical.

And first for a few negative ones.

1. Never *give in* to disobedience; and never threaten what you are not prepared to carry out.

2. Never lose your temper. I do not say *never be angry*. Anger is sometimes indispensable, especially where there has been any thing mean, dishonest, or cruel. But anger is very different from loss of temper. [Footnote: My Aunt Millicent is always saying, "I am *grieeeved* with you." But the announcement begets no sign of responsive grief on the face of the stolid child before her. She never whipped a child in her life. If she had, and it had but roused some positive anger in the child, instead of that undertone of complaint which is always oozing out of every one of them, I think It would have been a gain. But the poor lady is one of the whiny-piny people, and must be in preparation for a development of which I have no prevision. The only stroke of originality I thought I knew of her was this; to the register of her children's births, baptisms, and confirmations, entered on a grandly-ornamented fly-leaf of the family Bible, she has subjoined the record of every disease each has had, with the year, month, and day (and in one case the hour), when each distemper made its appearance. After most of the main entries, you may read, "*Cut his* (or her) *first tooth*"—at such a date. But, alas for the originality! she has just told me that her maternal grandmother did the same. How strange that she and my father should have had the same father I If they had had the same mother, too, I should have been utterly bewildered.]

3. Of all things, never sneer at them; and be careful, even, how you rally them.

4. Do not try to work on their feelings. Feelings are far too delicate things to be used for tools. It is like taking the mainspring out of your watch, and notching it for a saw. It may be a wonderful saw, but how fares your watch? Especially avoid doing so in connection with religious things, for so you will assuredly deaden them to all that is finest. Let your feelings, not your efforts on theirs, affect them with a sympathy the more powerful that it is not forced upon them; and, in order to do this, avoid being too English in the hiding of your feelings. A man's own family has a right to share in his *good* feelings.

5. Never show that you doubt, except you are able to convict. To doubt an honest child is to do what you can to make a liar of him; and to believe a liar, if he is not altogether shameless, is to shame him.

The common-minded masters in schools, who, unlike the ideal Arnold, are in the habit of *disbelieving* boys, have a large share in making the liars they so often are. Certainly the vileness of a lie is not the same in one who knows that whatever he says will be regarded with suspicion; and the master, who does not know an honest boy after he has been some time in his class, gives good reason for doubting whether he be himself an honest man, and incapable of the lying he is ready to attribute to all alike.

This last is my own remark, not my father's. I have an honest boy at school, and I know how he fares. I say honest; for though, as a mother, I can hardly expect to be believed, I have ground for believing that he would rather die than lie. I know *I* would rather he died than lied.

6. Instil no religious doctrine apart from its duty. If it have no duty as its necessary embodiment, the doctrine may well be regarded as doubtful.

7. Do not be hard on mere quarrelling, which, like a storm in nature, is often helpful in clearing the moral atmosphere. Stop it by a judgment between the parties. But be severe as to the *kind* of quarrelling, and the temper shown in it. Especially give no quarter to any unfairness arising from greed or spite. Use your strongest language with regard to that.

Now for a few of my father's positive rules:

1. Always let them come to you, and always hear what they have to say. If they bring a complaint, always examine into it, and dispense pure justice, and nothing but justice.

2. Cultivate a love of *giving* fair-play. Every one, of course, likes to *receive* fair-play; but no one ought to be left to imagine, therefore, that he *loves fair-play.*

3. Teach from the very first, from the infancy capable of sucking a sugar-plum, to share with neighbors. Never refuse the offering a child brings you, except you have a good reason,—and *give* it. And never *pretend* to partake: that involves hideous possibilities in its effects on the child.

The necessity of giving a reason for refusing a kindness has no relation to what is supposed by some to be the necessity of giving a reason with every command. There is no such necessity. Of course there ought to be a reason in every command. That it *may* be desirable, sometimes, to explain it, is all my father would allow.

4. Allow a great deal of noise,—as much as is fairly endurable; but, the moment they seem getting beyond their own control, stop the noise at once. Also put a stop at once to all fretting and grumbling.

5. Favor the development of each in the direction of his own bent. Help him to develop himself, but do not *push* development. To do so is most dangerous.

6. Mind the moral nature, and it will take care of the intellectual. In other words, the best thing for the intellect is the cultivation of the conscience, not in casuistry, but in conduct. It may take longer to arrive; but the end will be the highest possible health, vigor, and ratio of progress.

7. Discourage emulation, and insist on duty,—not often, but strongly.

Having written these out, chiefly from notes I had made of a long talk with my father, I gave them to Percivale to read.

"Rather—ponderous, don't you think, for weaving into a narrative?" was his remark.

"My narrative is full of things far from light," I returned. "I didn't say they were heavy, you know. That is quite another thing."

"I am afraid you mean generally uninteresting. But there are parents who might make them useful, and the rest of my readers could skip them."

"I only mean that a narrative, be it ever so serious, must not intrench on the moral essay or sermon."

"It is much too late, I fear, to tell me that. But, please, remember I am not giving the precepts as of my own discovery, though I *have* sought to verify them by practice, but as what they are,—my father's."

He did not seem to see the bearing of the argument.

"I want my book to be useful," I said. "As a mother, I want to share the help I have had myself with other mothers."

"I am only speaking from the point of art," he returned.

"And that's a point I have never thought of; any farther, at least, than writing as good English as I might."

"Do you mean to say you have never thought of the shape of the book your monthly papers would make?"

"Yes. I don't think I have. Scarcely at all, I believe."

"Then you ought."

"But I know nothing about that kind of thing. I haven't an idea in my head concerning the art of book-making. And it is too late, so far at least as this book is concerned, to begin to study it now."

"I wonder how my pictures would get on in that way."

"You can see how my book has got on. Well or ill, there it all but is. I had to do with facts, and not with art."

"But even a biography, in the ordering of its parts, in the arrangement of its light and shade, and in the harmony of the"—

"It's too late, I tell you, husband. The book is all but done. Besides, one who would write a biography after the fashion of a picture would probably, even without attributing a single virtue that was not present, or suppressing a single fault that was, yet produce a false book. The principle I have followed has been to try from the first to put as much value, that is, as much truth, as I could, into my story. Perhaps, instead of those maxims of my father's for the education of children, you would have preferred such specimens of your own children's sermons as you made me read to you for the twentieth time yesterday?"

Instead of smiling with his own quiet kind smile, as he worked on at his picture of St. Athanasius with "no friend but God and Death," he burst into a merry laugh, and said,—

"A capital idea! If you give those, word for word, I shall yield the precepts."

"Are you out of your five wits, husband?" I exclaimed. "Would you have everybody take me for the latest incarnation of the oldest insanity in the world,—that of maternity? But I am really an idiot, for you could never have meant it!"

"I do most soberly and distinctly mean it. They would amuse your readers very much, and, without offending those who may prefer your father's maxims to your children's sermons, would incline those who might otherwise vote the former a bore, to regard them with the clemency resulting from amusement."

"But I desire no such exercise of clemency. The precepts are admirable; and those need not take them who do not like them."

"So the others can skip the sermons; but I am sure they will give a few mothers, at least, a little amusement. They will prove besides, that you follow your own rule of putting a very small quantity of sage into the stuffing of your goslings; as also that you have succeeded in making them capable of manifesting what nonsense is indigenous in them. I think them very funny; that may be paternal prejudice: *you* think them very silly as well; that may be maternal solicitude. I suspect, that, the more of a philosopher any one of your readers is, the more suggestive will he find these genuine utterances of an age at which the means of expression so much exceed the matter to be expressed."

The idea began to look not altogether so absurd as at first; and a little more argument sufficed to make me resolve to put the absurdities themselves to the test of passing leisurely through my brain while I copied them out, possibly for the press.

The result is, that I am going to risk printing them, determined, should I find afterwards that I have made a blunder, to throw the whole blame upon my husband.

What still makes me shrink the most is the recollection of how often I have condemned, as too silly to repeat, things which reporting mothers evidently regarded as proofs of a stupendous intellect. But the folly of these constitutes the chief part of their merit; and I do not see how I can be mistaken for supposing them clever, except it be in regard of a glimmer of purpose now and then, and the occasional manifestation of the cunning of the stump orator, with his subterfuges to conceal his embarrassment when he finds his oil failing him, and his lamp burning low.

# CHAPTER XL.

## CHILD NONSENSE.

One word of introductory explanation.

During my husband's illness, Marion came often, but, until he began to recover, would generally spend with the children the whole of the time she had to spare, not even permitting me to know that she was in the house. It was a great thing for them; for, although they were well enough cared for, they were necessarily left to themselves a good deal more than hitherto. Hence, perhaps, it came that they betook themselves to an amusement not uncommon with children, of which I had as yet seen nothing amongst them.

One evening, when my husband had made a little progress towards recovery, Marion came to sit with me in his room for an hour.

"I've brought you something I want to read to you," she said, "if you think Mr. Percivale can bear it."

I told her I believed he could, and she proceeded to explain what it was.

"One morning, when I went into the nursery, I found the children playing at church, or rather at preaching; for, except a few minutes of singing, the preaching occupied the whole time. There were two clergymen, Ernest and Charles, alternately incumbent and curate. The chief duty of the curate for the time being was to lend his aid to the rescue of his incumbent from any difficulty in which the extemporaneous character of his discourse might land him."

I interrupt Marion to mention that the respective ages of Ernest and Charles were then eight and six.

"The pulpit," she continued, "was on the top of the cupboard under the cuckoo-clock, and consisted of a chair and a cushion. There were prayer-books in abundance; of which neither of them, I am happy to say, made other than a pretended use for reference. Charles, indeed, who was preaching when I entered, *can't* read; but both have far too much reverence to use sacred words in their games, as the sermons themselves will instance. I took down almost every word they said, frequent embarrassments and interruptions enabling me to do so. Ernest was acting as clerk, and occasionally prompted the speaker when his eloquence failed him, or reproved members of the congregation, which consisted of the two nurses and the other children, who were inattentive. Charles spoke with a good deal of *unction*, and had quite a professional air when he looked down on the big open book, referred to one or other of the smaller ones at his side, or directed looks of reprehension at this or that hearer. You would have thought he had cultivated the imitation of popular preachers, whereas he tells me he has been to church only three times. I am sorry I cannot give the opening remarks, for I lost them by being late; but what I did hear was this."

She then read from her paper as follows, and lent it me afterwards. I merely copy it.

"Once" (*Charles was proceeding when Marion entered*), "there lived an aged man, and another who was a *very* aged man; and the very aged man was going to die, and every one but the aged man thought the other, the *very* aged man, wouldn't die. I do this to *explain* it to you. He, the man who was *really* going to die, was—I will look in the dictionary" (*He looks in the book, and gives out with much confidence*), "was two thousand and eighty-eight years old. Well, the other man was—well, then, the other man 'at knew he was going to die, was about four thousand and two; not nearly so old, you see." (*Here Charles whispers with Ernest, and then announces very loud*),—"This is out of St. James. The *very* aged man had a wife and no children; and the other had no wife, but a *great many* children. The fact was—*this* was how it was—the wife *died*, and so *he* had the children. Well, the man I spoke of first, well, he died in the middle of the night." (*A look as much as to say, "There! what do you think of that?"*); "an' nobody but the aged man knew he was going to die. Well, in the morning, when his wife got up, she spoke to him, and he was dead!" (*A pause.*) "Perfectly, sure enough—*dead*!" (*Then, with a change of voice and manner*), "He wasn't really dead, because you know" (*abruptly and nervously*)—"Shut the door!—you know where he went, because in the morning next day" (*He pauses and looks round. Ernest, out of a book, prompts*—"The angels take him away"), "came the angels to take him away, up to where you know." (*All solemn. He resumes quickly, with a change of manner*), "They, all the rest, died of grief. Now, you must expect, as they all died of grief, that lots of angels must have come to take *them* away. Freddy *will* go when the sermon isn't over! That *is* such a bother!"

At this point Marion paused in her reading, and resumed the narrative form.

"Freddy, however, was too much for them; so Ernest betook himself to the organ, which was a chest of drawers, the drawers doing duty as stops, while Freddy went up to the pulpit to say 'Good-by,' and shake hands, for which he was mildly reproved by both his brothers."

My husband and I were so much amused, that Marion said she had another sermon, also preached by Charles, on the same day, after a short interval; and at our request she read it. Here it is.

"Once upon a time—a long while ago, in a little—Ready now?—Well, there lived in a rather big house, with *quite* clean windows: it was in winter, so nobody noticed them, but they were quite *white*, they were so clean. There lived some angels in the house: it was in the air, nobody knew why, but it did.

No: I don't think it did—I dunno, but there lived in it lots of children—two hundred and thirty-two—and they—Oh! I'm gettin' distracted! It is too bad!" (*Quiet is restored.*) "Their mother and father had died, but they were very rich. Now, you see what a heap of children,—two hundred and thirty-two! and yet it seemed like *one* to them, they were so rich. *That* was it! it seemed like *one* to them because they were so rich. Now, the children knew what to get, and I'll explain to you now *why* they knew; and *this* is how they knew. The angels came down on the earth, and told them their mother had sent messages to them; and their mother and father—*Don't* talk! I'm gettin' extracted!" (*Puts his hand to his head in a frenzied manner.*) "Now, my brother" (*This severely to a still inattentive member*), "I'll tell you what the angels told them—what to get. What—how—now I will tell you how,—yes, *how* they knew what they were to eat. Well, the fact was, that—Freddy's just towards my face, and he's laughing! I'm going to explain. The mother and father had the wings on, and so, of course—Ernest, I want you!" (*They whisper.*)—"they were he and she angels, and they told them what to have. Well, one thing was—shall I tell you what it was? Look at two hundred and two in another book—one thing was a leg of mutton. Of course, as the mother and father were angels, they had to fly up again. Now I'm going to explain how they got it done. They had four servants and one cook, so that would be five. Well, this cook did them. The eldest girl was sixteen, and her name was Snowdrop, because she had snowy arms and cheeks, and was a very nice girl. The eldest boy was seventeen, and his name was John. He always told the cook what they'd have—no, the girl did that. And the boy was now grown up. So they would be mother and father." (*Signs of dissent among the audience.*) "*Of course*, when they were so old, they would be mother and father, and master of the servants. And they were very happy, *but*—they didn't quite like it. And—and"—(*with a great burst*) "*you* wouldn't like it if *your* mother were to die! And I'll end it next Sunday. Let us sing."

"The congregation then sung 'Curly Locks,'" said Marion, "and dispersed; Ernest complaining that Charley gave them such large qualities of numbers, and there weren't so many in the whole of his book. After a brief interval the sermon was resumed."

"Text is No. 66. I've a good congregation! I got to where the children did not like it without their mother and father. Well, you must remember this was a long while ago, so what I'm going to speak about *could* be possible. Well, their house was on the top of a high and steep hill; and at the bottom, a little from the hill, was a knight's house. There were three knights living in it. Next to it was stables with three horses in it. Sometimes they went up to this house, and wondered what was in it. 'They never knew, but saw the angels come. The knights were out all day, and only came home for meals. And they wondered what *on earth* the angels were doin', goin' in the house. They found out *what*—what, and the question was—I'll explain what it was. Ernest, come here." (*Ernest remarks to the audience*, "I'm curate," *and to Charles*, "Well, but, Charles, you're going to explain, you know;" *and Charles resumes.*) "The fact was, that this was—if you'd like to explain it more to yourselves, you'd better look in your books, No. 1828. Before, the angels didn't speak loud, so the knights couldn't hear; *now* they spoke louder, so that the knights could visit them, 'cause they knew their names. They hadn't many visitors, but they had the knights in there, and that's all."

I am still very much afraid that all this nonsense will hardly be interesting, even to parents. But I may as well suffer for a sheep as a lamb; and, as I had an opportunity of hearing two such sermons myself not long after, I shall give them, trusting they will occupy far less space in print than they do in my foolish heart.

It was Ernest who was in the pulpit and just commencing his discourse when I entered the nursery, and sat down with the congregation. Sheltered by a clothes-horse, apparently set up for a screen, I took out my pencil, and reported on a fly-leaf of the book I had been reading:—

"My brother was goin' to preach about the wicked: I will preach about the good. Twenty-sixth day. In the time of Elizabeth there was a very old house. It was so old that it was pulled down, and a quite new one was built instead. Some people who lived in it did not like it so much now as they did when it was old. I take their part, you know, and think they were quite right in preferring the old one to the ugly, bare, new one. They left it—sold it—and got into another old house instead."

Here, I am sorry to say, his curate interjected the scornful remark,—

"He's not lookin' in the book a bit!"

But the preacher went on, without heeding the attack on his orthodoxy.

"This other old house was still more uncomfortable: it was very draughty; the gutters were always leaking; and they wished themselves back in the new house. So, you see, if you wish for a better thing, you don't get it so good after all."

"Ernest, that *is* about the bad, after all!" cried Charles.

"Well, it's *silly*," remarked Freddy severely.

"But I wrote it myself," pleaded the preacher from the pulpit; and, in consideration of the fact, he was allowed to go on.

"I was reading about them being always uncomfortable. At last they decided to go back to their own house, which they had sold. They had to pay so much to get it back, that they had hardly any money left; and then they got so unhappy, and the husband whipped his wife, and took to drinking. That's a lesson." (*Here the preacher's voice became very plaintive*), "that's a lesson to show you shouldn't try to get the better thing, for it turns out worse, and then you get sadder, and every thing."

He paused, evidently too mournful to proceed. Freddy again remarked that it was *silly*; but Charles interposed a word for the preacher.

"It's a good *lesson*, I think. A good *lesson*, I say," he repeated, as if he would not be supposed to consider it much of a sermon.

But here the preacher recovered himself and summed up.

"See how it comes: wanting to get every thing, you come to the bad and drinking. And I think I'll leave off here. Let us sing."

The song was "Little Robin Redbreast;" during which Charles remarked to Freddy, apparently by way of pressing home the lesson upon his younger brother,—

"Fancy! floggin' his wife!"

Then he got into the pulpit himself, and commenced an oration.

"Chapter eighty-eight. *The wicked.*—Well, the time when the story was, was about Herod. There were some wicked people wanderin' about there, and they—not *killed* them, you know, but—went to the judge. We shall see what they did to them. I tell you this to make you understand. Now the story begins—but I must think a little. Ernest, let's sing 'Since first I saw your face.'

"When the wicked man was taken then to the good judge—there were *some* good people: when I said I was going to preach about the wicked, I did not mean that there were no good, only a good lot of wicked. There were pleacemans about here, and they put him in prison for a few days, and then the judge could see about what he is to do with him. At the end of the few days, the judge asked him if he would stay in prison for life or be hanged."

Here arose some inquiries among the congregation as to what the wicked, of whom the prisoner was one, had done that was wrong; to which Charles replied,—

"Oh! they murdered and killed; they stealed, and they were very wicked altogether. Well," he went on, resuming his discourse, "the morning came, and the judge said, 'Get the ropes and my throne, and order the people *not* to come to see the hangin'.' For the man was decided to be hanged. Now, the people *would* come. They were the wicked, and they would *persist* in comin'. They were the wicked; and, if that was the *fact*, the judge must do something to them.

"Chapter eighty-nine. *The hangin'*.—We'll have some singin' while I think."

"Yankee Doodle" was accordingly sung with much enthusiasm and solemnity.
Then Charles resumed.

"Well, they had to put the other people, who persisted in coming, in prison, till the man who murdered people was hanged. I think my brother will go on."

He descended, and gave place to Ernest, who began with vigor.

"We were reading about Herod, weren't we? Then the wicked people *would* come, and had to be put to death. They were on the man's side; and they all called out that he hadn't had his wish before he died, as they did in those days. So of course he wished for his life, and of course the judge wouldn't let him have *that* wish; and so he wished to speak to his friends, and they let him. And the nasty wicked people took him away, and he was never seen in that country any more. And that's enough to-day, I think. Let us sing 'Lord Lovel he stood at his castle-gate, a combing his milk-white steed.'"

At the conclusion of this mournful ballad, the congregation was allowed to disperse. But, before they had gone far, they were recalled by the offer of a more secular entertainment from Charles, who re-ascended the pulpit, and delivered himself as follows:—

"Well, the play is called—not a proverb or a charade it isn't—it's a play called 'The Birds and the Babies.' Well!

"Once there was a little cottage, and lots of little babies in it. Nobody knew who the babies were. They were so happy! Now, I can't explain it to you how they came together: they had no father and mother, but they were brothers and sisters. They never *grew*, and they didn't like it. Now, *you* wouldn't like *not* to *grow*, would you? They had a little garden, and saw a great many birds in the trees. They *were* happy, but didn't *feel* happy—that's a funny thing now! The wicked fairies made them unhappy, and the good fairies made them happy; they gave them lots of toys. But then, how they got their living!

"Chapter second, called 'The Babies at Play.'—The fairies told them what to get—*that was it!*—and so they got their living Very nicely. And now I must explain what they played with. First was a house. *A house.* Another, dolls. They were very happy, and felt as if they had a mother and father; but they hadn't, and *couldn't* make it out. *Couldn't—make—it—out!*

"They had little pumps and trees. Then they had babies' rattles. *Babies' rattles.*—Oh! I've said hardly any thing about the birds, have I? an' it's called '*The Birds and the Babies!*' They had lots of little pretty robins and canaries hanging round the ceiling, and—*shall* I say?"—

Every one listened expectant during the pause that followed.

"*—And—lived—happy—ever—after.*"

The puzzle in it all is chiefly what my husband hinted at,—why and how both the desire and the means of utterance should so long precede the possession of any thing ripe for utterance. I suspect the answer must lie pretty deep in some metaphysical gulf or other.

At the same time, the struggle to speak where there is so little to utter can hardly fail to suggest the thought of some efforts of a more pretentious and imposing character.

But more than enough!

# CHAPTER XLI.

## "DOUBLE, DOUBLE, TOIL AND TROUBLE."

I had for a day or two fancied that Marion was looking less bright than usual, as if some little shadow had fallen upon the morning of her life. I say *morning*, because, although Marion must now have been seven or eight and twenty, her life had always seemed to me lighted by a cool, clear, dewy morning sun, over whose face it now seemed as if some film of noonday cloud had begun to gather. Unwilling at once to assert the ultimate privilege of friendship, I asked her if any thing was amiss with her friends. She answered that all was going on well, at least so far that she had no special anxiety about any of them. Encouraged by a half-conscious and more than half-sad smile, I ventured a little farther.

"I am afraid there is something troubling you," I said.

"There is," she replied, "something troubling me a good deal; but I hope it will pass away soon."

The sigh which followed, however, was deep though gentle, and seemed to indicate a fear that the trouble might not pass away so very soon.

"I am not to ask you any questions, I suppose," I returned.

"Better not at present," she answered. "I am not quite sure that"—

She paused several moments before finishing her sentence, then added,—

"—that I am at liberty to tell you about it."

"Then don't say another word," I rejoined. "Only when I can be of service to you, you *will* let me, won't you?"

The tears rose to her eyes.

"I'm afraid it may be some fault of mine," she said. "I don't know. I can't tell. I don't understand such things."

She sighed again, and held her peace.

It was enigmatical enough. One thing only was clear, that at present I was not wanted. So I, too, held my peace, and in a few minutes Marion went, with a more affectionate leave-taking than usual, for her friendship was far less demonstrative than that of most women.

I pondered, but it was not of much use. Of course the first thing that suggested itself was, Could my angel be in love? and with some mortal mere? The very idea was a shock, simply from its strangeness. Of course, being a woman, she *might* be in love; but the two ideas, *Marion* and *love*, refused to coalesce. And again, was it likely that such as she, her mind occupied with so many other absorbing interests, would fall in love unprovoked, unsolicited? That, indeed, was not likely. Then if, solicited, she but returned love for love, why was she sad? The new experience might, it is true, cause such commotion in a mind like hers as to trouble her greatly. She would not know what to do with it, nor where to accommodate her new inmate so as to keep him from meddling with affairs he had no right to meddle with: it was easy enough to fancy him troublesome in a house like hers. But surely of all women *she* might be able to meet her own liabilities. And if this were all, why should she have said she hoped it would soon pass? That might, however, mean only that she hoped soon to get her guest brought amenable to her existing household economy.

There was yet a conjecture, however, which seemed to suit the case better. If Marion knew little of what is commonly called love, that is, "the attraction of correlative unlikeness," as I once heard it defined by a metaphysical friend of my father's, there was no one who knew more of the tenderness of compassion than she; and was it not possible some one might be wanting to marry her to whom she could not give herself away? This conjecture was at least ample enough to cover the facts in my possession—which were scanty indeed, in number hardly dual. But who was there to dare offer love to my saint? Roger? Pooh! pooh! Mr. Blackstone? Ah! I had seen him once lately looking at her with an expression of more than ordinary admiration. But what man that knew any thing of her could help looking at her with such an admiration? If it was Mr. Blackstone—why, *he* might dare—yes, why should he not dare to love her?—especially if he couldn't help it, as, of course, he couldn't. Was he not one whose love, simply because he was a *true* man from the heart to the hands, would honor any woman, even Saint Clare—as she must be when the church has learned to do its business without the pope? Only he mustn't blame me, if, after all, I should think he offered less than he sought; or her, if, entertaining no question of worth whatever, she should yet refuse to listen to him as, truly, there was more than a possibility she might.

If it were Mr. Blackstone, certainly I knew no man who could understand her better, or whose modes of thinking and working would more thoroughly fall in with her own. True, he was peculiar; that is, he had kept the angles of his individuality, for all the grinding of the social mill; his manners were too abrupt, and drove at the heart of things too directly, seldom suggesting a *by-your-leave* to those whose prejudices he overturned: true, also, that his person, though dignified, was somewhat ungainly,—with an ungainliness, however, which I could well imagine a wife learning absolutely to love; but, on the whole, the thing was reasonable. Only, what would become of her friends? There, I could hardly doubt, there lay the difficulty! Ay, *there* was the rub!

Let no one think, when I say we went to Mr. Blackstone's church the next Sunday, that it had any thing to do with these speculations. We often went on the first Sunday of the month.

"What's the matter with Blackstone?" said my husband as we came home.

"What do *you* think is the matter with him?" I returned.

"I don't know. He wasn't himself."

"I thought he was more than himself," I rejoined; "for I never heard even *him* read the litany with such fervor."

"In some of the petitions," said Percivale, "it amounted to a suppressed agony of supplication. I am certain he is in trouble."

I told him my suspicions.

"Likely—very likely," he answered, and became thoughtful.

"But you don't think she refused him?" he said at length.

"If he ever asked her," I returned, "I fear she did; for she is plainly in trouble too."

"She'll never stick to it," he said.

"You mustn't judge Marion by ordinary standards," I replied. "You must remember she has not only found her vocation, but for many years proved it. I never knew her turned aside from what she had made up her mind to. I can hardly imagine her forsaking her friends to keep house for any man, even if she loved him with all her heart. She is dedicated as irrevocably as any nun, and will, with St. Paul, cling to the right of self-denial."

"Yet what great difficulty would there be in combining the two sets of duties, especially with such a man as Blackstone? Of all the men I know, he comes the nearest to her in his devotion to the well-being of humanity, especially of the poor. Did you ever know a man with such a plentiful lack of condescension? His feeling of human equality amounts almost to a fault; for surely he ought sometimes to speak as knowing better than they to whom he speaks. He forgets that too many will but use his humility for mortar to build withal the Shinar-tower of their own superiority."

"That may be; yet it remains impossible for him to assume any thing. He is the same all through, and—I had almost said—worthy of Saint Clare. Well, they must settle it for themselves. We can do nothing."

"We can do nothing," he assented; and, although we repeatedly reverted to the subject on the long way home, we carried no conclusions to a different result.

Towards evening of the same Sunday, Roger came to accompany us, as I thought, to Marion's gathering, but, as it turned out, only to tell me he couldn't go. I expressed my regret, and asked him why. He gave me no answer, and his lip trembled. A sudden conviction seized me. I laid my hand on his arm, but could only say, "Dear Roger!" He turned his head aside, and, sitting down on the sofa, laid his forehead on his hand.

"I'm so sorry!" I said.

"She has told you, then?" he murmured.

"No one has told me any thing."

He was silent. I sat down beside him. It was all I could do. After a moment he rose, saying,—

"There's no good whining about it, only she might have made a man of me. But she's quite right. It's a comfort to think I'm so unworthy of her. That's all the consolation left me, but there's more in that than you would think till you try it."

He attempted to laugh, but made a miserable failure of it, then rose and caught up his hat to go. I rose also.

"Roger," I said, "I can't go, and leave you miserable. We'll go somewhere else,—anywhere you please, only you mustn't leave us."

"I don't want to go somewhere else. I don't know the place," he added, with a feeble attempt at his usual gayety.

"Stop at home, then, and tell me all about it. It will do you good to talk. You shall have your pipe, and you shall tell me just as much as you like, and keep the rest to yourself."

If you want to get hold of a man's deepest confidence, tell him to smoke in your drawing-room. I don't know how it is, but there seems no trouble in which a man can't smoke. One who scorns extraneous comfort of every other sort, will yet, in the profoundest sorrow, take kindly to his pipe. This is more wonderful than any thing I know about our kind. But I fear the sewing-machines will drive many women to tobacco.

I ran to Percivale, gave him a hint of how it was, and demanded his pipe and tobacco-pouch directly, telling him he must content himself with a cigar.

Thus armed with the calumet, as Paddy might say, I returned to Roger, who took it without a word of thanks, and began to fill it mechanically, but not therefore the less carefully. I sat down, laid my hands in my lap, and looked at him without a word. When the pipe was filled I rose and got him a light, for which also he made me no acknowledgment. The revenge of putting it in print is sweet. Having whiffed a good many whiffs in silence, he took at length his pipe from his mouth, and, as he pressed the burning tobacco with a forefinger, said,—

"I've made a fool of myself, Wynnie."

"Not more than a gentleman had a right to do, I will pledge myself," I returned.

"She *has* told you, then?" he said once more, looking rather disappointed than annoyed.

"No one has mentioned your name to me, Roger. I only guessed it from what Marion said when I questioned her about her sad looks."

"Her sad looks?"

"Yes."

"What did she say?" he asked eagerly.

"She only confessed she had had something to trouble her, and said she hoped it would be over soon."

"I dare say!" returned Roger dryly, looking gratified, however, for a moment.

My reader may wonder that I should compromise Marion, even so far as to confess that she was troubled; but I could not bear that Roger should think she had been telling his story to me. Every generous woman feels that she owes the man she refuses at least silence; and a man may well reckon upon that much favor. Of all failures, why should this be known to the world?

The relief of finding she had not betrayed him helped him, I think, to open his mind: *he* was under no obligation to silence.

"You see, Wynnie," he said, with pauses, and puffs at his pipe, "I don't mean I'm a fool for falling in love with Marion. Not to have fallen in love with her would have argued me a beast. Being a man, it was impossible for me to help it, after what she's been to me. But I was worse than a fool to open my mouth on the subject to an angel like her. Only there again, I couldn't, that is, I hadn't the strength to help it. I beg, however, you won't think me such a downright idiot as to fancy myself worthy of her. In that case, I should have deserved as much scorn as she gave me kindness. If you ask me how it was, then, that I dared to speak to her on the subject, I can only answer that I yielded to the impulse common to all kinds of love to make itself known. If you love God, you are not content with his knowing it even, but you must tell him as if he didn't know it. You may think from this cool talk of mine that I am very philosophical about it; but there are lulls in every storm, and I am in one of those lulls, else I shouldn't be sitting here with you."

"Dear Roger!" I said, "I am very sorry for your disappointment. Somehow, I can't be sorry you should have loved"—

"*Have loved!*" he murmured.

"*Should love* Marion, then," I went on. "That can do you nothing but good, and in itself must raise you above yourself. And how could I blame you, that, loving her, you wanted her to know it? But come, now, if you can trust me, tell me all about it, and especially what she said to you. I dare not give you any hope, for I am not in her confidence in this matter; and it is well that I am not, for then I might not be able to talk to you about it with any freedom. To confess the real truth, I do not see much likelihood, knowing her as I do, that she will recall her decision."

"It could hardly be called a decision," said Roger. "You would not have thought, from the way she took it, there was any thing to decide about. No more there was; and I thought I knew it, only I couldn't be quiet. To think you know a thing, and to know it, are two very different matters, however. But I don't repent having spoken my mind: if I am humbled, I am not humiliated. If she *had* listened to me, I fear I should have been ruined by pride. I should never have judged myself justly after it. I wasn't humble, though I thought I was. I'm a poor creature, Ethelwyn."

"Not too poor a creature to be dearly loved, Roger. But go on and tell me all about it. As your friend and sister, I am anxious to hear the whole."

Notwithstanding what I had said, I was not moved by sympathetic curiosity alone, but also by the vague desire of rendering some help beyond comfort. What he had now said, greatly heightened my opinion of him, and thereby, in my thoughts of the two, lessened the distance between him and Marion. At all events, by hearing the whole, I should learn how better to comfort him.

And he did tell me the whole, which, along with what I learned afterwards from Marion, I will set down as nearly as I can, throwing it into the form of direct narration. I will not pledge myself for the accuracy of every trifling particular which that form may render it necessary to introduce; neither, I am sure, having thus explained, will my reader demand it of me.

# CHAPTER XLII.

## ROGER AND MARION.

During an all but sleepless night, Roger had made up his mind to go and see Marion: not, certainly, for the first time, for he had again and again ventured to call upon her; but hitherto he had always had some pretext sufficient to veil his deeper reason, and, happily or unhappily, sufficient also to prevent her, in her more than ordinary simplicity with regard to such matters, from suspecting one under it.

She was at home, and received him with her usual kindness. Feeling that he must not let an awkward silence intervene, lest she should become suspicious of his object, and thus the chance be lost of interesting, and possibly moving her before she saw his drift, he spoke at once.

"I want to tell you something, Miss Clare," he said as lightly as he could.

"Well?" she returned, with the sweet smile which graced her every approach to communication.

"Did my sister—in—law ever tell you what an idle fellow I used to be?"

"Certainly not. I never heard her say a word of you that wasn't kind."

"That I am sure of. But there would have been no unkindness in saying that; for an idle fellow I was, and the idler because I was conceited enough to believe I could do any thing. I actually thought at one time I could play the violin. I actually made an impertinent attempt in your presence one evening, years and years ago, I wonder if you remember it."

"I do; but I don't know why you should call it impertinent."

"Anyhow, I caught a look on your face that cured me of that conceit. I have never touched the creature since,—a Cremona too!"

"I am very sorry, indeed I am. I don't remember—Do you think you could have played a false note?"

"Nothing more likely."

"Then, I dare say I made an ugly face. One can't always help it, you know, when something unexpected happens. Do forgive me."

"Forgive *you*, you angel!" cried Roger, but instantly checked himself, afraid of reaching his mark before he had gathered sufficient momentum to pierce it. "I thought you would see what a good thing it was for me. I wanted to thank you for it."

"It's such a pity you didn't go on, though. Progress is the real cure for an overestimate of ourselves."

"The fact is, I was beginning to see what small praise there is in doing many things ill and nothing well. I wish you would take my Cremona. I could teach you the A B C of it well enough. How you would make it talk! That *would* be something to live for, to hear *you* play the violin! Ladies do, nowadays, you know."

"I have no time, Mr. Roger. I should have been delighted to be your pupil; but I am sorry to say it is out of the question."

"Of course it is. Only I wish—well, never mind, I only wanted to tell you something. I was leading a life then that wasn't worth leading; for where's the good of being just what happens,—one time full of right feeling and impulse, and the next a prey to all wrong judgments and falsehoods? It was you made me see it. I've been trying to get put right for a long time now. I'm afraid of seeming to talk goody, but you will know what I mean. You and your Sunday evenings have waked me up to know what I am, and what I ought to be. I am a little better. I work hard now. I used to work only by fits and starts. Ask Wynnie."

"Dear Mr. Roger, I don't need to ask Wynnie about any thing you tell me. I can take your word for it just as well as hers. I am very glad if I have been of any use to you. It is a great honor to me."

"But the worst of it is, I couldn't be content without letting you know, and making myself miserable."

"I don't understand you, I think. Surely there can be no harm in letting me know what makes me very happy! How it should make you miserable, I can't imagine."

"Because I can't stop there. I'm driven to say what will offend you, if it doesn't make you hate me—no, not that; for you don't know how to hate. But you must think me the most conceited and presumptuous fellow you ever knew. I'm not that, though; I'm not that; it's not me; I can't help it; I can't help loving you—dreadfully—and it's such impudence! To think of you and me in one thought! And yet I can't help it. O Miss Clare! don't drive me away from you."

He fell on his knees as he spoke, and laid his head on her lap, sobbing like a child who had offended his mother. He almost cried again as he told me this. Marion half started to her feet in confusion, almost in terror, for she had never seen such emotion in a man; but the divine compassion of her nature conquered: she sat down again, took his head in her hands, and began stroking his hair as if she were indeed a mother seeking to soothe and comfort her troubled child. She was the first to speak again, for Roger could not command himself.

"I'm very sorry, Roger," she said. "I must be to blame somehow."

"To blame!" he cried, lifting up his head. "*You* to blame for my folly! But it's not folly," he added impetuously: "it would be downright stupidity not to love you with all my soul."

"Hush! hush!" said Marion, in whose ears his language sounded irreverent. "You *couldn't* love me with all your soul if you would. God only *can* be loved with all the power of the human soul."

"If I love him at all, Marion, it is you who have taught me. Do not drive me from you—lest—lest—I should cease to love him, and fall back into my old dreary ways."

"It's a poor love to offer God,—love for the sake of another," she said very solemnly.

"But if it's all one has got?"

"Then it won't do, Roger. I wish you loved me for God's sake instead. Then all would be right. That would be a grand love for me to have."

"Don't drive me from you, Marion," he pleaded. It was all he could say.

"I will not drive you from me. Why should I?"

"Then I may come and see you again?"

"Yes: when you please."

"You *don't* mean I may come as often as I like?"

"Yes—when I have time to see you."

"Then," cried Roger, starting to his feet with clasped hands, "—perhaps—is it possible?—you will—you will let me love you? O my God!"

"Roger," said Marion, pale as death, and rising also; for, alas! the sunshine of her kindness had caused hopes to blossom whose buds she had taken only for leaves, "I thought you understood me! You spoke as if you understood perfectly that that could never be which I must suppose you to mean. Of course it cannot. I am not my own to keep or to give away. I belong to this people,—my friends. To take personal and private duties upon me, would be to abandon them; and how dare I? You don't know what it would result in, or you would not dream of it. Were I to do such a thing, I should hate and despise and condemn myself with utter reprobation. And then what a prize you would have got, my poor Roger!"

But even these were such precious words to hear from her lips! He fell again on his knees before her as she stood, caught her hands, and, hiding his face in them, poured forth the following words in a torrent,—

"Marion, do not think me so selfish as not to have thought about that. It should be only the better for them all. I can earn quite enough for you and me too, and so you would have the more time to give to them. I should never have dreamed of asking you to leave them. There are things in which a dog may help a man, doing what the man can't do: there may be things in which a man might help an angel."

Deeply moved by the unselfishness of his love, Marion could not help a pressure of her hands against the face which had sought refuge within them. Roger fell to kissing them wildly.

But Marion was a woman; and women, I think, though I may be only judging by myself and my husband, look forward and round about, more than men do: they would need at all events; therefore Marion saw other things. A man-reader may say, that, if she loved him, she would not have thus looked about her; and that, if she did not love him, there was no occasion for her thus to fly in the face of the future. I can only answer that it is allowed on all hands women are not amenable to logic: look about her Marion did, and saw, that, as a married woman, she might be compelled to forsake her friends more or less; for there might arise other and paramount claims on her self-devotion. In a word, if she were to have children, she would have no choice in respect to whose welfare should constitute the main business of her life; and it even became a question whether she would have a right to place them in circumstances so unfavorable for growth and education. Therefore, to marry might be tantamount to forsaking her friends.

But where was the need of any such mental parley? Of course, she couldn't marry Roger. How could she marry a man she couldn't look up to? And look up to him she certainly did not, and could not.

"No, Roger," she said, this last thought large in her mind; and, as she spoke, she withdrew her hands, "it mustn't be. It is out of the question: I can't look up to you," she added, as simply as a child.

"I should think not," he burst out. "That *would* be a fine thing! If you looked up to a fellow like me, I think it would almost cure me of looking up to you; and what I want is to look up to you every day and all day long: only I can do that whether you let me or not."

"But I don't choose to have a—a—friend to whom I can't look up."

"Then I shall never be even a friend," he returned sadly. "But I would have tried hard to be less unworthy of you."

At this precise moment, Marion caught sight of a pair of great round blue eyes, wide open under a shock of red hair, about three feet from the floor, staring as if they had not winked for the last ten minutes. The child looked so comical, that Marion, reading perhaps in her looks the reflex of her own position, could not help laughing. Roger started up in dismay, but, beholding the apparition, laughed also.

"Please, grannie," said the urchin, "mother's took bad, and want's ye."

"Run and tell your mother I shall be with her directly," answered Marion; and the child departed.

"You told me I might come again," pleaded Roger.

"Better not. I didn't know what it would mean to you when I said it."

"Let it mean what you meant by it, only let me come."

"But I see now it can't mean that. No: I will write to you. At all events, you must go now, for I can't stop with you when Mrs. Foote"—

"Don't make me wretched, Marion. If you can't love me, don't kill me. Don't say I'm not to come and see you. I *will* come on Sundays, anyhow."

The next day came the following letter:—

Dear Mr. Roger,—I am very sorry, both for your sake and my own, that I did not speak more plainly yesterday. I was so distressed for you, and my heart was so friendly towards you, that I could hardly think of any thing at first but how to comfort you; and I fear I allowed you, after all, to go away with the idea that what you wished was not altogether impossible. But indeed it is. If even I loved you in the way you love me, I should yet make every thing yield to the duties I have undertaken. In listening to you, I should be undermining the whole of my past labors; and the very idea of becoming less of a friend to my friends is horrible to me.

But much as I esteem you, and much pleasure as your society gives me, the idea you brought before me yesterday was absolutely startling; and I think I have only to remind you, as I have just done, of the peculiarities of my position, to convince you that it could never become a familiar one to me. All that friendship can do or yield, you may ever claim of me; and I thank God if I have been of the smallest service to you: but I should be quite unworthy of that honor, were I for any reason to admit even the thought of abandoning the work which has been growing up around me for so many years, and is so peculiarly mine that it could be transferred to no one else. Believe me yours most truly,

**MARION CLARE**

# CHAPTER XLIII.

## A LITTLE MORE ABOUT ROGER, AND ABOUT MR. BLACKSTONE.

After telling me the greater part of what I have just written, Roger handed me this letter to read, as we sat together that same Sunday evening.

"It seems final, Roger?" I said with an interrogation, as I returned it to him.

"Of course it is," he replied. "How could any honest man urge his suit after that,—after she says that to grant it would be to destroy the whole of her previous life, and ruin her self-respect? But I'm not so miserable as you may think me, Wynnie," he went on; "for don't you see? though I couldn't quite bring myself to go to-night, I don't feel cut off from her. She's not likely, if I know her, to listen to anybody else so long as the same reasons hold for which she wouldn't give me a chance of persuading her. She can't help me loving her, and I'm sure she'll let me help her when I've the luck to find a chance. You may be sure I shall keep a sharp lookout. If I can be her servant, that will be something; yes, much. Though she won't give herself to me—and quite right, too!—why should she?—God bless her!—she can't prevent me from giving myself to her. So long as I may love her, and see her as often as I don't doubt I may, and things continue as they are, I sha'n't be down-hearted. I'll have another pipe, I think." Here he half-started, and hurriedly pulled out his watch, "I declare, there's time yet!" he cried, and sprung to his feet. "Let's go and hear what she's got to say to-night."

"Don't you think you had better not? Won't you put her out?" I suggested.

"If I understand her at all," he said, "she will be more put out by my absence; for she will fear I am wretched, caring only for herself, and not for what she taught me. You may come or stay—*I*'m off. You've done me so much good, Wynnie!" he added, looking back in the doorway. "Thank you a thousand times. There's no comforter like a sister!"

"And a pipe," I said; at which he laughed, and was gone.

When Percivale and I reached Lime Court, having followed as quickly as we could, there was Roger sitting in the midst, as intent on her words as if she had been, an old prophet, and Marion speaking with all the composure which naturally belonged to her.

When she shook hands with him after the service, a slight flush washed the white of her face with a delicate warmth,—nothing more. I said to myself, however, as we went home, and afterwards to my husband, that his case was not a desperate one.

"But what's to become of Blackstone?" said Percivale.

I will tell my reader how afterwards he seemed to me to have fared; but I have no information concerning his supposed connection with this part of my story. I cannot even be sure that he ever was in love with Marion. Troubled he certainly was, at this time; and Marion continued so for a while,—more troubled, I think, than the necessity she felt upon her with regard to Roger will quite account for. If, however, she had to make two men miserable in one week, that might well cover the case.

Before the week was over, my husband received a note from Mr. Blackstone, informing him that he was just about to start for a few weeks on the Continent. When he returned I was satisfied from his appearance that a notable change had passed upon him: a certain indescribable serenity seemed to have taken possession of his whole being; every look and tone indicated a mind that knew more than tongue could utter,—a heart that had had glimpses into a region of content. I thought of the words, "He that dwelleth in the secret place of the Most High," and my heart was at rest about him. He had fared, I thought, as the child who has had a hurt, but is taken up in his mother's arms and comforted. What hurt would not such comforting outweigh to the child? And who but he that has had the worst hurt man can receive, and the best comfort God can give, can tell what either is?

I was present the first time he met Marion after his return. She was a little embarrassed: he showed a tender dignity, a respect as if from above, like what one might fancy the embodiment of the love of a wise angel for such a woman. The thought of comparing the two had never before occurred to me; but now for the moment I felt as if Mr. Blackstone were a step above Marion. Plainly, I had no occasion to be troubled about either of them.

On the supposition that Marion had refused him, I argued with myself that it could not have been on the ground that she was unable to look up to him. And, notwithstanding what she had said to Roger, I was satisfied that any one she felt she could help to be a nobler creature; must have a greatly better chance of rousing all the woman in her; than one whom she must regard as needing no aid from her. All her life had been spent in serving and sheltering human beings whose condition she regarded with hopeful compassion: could she now help adding Roger to her number of such? and if she once looked upon him thus tenderly, was it not at least very possible, that, in some softer mood, a feeling hitherto unknown to her might surprise her consciousness with its presence,—floating to the surface of her sea from its strange depths, and leaning towards him with the outstretched arms of embrace?

But I dared not think what might become of Roger should his divine resolves fail,—should the frequent society of Marion prove insufficient for the solace and quiet of his heart. I had heard how men will seek to drown sorrow in the ruin of the sorrowing power,—will slay themselves that they may cause their hurt to cease, and I trembled for my husband's brother. But the days went on, and I saw no sign of failure or change. He was steady at his work, and came to see us as constantly as before; never missed a chance of meeting Marion: and at every treat she gave her friends, whether at the house of which I have already spoken, or at Lady Bernard's country-place in the neighborhood of London, whether she took them on the river, or had some one to lecture or read to them, Roger was always at hand for service and help. Still, I was uneasy; for might there not come a collapse, especially if some new event were to destroy the hope which he still cherished, and which I feared was his main support? Would his religion then prove of a quality and power sufficient to keep him from drifting away with the receding tide of his hopes and imaginations? In this anxiety perhaps I regarded too exclusively the faith of Roger, and thought too little about the faith of God. However this may be, I could not rest, but thought and thought, until at last I made up my mind to go and tell Lady Bernard all about it.

# CHAPTER XLIV.

## THE DEA EX.

"And you think Marion likes him?" asked Lady Bernard, when she had in silence heard my story.

"I am sure she *likes* him. But you know he is so far inferior to her,—in every way."

"How do you know that? Questions are involved there which no one but God can determine. You must remember that both are growing. What matter if any two are unequal at a given moment, seeing their relative positions may be reversed twenty times in a thousand years? Besides, I doubt very much if any one who brought his favors with him would have the least chance with Marion. Poverty, to turn into wealth, is the one irresistible attraction for her; and, however duty may compel her to act, my impression is that she will not escape *loving* Roger."

I need not say I was gratified to find Lady Bernard's conclusion from Marion's character run parallel with my own.

"But what can come of it?" I said.

"Why, marriage, I hope."

"But Marion would as soon think of falling down and worshipping Baal and Ashtoreth as of forsaking her grandchildren."

"Doubtless. But there would be no occasion for that. Where two things are both of God, it is not likely they will be found mutually obstructive."

"Roger does declare himself quite ready to go and live amongst her friends, and do his best to help her."

"That is all as it should be, so far as he—as both of them are concerned; but there are contingencies; and the question naturally arises, How would that do in regard of their children?"

"If I could imagine Marion consenting." I said, "I know what she would answer to that question. She would say, Why should her children be better off than the children about them? She would say that the children must share the life and work of their parents."

"And I think she would be right, though the obvious rejoinder would be, 'You may waive your own social privileges, and sacrifice yourselves to the good of others; but have you a right to sacrifice your children, and heap disadvantages on their future?'"

"Now give us the answer on the other side, seeing you think Marion would be right after all."

"Marion's answer would, I think, be, that their children would be God's children; and he couldn't desire better for them than to be born in lowly conditions, and trained from the first to give themselves to the service of their fellows, seeing that in so far their history would resemble that of his own Son, our Saviour. In sacrificing their earthly future, as men would call it, their parents would but be furthering their eternal good."

"That would be enough in regard of such objections. But there would be a previous one on Marion's own part. How would her new position affect her ministrations?"

"There can be no doubt, I think," Lady Bernard replied, "that what her friends would lose thereby—I mean, what amount of her personal ministrations would be turned aside from them by the necessities of her new position—would be far more than made up to them by the presence among them of a whole well-ordered and growing family, instead of a single woman only. But all this jet leaves something for her more personal friends to consider,—as regards their duty in the matter. It naturally sets them on the track of finding out what could be done to secure for the children of such parents the possession of early advantages as little lower than those their parents had as may be; for the breed of good people ought, as much as possible, to be kept up. I will turn the thing over in my mind, and let you know what comes of it."

The result of Lady Bernard's cogitations is, in so far, to be seen in the rapid rise of a block of houses at no great distance from London, on the North-western Railway, planned under the instructions of Marion Clare. The design of them is to provide accommodation for all Marion's friends, with room to add largely to their number. Lady Bernard has also secured ground sufficient for great extension of the present building, should it prove desirable. Each family is to have the same amount of accommodation it has now, only far better, at the same rent it pays now, with the privilege of taking an additional room or rooms at a much lower rate. Marion has undertaken to collect the rents, and believes that she will thus in time gain an additional hold of the people for their good, although the plan may at first expose her to misunderstanding. From thorough calculation she is satisfied she can pay Lady Bernard five per cent for her money, lay out all that is necessary for keeping the property in thorough repair, and accumulate a fund besides to be spent on building more houses, should her expectations of these be answered. The removal of so many will also make a little room for the accommodation of the multitudes constantly driven from their homes by the wickedness of those, who, either for the sake of railways or fine streets, pull down crowded houses, and drive into other courts and alleys their poor inhabitants, to double the wretchedness already there from overcrowding.

In the centre of the building is a house for herself, where she will have her own private advantage in the inclusion of large space primarily for the entertainment of her friends. I believe Lady Bernard intends to give her a hint that a married couple would, in her opinion, be far more useful in such a position than a single woman. But although I rejoice in the prospect of greater happiness for two dear friends, I must in honesty say that I doubt this.

If the scheme should answer, what a strange reversion it will be to something like a right reading of the feudal system!

Of course it will be objected, that, should it succeed ever so well, it will all go to pieces at Marion's death. To this the answer lies in the hope that her influence may extend laterally, as well as downwards; moving others to be what she has been; and, in the conviction that such a work as hers can never be lost, for the world can never be the same as if she had not lived; while in any case there will be more room for her brothers and sisters who are now being crowded out of the world by the stronger and richer. It would be sufficient answer, however, that the work is worth doing for its own sake and its immediate result. Surely it will receive a *well-done* from the Judge of us all; and while his idea of right remains above hers, high as the heavens are above the earth, his approbation will be all that either Lady Bernard or Marion will seek.

If but a small proportion of those who love the right and have means to spare would, like Lady Bernard, use their wealth to make up to the poor for the wrongs they receive at the hands of the rich,—let me say, to defend the Saviour in their persons from the tyranny of Mammon, how many of the poor might they not lead with them into the joy of their Lord!

Should the plan succeed, I say once more, I intend to urge on Marion the duty of writing a history of its rise and progress from the first of her own attempts. Then there would at least remain a book for all future reformers and philanthropists to study, and her influence might renew itself in other ages after she was gone.

I have no more to say about myself or my people. We live in hope of the glory of God.

Here I was going to write, THE END; but was arrested by the following conversation between two of my children,—Ernest, eight, and Freddy, five years of age.

*Ernest.*—I'd do it for mamma, of course.

*Freddy.*—Wouldn't you do it for Harry?

*Ernest.*—No: Harry's nobody.

*Freddy.*—Yes, he is somebody.

*Ernest.*—You're nobody; I'm nobody; we are all nobody, compared to mamma.

*Freddy. (stolidly).*—Yes, I am somebody.

*Ernest.*—You're nothing; I'm nothing; we are all nothing in mamma's presence.

*Freddy.*—But, Ernest, *every thing* is something; so I must be something.

*Ernest.*—Yes, Freddy, but you're *no thing*; so you're nothing. You're nothing to mamma.

*Freddy.—But I'm mamma's.*

Milton Keynes UK
Ingram Content Group UK Ltd.
UKHW031953281024
450365UK00009B/561